The Poetics and Politics of Hospitality in US Literature and Culture

Critical Approaches to Ethnic American Literature

General Editors

Jesús Benito Sánchez (*Universidad de Valladolid*)
Ana María Manzanas (*Universidad de Salamanca*)

Editorial Board

Babs Boter (*Vrije Universiteit Amsterdam*)
Isabel Caldeira (*University of Coimbra*)
Nathalie Cochoy (*Université Toulouse*)
Astrid Fellner (*Universität des Saarlandes*)
Markus Heide (*Uppsala University*)
Paul Lauter (*Trinity College, Hartford, Connecticut*)
Shirley Lim (*University of California, Santa Barbara*)
Angel Mateos-Aparicio (*University of Castilla-La Mancha*)
Silvia Schultermandl (*University of Graz*)

Assistant Editors

Amanda Gerke
Paula Barba

VOLUME 7

The titles published in this series are listed at *brill.com/aeal*

The Poetics and Politics of Hospitality in US Literature and Culture

Edited by

Amanda Ellen Gerke, Santiago Rodríguez
Guerrero-Strachan and Patricia San José Rico

BRILL
RODOPI

LEIDEN | BOSTON

Cover illustration: "Post Office" by SRGS.

Library of Congress Cataloging-in-Publication Data

Names: Gerke, Amanda Ellen, editor. | Rodríguez Guerrero-Strachan, Santiago, editor. | San José Rico, Patricia, editor.
Title: The poetics and politics of hospitality in US literature and culture / edited by Amanda Ellen Gerke, Santiago Rodríguez Guerrero-Strachan, and Patricia San José Rico.
Description: Leiden ; Boston : Brill, 2020. | Series: Critical approaches to ethnic American literature ; volume 7 | Includes bibliographical references and index. | Summary: "The introduction to this volume makes a brief survey of the concept of hospitality in history, focusing on Emmanuel Levinas and Jacques Derrida, and describes the content of the chapters. Starting with Immanuel Kant and his notion of hospitality based on reciprocity, the authors of the introduction move towards Levinas's ethical hospitality as it shapes our identity, since we are constituted by the Other's self. For Levinas, hospitality is defined in terms of space and of care, while Jacques Derrida attempted to reconcile the ethical and the political in his theorization of the concept in the light of contemporary needs. For him, it is absolutely necessary a negotiation between the law of the nation and the law of hospitality, otherwise hospitality will always be conditioned"– Provided by publisher.
Identifiers: LCCN 2020014368 | ISBN 9789004407930 (hardback) | ISBN 9789004408043 (ebook)
Subjects: LCSH: Hospitality in literature. | American literature–History and criticism.
Classification: LCC PS169.H67 P64 2020 | DDC 810.9/353–dc23
LC record available at https://lccn.loc.gov/2020014368

Typeface for the Latin, Greek, and Cyrillic scripts: "Brill". See and download: brill.com/brill-typeface.

ISSN 1871-6067
ISBN 978-90-04-40793-0 (hardback)
ISBN 978-90-04-40804-3 (e-book)

Copyright 2020 by Koninklijke Brill NV, Leiden, The Netherlands.
Koninklijke Brill NV incorporates the imprints Brill, Brill Hes & De Graaf, Brill Nijhoff, Brill Rodopi, Brill Sense, Hotei Publishing, mentis Verlag, Verlag Ferdinand Schöningh and Wilhelm Fink Verlag.
All rights reserved. No part of this publication may be reproduced, translated, stored in a retrieval system, or transmitted in any form or by any means, electronic, mechanical, photocopying, recording or otherwise, without prior written permission from the publisher.
Authorization to photocopy items for internal or personal use is granted by Koninklijke Brill NV provided that the appropriate fees are paid directly to The Copyright Clearance Center, 222 Rosewood Drive, Suite 910, Danvers, MA 01923, USA. Fees are subject to change.

This book is printed on acid-free paper and produced in a sustainable manner.

Amanda dedicates this book to VAG, PTG, LGG, GGG, NGG, and "Doña K": the roots, the trunk, and the branches. Santiago wishes to dedicate this volume to those teachers, now sadly fallen into oblivion, who taught him to read and write and revealed for him the unforeseen province of the written word. Patricia dedicates this book to the two pillars of her life; and to Luis, the third one.

Contents

Acknowledgments ix
Note on Contributors x

1 Introduction: Hospitality in American Literature and Culture 1
   Santiago Rodríguez Guerrero-Strachan, Amanda Ellen Gerke and Patricia San José Rico

2 Hospitality from Below? Native Americans in the Host-Guest Binary 20
   Puspa Damai

3 Language Interaction and Hospitality: Combating the *Hosted-Host* Figure 36
   Amanda Ellen Gerke

4 Latino Immigrants at the Threshold: a Sociolinguistic Approach to Hospitality in US *Barriocentric* Narratives 57
   Luisa María González Rodríguez

5 (In)Hospitable Languages and Linguistic Hospitality in Hyphenated American Literature: the Case of Ha Jin 77
   José R. Ibáñez

6 The Contention for Jollity and Gloom: Hospitality in Nathaniel Hawthorne's Historical Short Fiction 94
   Santiago Rodríguez Guerrero-Strachan

7 (In)Hospitable Encounters in Herman Melville's *Clarel* 113
   Laura López Peña

8 Eating, Ethics, and Strangers: Hospitality and Food in Ruth Ozeki's Novels 134
   Cristina Garrigós

9 "It's a Long Way to Tipperary": the Relation between Race and Hospitality in the Irish-American Experience and its Literary Representation 154
   Patricia San José Rico

10 Hospitality Rituals and Caribbean Migrants: Tom Wolfe's *Back to Blood*, Ana Lydia Vega's "Encancaranublado," and Francisco Goldman's *The Ordinary Seaman*   176
    Ana María Manzanas Calvo

11 Tim Z. Hernandez's *Mañana Means Heaven*: Love on the Road and the Challenge of Multicultural Hospitality   194
    Maria Antònia Oliver-Rotger

12 "Parasites in a Host Country": Migrants, Refugees, Asylum Seekers and Other Zombies in *The Walking Dead*   211
    Ángel Mateos-Aparicio and Jesús Benito Sánchez

Index   233

Acknowledgments

Many people and organizations have helped make this volume possible. First and foremost, the editors would like to thank Ana Manzanas and Jesús Benito for their support and assistance during the editorial process. We would also like to thank all the authors of the individual chapters for their valuable contributions and commitment to this project as well as for their patience and understanding through all the deadlines, edits, and even rewritings. Also, special thanks must go towards our friends and family for their support and the occasional shoulder to cry on.

On a more personal note, Santiago Rodríguez Guerrero-Strachan wants to thank the Center for Humanities and the Arts at the University of Colorado at Boulder for the short-term stay at the Center to research hospitality. Likewise, Patricia San José is indebted to the English Department at Michigan State University for the time spent there as a visiting scholar. She would especially thank Dr. Gordon Henry, Dr. Jyotsna Singh, and all the lovely people she met there through the MSU Office for International Students and Scholars for showing her what true, unconditional hospitality feels like.

Finally, this book is part of the research project "Historia crítica de la literatura étnica norteamericana: una aproximación intercultural" (MINECO FFI2015-64137-P), funded by the Spanish Ministerio de Economía y Competitividad; without the economic help derived from it, this volume would not have been possible. Additional funding has been secured through the "Hostfilm: Hospitality in European Film" (2017-1-ES01-KA203-038181) research project, funded by the Erasmus + KA2: Strategic Partnership program of the European Union, and the "Las fronteras de la hospitalidad en los estudios culturales de Estados Unidos y Europa" (SA342U1) Research Project, funded by the Junta de Castilla y León.

Note on Contributors

Jesús Benito Sánchez
is Full Professor of American literature and culture at Universidad de Valladolid, and formerly, literary theory and English and American literature at the Universidad de Castilla-La Mancha (Spain). His main field of research is the ethnic American literatures, which he approaches from a comparative perspective, focusing on interethnic cultural analysis, as well as on transnational perspectives. He is General Editor of the Brill series "Critical Approaches to Ethnic American Literature" with Ana Mª Manzanas. He has authored three books: H*ospitality in American Literature and Culture* (Routledge 2017); *Occupying Space in American Literature and Culture* (Routledge 2014); and *Cities, Borders, and Spaces in Intercultural American Literature and Film* (Routledge 2011). He has served in the executive of different academic associations of English and American studies, including SAAS, EAAS, and AEDEAN.

Puspa Damai
is an Associate Professor of English at Marshall University, US. Dr. Damai has published articles in journals including *CR: The New Centennial Review, Discourse, Postcolonial Text, Sanglap,* and *Postcolonial Interventions*. He is currently working on two research projects: a book-length study of hospitality in American multi-ethnic literature, and a collection of essays on South Asian literature.

Cristina Garrigós
is Professor of American Literature at the National University of Distance Education (UNED) in Spain, where she has been teaching since 2015. She has taught at different universities in Spain (University Autonomous of Madrid, University of León) and the USA (UNC-Chapel Hill, University of Mississippi (Ole Miss), and Texas A&M International). Her research interests include US contemporary literature, film, music, and gender. She has published on authors such as John Barth, Kathy Acker, Gloria Anzaldúa, Giannina Braschi, Rabih Alameddine, Don DeLillo, or Ruth Ozeki. Currently she is working on memory loss in contemporary US fiction. She has been a member of several funded research projects on multiculturalism in the US, ethnic literature, and hospitality.

Amanda Ellen Gerke
is Assistant Professor at the University of Salamanca where she teaches classes on English language, culture and linguistics at the undergrad and postgraduate

levels. She has teaching and research experience in various international universities, both in the United States, and in Europe, including George Fox University (US), Portland State University (US) the University of Cambridge (UK), and the University of Coimbra (Portugal), among others. Her work in sociolinguistics started in Portland, Oregon, US, as the director of a non-profit organization that assisted women in prostitution and sex-work, and gave various talks and conference presentations for the government and other NGO s, with an emphasis on the ways in which sex-workers and other marginalized people are portrayed and understood through various social lenses, including social discourse. Her research trajectory has included a multidisciplinary focus on approaches in cognition, linguistics, sociolinguistics, and ties these together with cultural studies including border studies, cultures in contact, and hospitality. Gerke has formed part of multiple national and international research groups on hospitality and is currently a linguistic analyst and researcher addressing educational policy according to sociolinguistic representations of students with special needs in the Spanish education system.

Luisa María González Rodríguez
is an Associate Professor in English language and linguistics at the University of Salamanca (Spain), where she combines research on literature and linguistics. Her main field of research is American literature, with an emphasis on the politics and aesthetics of postmodernism and postmodern short fiction and poetry. She is also interested in the use of multicultural literature to develop intercultural competence in foreign language contexts, and in the use of dialect in fiction. She has written on a variety of authors, including John Fowles, Barth, Barthelme, W. H. Gass, Lyn Hejinian, and Sandra Cisneros. Her latest research is related to the topic of hospitality and the poetics of space in Sandra Cisneros and Piri Thomas. She is currently editing a volume entitled *Towards New Perspectives on Latinidad in American Literature and Culture* to be published by Brill Publishers. She has also participated in numerous research projects on American short story, American poetry and the frontiers of hospitality in US and Europe.

Santiago Rodríguez Guerrero-Strachan
is a Senior Lecturer at the University of Valladolid. He has published extensively on the relations between Spanish and American literatures and on the short story. His research interests include American literature of the Romantic and Modernist periods. He has written extensively on the reception of Edgar Allan Poe in Spain, on the readings of Wallace Stevens's work by Spanish poets, and has translated and edited several anthologies of American short fiction.

José R. Ibáñez
is Associate Professor of American Literature and English Studies at the University of Almeria, Spain. He is coeditor of *Contemporary Debates on the Short Story* (Peter Lang 2007). With Blasina Cantizano, he has published *Una llegada inesperada y otras historias* (Encuentro 2015), an anthology in Spanish of thirteen stories by Ha Jin. He has also published articles and book chapters on American Southern literature (Flannery O'Connor, André Dubus, Moira Crone, and Tim Gautreaux), the Jewish American short story (Bernard Malamud, Nathan Englander), and on the translation and reception of Edgar Allan Poe among nineteenth and twentieth century Spanish authors.

Laura López Peña
(PhD Universitat de Barcelona, 2013) is currently a lecturer at EU Mediterrani, Universitat de Girona (Spain), where she centers her teaching within the degrees in Tourism and Marketing. She has based her research on the works of Herman Melville, particularly his post-civil war poetry volumes *Battle-Pieces* (1866) and *Clarel: A Poem and Pilgrimage in the Holy Land* (1876), on which she has published book chapters and articles such as "Dressing Uncivil Neighbor(hood)s. Walt Whitman's Adhesive Democracy in "Calamus" and *Drum-Taps*" (2014), "The Fate of Democracy in *Clarel* and the Creation of a Democratic Poem" (2014); "From Battle-Fields to Mounts of Stones: The Failed Promise of National Renewal in Herman Melville's *Battle-Pieces* and *Clarel*" (2014), and "The 'fatal embrace of the Deity': The Critique of American Exceptionalism in Herman Melville's *Clarel* (1876)" (2012), among other titles, together with the article on contemporary British playwrights Edward Bond and Sara Kane "Witnesses Inside/Outside the Stage. The Purpose of Representing Violence in Edward Bond's *Saved* (1965) and Sara Kane's *Blasted* (1995)" (2009). Last but not least, she has also published the book *Beyond the Walls. Being with Each Other in Herman Melville's Clarel* (2015), dedicated exclusively to *Clarel* as a literary space analyzing the political potentiality of intersubjectivity for the creation of forms of togetherness that radically question traditionally dividing categorizations of both personal and communitarian identities. In 2011, she was awarded the Melville Society Archive Fellowship, which allowed her to enrich her research on the works of Herman Melville in New Bedford, MA.

Ana María Manzanas Calvo
is Full Professor of American Literature and Culture at University of Salamanca (Spain). Her publications include *Hospitality in American Literature and Culture: Spaces, Bodies* (Routledge 2017), *Borders Occupying Space in*

American Literature and Culture: Social Movements, Occupation, and Empowerment (Routledge 2014), *Cities, Borders, and Spaces in Intercultural American Literature and Film* (Routledge 2011), *Uncertain Mirrors: Magical Realism in US Ethnic Literatures* (Rodopi 2009), and *Intercultural Mediations: Mimesis and Hybridity in American Literatures* (LIT Verlag 2003), all of them coauthored with J. Benito. She has edited and coedited collections of essays, such as *Literature and Ethnicity in the Cultural Borderlands* (Rodopi 2002), and *Border Transits: Literature and Culture across the Line* (Rodopi 2007). With J. Benito she is general editor of the Brill Series "Critical Approaches to Ethnic American Literature."

Ángel Mateos-Aparicio
obtained his Ph.D. at the University of Castilla-La Mancha (Ciudad Real, Spain), where he currently teaches as an Associate Professor. His main research interests focus on the intersection of science fiction, mainstream postmodern literature, and postmodern culture. Among his recent publications are the articles "Popularizing Postmodern Utopian Thinking in Science Fiction Film: *Matrix, V for Vendetta, In Time* and *Verbo*," in María del Mar Ramón Torrijos and Eduardo de Gregorio-Godeo (eds.), *Making Sense of Popular Culture* (2017); "Perfect Cities, Permanent Hells: The Ideological Coordinates of Urban Space in Postmodern Science Fiction," in David Walton y Juan Suárez (eds.), *Borders, Networks, Escape Lines: Contemporary Writing and the Politics of Space* (2017), and "The Frontier Myth and Racial Politics," in Masood Ashraf Raja, Jason W. Ellis and Swarapili Nandi (eds.), *The Postnational Fantasy: Essays on Postcolonialism, Cosmopolitics and Science Fiction* (2011).

Maria Antònia Oliver-Rotger
is an Associate Professor in the Department of Humanities at the Universitat Pompeu Fabra (Barcelona, Spain) where she teaches courses on English and American literature. Her main research interest is Chican@ Latin@ Literature with two specific focuses: The literary representation of the borderlands as lived and existential space, and, more recently, the testimonial, documentary, and auto ethnographic aspects of Chican@literature. She is a member of the state-funded research project "A Critical History of Ethnic American Literature: An Intercultural Approach (I-V) MINECO (2003-2019). Her publications include academic essays in journals such as *Journal of American Studies, Melus, Aztlán, Signs,* and *Interdisciplinary Literary Studies,* the monograph *Battlegrounds and Crossroads: Social and Imaginary Space in Writings by Chicanas* (Rodopi 2003), and the edited volume *Identity, Diaspora and Return in American Literature* (Routledge 2015).

Patricia San José Rico
is an Associate Professor in the Department of English Studies at the University of Valladolid. In 2013 she defended her thesis on the representation of trauma in contemporary African American literature, which has since become her main research interest. She has published several book chapters including " 'It's Black, It's White, It's Hard for you to Get By': Discourses of Race, Color, and Ugliness in Contemporary African-American Novels" in *Discourses that Matter: Selected Essays on English and American Studies* (Cambridge Scholars 2013); "The writer as translator: Langston Hughes and his transcultural racial interpretation of the Spanish Civil War" in *Translation and Conflict—Narratives of the Spanish Civil War and the Dictatorship* (Palgrave Macmillan 2019), and a monograph entitled *Creating Memory and Cultural Identity in African American Trauma Fiction* (Brill 2019).

CHAPTER 1

Introduction: Hospitality in American Literature and Culture

Santiago Rodríguez Guerrero-Strachan, Amanda Ellen Gerke and Patricia San José Rico

Abstract

The introduction to this volume makes a brief survey of the concept of hospitality in history, focusing on Emmanuel Levinas and Jacques Derrida, and describes the content of the chapters. Starting with Immanuel Kant and his notion of hospitality based on reciprocity, the authors of the introduction move towards Levinas's ethical hospitality as it shapes our identity, since we are constituted by the Other's self. For Levinas, hospitality is defined in terms of space and of care, while Jacques Derrida attempted to reconcile the ethical and the political in his theorization of the concept in the light of contemporary needs. For him, it is absolutely necessary a negotiation between the law of the nation and the Law of hospitality, otherwise hospitality will always be conditioned.

This first chapter also summarizes how the authors of the book have written on the reflection of hospitality in American literature and culture, the way it has shifted to a discussion on race, culture and identity, and also the way it explains a new Other. The authors agree that literature and culture create a space that becomes a refuge for hospitality. Thus, language, space, and hospitality structure the book, since hospitality, though represented in terms of space, starts with linguistic interaction. The introduction also deals with the construction of dominant and subordinate identities in a space that is familiar and that eventually becomes the place of interaction, negotiation, social action, and linguistic hospitality. Finally, it also surveys briefly how hospitality has been represented in American literature across the centuries, and the ways in which American authors have responded to the political pressures of their times by representing either conditioned or unconditioned hospitality.

Keywords

American literature – American culture – hospitality – Jacques Derrida – Emmanuel Levinas

⋯

> America has its purpose: it must serve that purpose to the end: I look upon the future as certain: our people will in the end read all these lessons right: America will stand opposed to everything which means restriction—stand against all policies of exclusion: accept Irish, Chinese—knowing it must not question the logic of its hospitality. [...] Our conditions, ideals, causes, all point one way: that way cannot but be the way of freedom.
>
> WALT WHITMAN
> *With Walt Whitman in Camden*. Nov. 9, 1888

⋮

Despite Walt Whitman's expectations, more than a hundred years later policies of exclusion are widespread across the world. Recent political and social events have shown several migratory and refugee crises that prove that countries are reinforcing their conditions on hospitality. Thousands of Syrian refugees remain in unwelcoming and almost uninhabitable refugee camps in Turkey. Simultaneously, laws restricting immigration have been passed in countries such as Denmark and Hungary, while other countries such as Italy ban rescue ships from entering their territorial waters in the Mediterranean. The American sphere is no stranger to these global circumstances. The implementation of migratory restrictions, as well as a calculated and outspoken campaign to stigmatize and criminalize migrants are sparking heated debates in the US. Since the summer of 2018, for instance, the family separation policy at the Mexican-American border, in which immigrant families are broken up and held in detention facilities likened to concentration camps, has caused controversy and uproar. Although "Family values do not stop at the Rio Grande," as former President George W. Bush claimed, such a pronouncement bifurcates depending on which bank of the river you have in mind.[1] The "zero tolerance" approach of

---

[1] *The Economist* https://www.economist.com/leaders/2018/06/02/a-cruel-and-unusual-border-policy.

INTRODUCTION

the Trump administration is ostensibly intended to deter illegal immigration and enforce harsher legislation concerning border crossing. However, the accompanying cruelty and inhumane treatment seem to have become an end in themselves. Although some families have been reunited, many remain apart, housed in the numerous detention facilities that have popped up along the border, many of which remain unfit and unsafe for habitation since they were initially intended only for short-term use. Cases of physical and sexual abuse against detained adults and children continue to emerge, and it is still unclear whether some of these children will ever be reunited with their parents and guardians or will remain effectively orphaned. Reactions to these policies were, and continue to be, an indication of a profound rift in American society; some Americans are outraged, while others strongly defend and praise this practice. The ethical underpinnings of such policies were brushed aside by a Fox News commentator who defended the family separation claiming, "these are not *our* kids."[2] These mixed responses reflect the different ways in which hospitality is understood and approached, and to what extent it is constantly mediated by hostility and cruelty. How can a part of American society hold a group of people to humanitarian standards while others actively support policies that dehumanize an entire group and make them unworthy of humane treatment? What exactly does welcoming the Other entail, and how does the act of welcoming manifest across cultures, communities, and policies? It seems clear by now that America, in spite of Whitman's words, does not stand fully "opposed to everything which means restriction—stand against all policies of exclusion: accept Irish, Chinese." America, in fact, repeatedly questions the logic of its hospitality.

The border becomes the site *par excellence* to test this logic of hospitality. At the border, countries exert the right of admission and dispense welcoming or unwelcoming protocols against an outsider that, due to its difference, is often feared and unwelcome. In the words of Levinas, "[t]he other's entire being is constituted by its exteriority, or rather, its alterity" (1987, 76). This exteriority is perceived as inimical to the creation of a national identity, a "We the People," and a sense of belonging to a community or group. As Manzanas Calvo (2017) reflects, borders are "sites where political systems fortify the notions of nationality and national identity," and "speak volumes about the country's or the continent's values" (42). Questions of whom we welcome and how, are now being regressively redefined as American politics moves towards a future that may be either the end of the period marked by Reaganism or the beginning of

---

[2] https://www.washingtonpost.com/news/the-fix/wp/2018/06/22/fox-news-hosts-not-our-kids-statement-and-the-limits-of-compassion/?noredirect=on&utm_term=.5a1164edb45f.

a completely unknown era shaped by Trumpism, as Mark Lilla argues in *The Once and Future Liberal* (2018, 53–55). Trump's domestic politics, and the heated conversation between supporters and detractors have brought the notion of hospitality to the center of American politics.

Stemming from Jacques Derrida's and Emmanuel Levinas's notions of hospitality, as well as the contributions of more recent scholars such as Ana Mª Manzanas, Jesús Benito, and Puspa L. Damai, this volume tackles hospitality in American cultural, linguistic, and literary productions. Our aim is to discuss and analyze the intersubjective relations that hospitality creates and the ways in which hospitality and its modalities are generated by these relations. From Gayatri Spivak's notion of "hospitality from below," as discussed by Puspa Damai (this volume), to the different rings of conditionality that plague hospitality, according to Derrida, as well as the different manifestations of hospitality and hostility and their cultural and linguistic implications, this volume aims to explore hospitality and its relation to historical and contemporary politics in the United States, including immigration, minority communities, and questions of national identity construction through 'othering' processes.

1   An Overview of Hospitality

Emmanuel Levinas and Jacques Derrida were prominent in delving into notions of hospitality in the twentieth century. Long before them, in the eighteenth century, Immanuel Kant set down the bases of hospitality in *Perpetual Peace*, a text originally published in 1795. For Kant, the law of hospitality concerns the "right of a stranger not to be treated with hostility when he arrives on someone else's territory" (1991, 105) provided that he "behaves in a peaceable manner in the place he happens to be in" (106). As Garrett W. Brown has pointed out, Kant's notion of hospitality is not universal since it imposes severe limits on the rights of the guest (2010, 309–310). Kantian hospitality responds to Bartolomé de las Casas's experience in America, where European colonizers justified their pillaging of the New World on the basis that they had not been offered enough hospitality (313–314). For de las Casas, writing in *A Short Account of the Destruction of the Indies* in 1552, the natives had the right to be treated with respect and, more importantly, according to the principles of mutual hospitality (1992, 14). While for Kant the host has the obligation to treat his guest without hostility, the guest cannot threaten the host's material and spiritual life. Kant's hospitality is thus based on reciprocity insomuch as both hosts and guests are equally obliged to respect everyone else's "right to the earth's surface, which the human race shares in common" (106). In turn, this respect would not only grant the temporary right of visitation to foreign travelers, but would also guarantee the absence of violence and abuse of power in international relations. It was Kant's early meditations on political hospitality across borders that triggered Levinas's and Derrida's contemporary theories of hospitality, which have turned into a lens to address the experiences of migrants, refugees, and asylum seekers in a globalized world.

Emmanuel Levinas's concept of hospitality—directly related to his position as a Jewish post-Holocaust thinker—shifts the Kantian idea of reciprocity from the political to the ethical realm. Levinas argues in "Ethics of the Infinite" that we are not autonomous selves, but hold an inescapable obligation to and responsibility for the Other. Identity and alterity are intertwined to the point where "the Other haunts our ontological existence" (1984, 63). Subjectivity is shaped by the welcoming of the Other, as theorized in *Totality and Infinity* (1969, 51). This exposure to alterity, which is the foundation of ethics, takes the form of an epiphany in which the inwardness of the self meets the outwardness of the Other (51). For Levinas hospitality can only be possible if the private space of the home opens to the outside, if the individual ventures outside, becoming then an ethical subject. As the individual dwelling opens to exteriority, it facilitates "a coming to oneself, a retreat home with oneself as in a land of refuge, which answers to a hospitality, an expectancy, a human welcome" of the Other (155). In this circumstance, the 'I' becomes a hostage that can experience pity, compassion and proximity while being hospitable to the Other, as pointed out in *Otherwise Than Being* (1998, 177). Thus, hospitality for Levinas is based on care, since the self is obliged to respond to the Other, though the extent of that obligation to respond is never clearly stated, as Clive Barnett discusses (2005, 6).

Relying on Kant's and Levinas's theories of hospitality, Jacques Derrida revisited the concept in order to reconcile the political and the ethical in light of the needs of contemporary society. Derrida was aware of the aporia that Kant had circumvented in the eighteenth century, for he limited hospitality to the right of visitation but not of residence (22). In *Of Hospitality* (1997) Derrida addresses the ethics of welcoming (or not) the Other in his assertion of the double law of hospitality. He states that there must be a negotiation between the law of the land, and the intrinsic laws of hospitality. The policies and actions of border control must take into account the double notions of hospitality that simultaneously protect the host but also allow an unrestricted welcoming of the Other (66). Therefore, and according to Derrida ([1997] 2000, 25–27), if we are to apply the law of unlimited hospitality, then all strangers asking—or even not asking—for shelter should be welcomed and accepted regardless of the repercussions that such an act could have for the host and the community. This unconditional welcoming could go against the spirit of self-preservation (the law of the land) if the stranger poses—or is perceived to pose—a threat to the host country and its inhabitants, which immediately establishes the difference between acceptable and unacceptable guests.

In "Hostipitality" (2000), Derrida continues to revisit Kant's assessment of the conditions of universal hospitality in *Perpetual Peace*, in order to address "the historical, ethical, juridical, political, and economic questions of hospitality" (3). Although Derrida begins by stating that Kant's words hover over the essence of hospitality, in this same essay, he also admits that we do not know what hospitality is, "not yet" (6). In discussing Kant's essay, Derrida describes hospitality as a right and a duty to greet the Other as a friend, but always on the condition that the host remains the master of the domain (6). Derrida realizes that hospitality is intrinsically aporetic and binary by nature, as it is based on notions of friend/enemy or hospitality/hostility, which makes the host/guest relationship both precarious and hazardous for host and guest. The host risks invasion from the Other, and the guest may be in danger of becoming oppressed and controlled by the host: "there is a history of hospitality, an always possible perversion of the law of hospitality," as he pointed out in *On Cosmopolitanism* (2001, 17). Hospitality then becomes impossible. It is only through the conditional that the unconditional can happen, an aporia that gives way to the paradox he termed *hostipitality*,[3] a blend of 'hospitality' and 'hostility.'

Though Derrida initially reassessed the concept of hospitality in its religious and ethical overtones, his theories were particularly useful for casting hospitality onto the political arena. In fact, he wrote *On Cosmopolitanism* based on his address to the European Parliament, requesting the establishment of cities across Europe in which refugees could live safely (Damai 2005, 68–94). Clearly, hospitality has now absorbed the challenges that immigration is posing all over the world, be it in the Mediterranean or at the Mexican-American border, among many other regions. And yet we cannot simply circumscribe hospitality to refugees—that is, those strangers asking for asylum to which Derrida referred. Contemporary political experiences within and across national

---

[3] In an article published in 2000, Derrida articulated the term *hostipitality*, a portmanteau word which subverts the traditional meaning of hospitality, that of an unconditional welcoming which can never be fully accomplished, and which at the same time produces *a priori* a sentiment that such hospitality aims to mitigate (Still 2010, 18).

boundaries require that we include other groups (ethnic, religious, linguistic) that, due to historical and political circumstances, emerge as the almost invisible presence that allegedly menaces our personal and national identity. Similarly, it is imperative to extend the concept of hospitality beyond welcoming and unwelcoming protocols, as the field of post-migration studies claims. The field emphasizes the plurality of the post-migrant narrative arguing that it constitutes a crossroads that allows for an overcoming of binary identities concerning the migrant. The point at which a migrant becomes a post-migrant happens at the border, either physically or metaphorically, and yet, as this volume contends, the post-migrant, or the 'post-Other' is really what is of concern in terms of hospitality as a cultural concept. How is the post-migrant incorporated, tolerated, assimilated, excluded? How does the post-migrant find a place in the host society, or how are they allocated a place there? As the volume illustrates, there are many facets of the Other; each encounter entails a complex weaving of movement, decisions, morality, and interaction, hence our contention that hospitality takes place, or fails to take place during those encounters. Through analysis of the terms on which hospitality is granted or denied, we can extrapolate the terms by which the Other is recognized by those offering or denying hospitality.

This is the philosophical framework and the historical context that this volume converses with. *The Poetics and Politics of Hospitality in US Literature and Culture* draws from Levinas's and Derrida's tenets and attempts to address hospitality and its counterpart, hostility, by focusing on how both concepts relate to the perception and representation of the Other. The volume highlights how hospitality is reflected in American literature, how it has shifted to a contemporary discussion on race, culture, and identity, and how hospitality explains a 'new Other'—an Other that transculturalizes, transnationalizes, and transconceptualizes hospitality in our current world.

The volume also aims to follow Manzanas Calvo and Benito Sánchez's work (2017) by highlighting Michaud's statement that literature is a resource for hospitality because it is literature itself that provides a refuge for hospitality, giving it agency and its own language (in Manzanas Calvo and Benito Sánchez, 7). We claim, therefore, that literature acts as a bridge between a culture, its politics, and its diverse ideologies. Literature and culture create a responsibility to discuss hospitality. As Vidal Claramonte argues, "human beings are continually translating, inhabiting the other's language" (2014, 248), which in the end makes language a home where the writer may find a hospitable refuge. Hospitable languages and literatures go beyond the polyglot transit between languages that Braidotti identifies (1994, 11–12) and create hospitable spaces.

2 Hospitality and Language Interaction

Language, space, and hospitality create a conceptual triangle that is crucial for this volume because hospitality starts with an encounter and a linguistic interaction. In the encounter between host and guest, Derrida states that the guest

> has to ask for hospitality in a language which by definition is not his own, the one imposed on him by the master of the house, the host, the king, the lord, the authorities, the nation, the State, the father, etc. This personage imposes on him translation into their own language, and that is the first act of violence. That is where the question of hospitality begins: must we ask the foreigner to understand us, to speak our language, in all the senses of this term, in all its possible extensions, before being able and so as to be able to welcome him into our country? ([1997] 2000, 15)

The concept of hospitality is directly related to the process of constructing dominant and subordinate identities and the epistemological systems that promote these processes. For Levinas, language is fundamentally connected to hospitality, as it enables us to share our world with the Other. Sharing, welcoming, and inviting is at the heart of language interaction and the cognitive structures from which agency in language is created, as the language and the user both draw from and form each other. Jacques Derrida, in *Adieu to Emmanuel Levinas* (1999a), reflects that the one who receives (the host) is often transformed into the guest himself, as what he thinks of as his home—and therefore where he is able to receive guests—is not actually his home but a private space that changes from his own, to a space shared with the Other as soon as he opens the door. The home becomes a place of interaction, negotiation, social action, and linguistic hospitality. As soon as there is an open door for communication, the agency shifts from the host language to a new negotiation of meaning-making that includes the guest language.

Paul Ricoeur's concept of "linguistic hospitality" (2006, 6) breaks down the power of the dominant host and gives agency to the guest. In his work on translation, Ricoeur seeks to "chart a middle way which combine[s] both the empathy and conviction" of critical theory and the hermeneutics of deconstruction, giving way to a third path in translation studies (Kearney 2006, vii). This third path opens a gateway to a concept of translating *experience* (Ricoeur 2006, 6), where the act of translation allows an encounter between what is one's own and what is foreign. According to Ricoeur, this is "where the pleasure of dwelling in the other's language is balanced by the pleasure of receiving the foreign word at home, in one's own welcoming house" (2006, 10). Ricoeur's theories strive to break down power relations at the language level. The goal is to disappropriate the reader from the host language and culture by taking him or her to the language and culture of the guest and to a sympathetic understanding of the Other. This is most often seen in the literary use of code-switching in Latino and other US minority literatures where the phenomenon contributes to group identity-construction alongside their narrative contexts. Authors such as Junot Díaz, Gloria Anzaldúa, Elizabeth Acevedo, Helena Viramontes, and Sandra Cisneros, among many others, employ a type of code-switching and 'non-translation' that alludes to the uncomfortable confines of characters in a multicultural and multilingual space, and confront displacement with characters in conflict with traditional identities. These authors forge power through gaining 'actor/agent' status, since they shape not only the readers' notions of culture, identity, and value-systems, but also contribute to the overarching communities' sense of selfhood and experience.

Language interaction asserts that at the point of encounter with the Other, the language space that this encounter occupies transforms into a site of negotiation which occurs even in a monolingual situation where the guest takes on the language of the host. This connectedness of language and hospitality can be further explained by established notions in cognition. Through this understanding of social consciousness, the connections between hospitality and language interaction can be affirmed, as has been asserted by cognitive linguists. In essence, this is an intricate weaving of shared knowledge and a cognitive structure which, in turn, gives language users discourse strategies and a way to organize and maintain interaction. The sharing of these knowledge systems, both old and new, yields the communication that takes place inside the community. Knowledge structures, as Teun van Dijk argues, broaden the scope of focus from the processing of words and sentences to the experimental study of language production. This translates to how language users are able to "strategically produce, understand, store and recall complex discourse, establish local and global coherence and activate and apply knowledge in the construction of mental models" (2014, 11). One cannot hold the capacity for language without the input and interaction of another, whether that is from their in-group or out-group. In simpler terms, when imagining two language users (regardless of their reliance on the host-language, the guest-language, or something in-between), the two create a blended space that consists of connective experiences, thus forging a new and unique fusion of social schemata. The mental spaces and connections are constructed as the new discourse unfolds, and all the while the participants are making use of a particular schema. So, what happens in language at the point of the encounter with the Other? Who, then, is the dominant and who is the conformer? Is translation, or writing in the Other's language always a point of submission? And is conveying experience, despite the language employed, more powerful than the 'submission' of translation? In this volume, we aim to uncover some of the ways in which Derrida's "first act of violence" can be understood on broader terms of language interaction (translation, speech communities, and multimodal expressions, among others). These language interactions suggest that the primary host may not have as much power over the guest as it may seem.

3 Hospitality in Early American Literature

The creation of blended spaces resulting from linguistic displacement combines, in early American experiences, with the need to engage in forms of hospitality in dislocation. Hospitality during the Colonial period, the times of the Early Republic and Romanticism, is built around a significant reversal, insomuch as the Native Americans will figure as the emplaced guests, whereas the English colonists play the displaced hosts. This problematic reversal explains some features of hospitality in the early periods of American history. Though Brian Treanor argues that a displaced host cannot offer hospitality (2011, 50), the representations of hospitality in American literature show that it is indeed possible, as Hawthorne's fiction attests, but that the displaced host creates a different way of understanding hospitality.

Rather than connecting the experience of hosting to the act of giving space to a visiting Other, early American experiences articulate a particular narrative of place and belonging. Hospitality is then subordinated to the issue of inclusion within a body politic and a national identity. In this context, hospitality becomes an instrument of discrimination which endows displaced hosts with the capacity to incorporate/exclude foreigners as part of a restrictive body politic, which was largely a religious body in colonial days. As Manzanas and Benito discuss, John Winthrop's arguments about the necessity of establishing limits for strangers was the first attempt to limit hospitality (2017, 18). Winthrop's "A Declaration in Defense of an Order of Court Made in May, 1637" would be one of the many attempts to discriminate against strangers who arrived in America with the aim of creating a 'Christian Utopia.' This kingdom of the Chosen People would be created, however, by legislating against the Christian doctrine of hospitality and putting the most radical doctrine of Puritanism at the forefront, as Nathaniel Hawthorne would show in his fiction.

John Hector Saint John of Crèvecoeur's *Letters of an American Farmer* (1782) is a fitting example of the displaced host. James represents the person who has settled in the country with the aim of living a self-sufficient life. For Crèvecoeur, he is the model of the new American, and in such a role he travels across the new nation describing its natural beauties, its wealth, and its resources. Rightfully enough, the jaunt in the South and the discovery of a black slave in a cage tinges the rest of the book with somber pessimism. The last letter is somewhat darker. James moves to the frontier to live with the Native Americans but eventually realizes that he is not a member of the tribe but rather an alien in that civilization. In a similar vein James Fennimore Cooper and Herman Melville deal with the same issue of Native hospitality to the Americans from the Americans' point of view.

Walt Whitman offers a different side of hospitality in the 1855 preface to *Leaves of Grass*: "Of them a bard is to be commensurate with a people. To him the other continents arrive as contributions … he gives them reception for their sake and his own sake" (1982, 7). Whitman, who regarded America as a nation composed of peoples from all over the world who would make America their home, did not regard himself as displaced. For him America is his native place, which is the soil, both geographic and cultural, from which he writes (Rodríguez Guerrero-Strachan 2018), and in which he offers unconditional hospitality to all the people who live in and come to America.

4   From Linguistics to Zombies: an Analysis of Hospitality in the American Scene

In this volume, the ethics and aesthetics of hospitality explore a matrix of understandings, approaches, and conditions that form part of the current conversation about hospitality. Through a focused study on different literary and cultural manifestations, we aim to continue a conversation that can identify moments or hospitality versus hostility, and, at the same time, see how those illustrations can redraw the concept of hospitality itself. As a point of departure, the volume opens with two chapters that challenge the classical understandings of the host-guest relationship by offering new approaches to the underlying dynamics that each role encompasses. The first of these, "Hospitality from Below? Native Americans in the Host-Guest Binary" by Puspa Damai focuses on Gayatri Spivak's concept of hospitality from below according to which a colonized subject acts as host to a colonizer guest. A new approach to the resident alien—a figure invisible in the immigrant model of hospitality—this chapter offers a postcolonial view on hospitality examining the place of Native America in the guest-host binary. It studies three novels dealing with the challenges faced by Native Americans in nineteenth-, twentieth-, and twenty-first century America: *The Life and Adventure of Joaquin Murieta* (1854); *Ceremony* (1977);

and *Flight* (2007). While this chapter follows Spivak in tracing the notion of hospitality from below in these three novels, it also interrogates Spivak's anthropocentric premise that flipping the roles and reinstating the colonized as host would be more hospitable, and constitute some form of decolonization. It argues that all three Native American novels mimic the immigrant/refugee model of hospitality. They depict hospitality from below not because Native Americans act as hosts but because a more immanent form of hospitality, of contiguity, cosmopolitanism and planetarity emerges from these narratives.

The idea of 'flipping roles' presented in the previous chapter gives way in Chapter 3 to another type of examination of role reversal, or rather, one that allows for a third plane of occupation. "Language Interaction and Hospitality: Combating the *Hosted-host* Figure" by Amanda Ellen Gerke opens the discussion of hospitality from a sociolinguistic point of view by demonstrating how the tensions within immigrant families can be seen as second-degree host-guest power relations. The chapter focuses on the concept of hospitality as rooted in the interactions, or non-actions between both the host and the guest. Hospitality is understood in this chapter through the dynamics of knowledge and power in which power is generated in relation to the Other, where one member has power and the other does not. Knowledge, or its lack, manifests in actions, and constitutes what pushes and pulls the hosts. Through readings of Junot Díaz's "Invierno" in *This is How You lose Her*, and Sandra Cisneros's *The House on Mango Street*, Gerke explores the notion of speech acts and knowledge systems that create language interaction and, in turn, shake up the rules of engagement between the host and guest, lending a conceptualization of the *hosted-host*. This figure, once a primary-guest but converted to a 'host of guests' (migrant women and children who comprise his family) creates a subdivision of roles, fulfilling a need to exert power over subaltern figures and exercise control over the matriarchal group. These notions are presented from a sociolinguistic and sociocognitive approach, demonstrating that, in terms of designated spatial and epistemic systems, the migrant males in these two collections have reacted to their own guest-status, and as a recompense, have taken on the role of the violent host in order to achieve supremacy. This chapter also contends that where the secondary guests observe that the lack of linguistic agency creates powerlessness, the ability to pass through planes of linguistic space will enable their powerful emergence.

Following the sociolinguistic discussion of hospitality offered in the volume, Chapter 4, "Latino Immigrants at the Threshold: A Sociolinguistic Approach to Hospitality in US *Barriocentric* Narratives," by Luisa González Rodríguez, draws on Levinas's predicament that language is inextricably connected to hospitality because it allows us to share the world with the Other. González

Rodríguez explores controversial issues related to language exchanges and linguistic tensions that arise when power, hospitality, and space are questioned and contested. US *barriocentric* novels vividly portray how linguistic boundaries separate outsiders from insiders by delimiting a psychic and linguistic territory where the immigrant is at a disadvantage in a decidedly monolingual host country. Like the preceding chapter, this chapter focuses on Sandra Cisneros's *The House on Mango Street*, but this time it is coupled with Piri Thomas's *Down these Mean Streets* and analyzed through the magnifying lens of language use and code-switching. The analysis seeks a deeper insight into the ways in which ethnolinguistic identities are constructed, and how power relationships are negotiated and challenged. In these novels, concepts of host/guest languages bring to the fore other concerns connected to displacement and unstable resettlement as well as identity issues that reflect a fractured mode of belonging. By challenging the power expressed through language, these characters also question the possibility of experiencing "migrant sites" (Kandiyoti 2009) as habitable places. Their refusal to use Standard English clearly proves they know that the spatial limitations are also linguistic barricades. Furthermore, by refraining from crossing the linguistic threshold, the viability of experiencing hospitable encounters and the host country's capacity to open up spaces of hospitality are seriously questioned.

Derrida's preoccupation with the act of violence that comes from a host imposing linguistic conditions on the guest, together with other sociolinguistic concerns about linguistic hospitality, may result in a particular case of violence inflicted on a guest. This is the type of violence that may occur not only when the guest is forced into an imposed linguistic situation, but also the type of violence that is inflicted by part of the guest's home-culture. Chapter 5, "(In)Hospitable Languages and Linguistic Hospitality in Hyphenated American Literature: The Case of Ha Jin" by José Ramón Ibáñez presents the inner conflict of a Chinese author, Ha Jin, who finds himself in a dichotomous inhospitable refuge. In its approach to hospitality from a sociolinguistic point of view, the chapter serves as a hinge between the discussion of hospitality from the realm of linguistic interaction and the analysis of hospitality in the American literary sphere. Forced to remain in the United States after seeing the response of Chinese authorities to the demonstration at Tiananmen Square in 1989, Ha Jin developed his entire literary career in English, a language that he learned after the end of Mao Zedong's Cultural Revolution. Writing in this language became a matter of survival and a safe haven to which this author retreated in an attempt to exile himself from Chinese, a language loaded with political jargon and unsuitable for the representation of his fictional worlds. Having accepted being an outcast from his native language—Chinese—Ha Jin's adopted language became, metaphorically speaking, both a *hospitable* and an *inhospitable space* in which he could secure a successful literary career at the expense of being accused of betrayal by both Chinese intellectuals and authorities, and through criticism of his particular use of English. This chapter examines Ha Jin's *exilic* condition and pays close attention to some of Ha Jin's best known essays: "In Defence of Forgiveness" and *The Writer as Migrant*. Ibáñez puts a particular emphasis on language and spaces of exile, and questions the double nature of rejecting one's own language and adopting another.

From the sociolinguistic approach the volume moves on to literary representations of hospitality. The next two chapters dissect the vision of hospitality in two key figures of early American Literature: Nathaniel Hawthorne and Herman Melville. In Chapter 6, "The Contention for Jollity and Gloom: Hospitality in Nathaniel Hawthorne's Historical Short Fiction," Santiago Rodríguez Guerrero-Strachan focuses on the author's short fiction, written at an early stage of his career. These stories, though popular, do not always appear as the first choices in anthologies or discussions of Hawthorne's works. The ambiguous status of being part of the canon while standing at its margin helps Rodríguez Guerrero-Strachan discuss hospitality through a new reading of Hawthorne's political ideas where hospitality is at the core of his narratives. Hawthorne was well acquainted with German Idealist philosophers, central among whom was Immanuel Kant. Rodríguez's reading of hospitality revolves around Kant's principles as expressed in *Perpetual Peace*. More specifically, the principle that the guest not be allowed to use hospitality to inflict harm on the host. In "The May-Pole of Merry Mount" and "John Endicott and the Red Cross," Hawthorne discusses, in a typically ironical manner, the problems that hospitality posed to the Americans by fictionalizing the Puritans' encounters with native inhabitants and other colonists, while playing the role of the displaced host that does not take into account the Kantian law of hospitality. In "The Gentle Boy" Hawthorne adds new nuances to the topic of hospitality and the question of national identity. Whether America would be a nation built upon religious tolerance or upon the strict principles of a single religion was an excuse to talk about concepts such as 'Manifest Destiny' and the 'empire for liberty.'

Laura López Peña chooses a much-neglected text of Herman Melville, the long poem *Clarel*, to discuss the issue of hospitality in "(In)Hospitable Encounters in Herman Melville's *Clarel*." Melville, along with Hawthorne, is rightly regarded as a 'dissenter' from his contemporary American society. In her approach to hospitality, López Peña addresses the multiplicity of subjectivities that unfold in Melville's works. Drawing from Derridean and Levinasian versions of hospitality, she converses with Martin Buber's concept of openness towards the Other and Hannah Arendt's ideas about the dialogic process by which people make sense of the world together. Thus, the dialogic nature of *Clarel*, and of *Moby-Dick*, accounts for the plural encounter of the characters where the 'you' is always an 'I.' Through the awareness that the Other's strangeness is not so, unconditional hospitality is vindicated in Melville's poem. The setting of the poem, Jerusalem, represents both the potentiality of unconditional hospitality and the site of inhospitable encounters.

The next chapter, "Eating, Ethics, and Strangers: Hospitality and Food in Ruth Ozeki's Novels" by Cristina Garrigós, focuses on yet one more aspect of hospitality: food and food offerings and analyzes it in the, to date, three novels published by the American-Canadian author, filmmaker, and Zen Buddhist priest Ruth Ozeki. By highlighting tropes of food preparation, food consumption, and even metaphorical cannibalism in the three novels analyzed, Garrigós shows how hospitality is very much related to food and to culture clash in Ozeki's literary production, and she explores how offering or denying hospitality across different cultures and among strangers, as well as through and around food and food rituals, often results in the creation of specific host-guest relationships and even in the reversal of those relationships. This chapter, therefore, goes back to previously explored notions of conditional/unconditional hospitality and host/guest binaries by tackling the acceptance or rejection of difference in terms of differing cultures, ideologies, and food rituals.

Chapters 9, 10, and 11 also explore culture clash and hostility as portrayed in contemporary novels, but this time with a focus on race as a marker of otherness by taking into account that race, while an obvious marker of 'othering,' is not always construed in terms of mere physical difference. Chapter 9, "'It's a Long Way to Tipperary': The Relation Between Race and Hospitality in the Irish-American Experience and its Literary Representation" by Patricia San José Rico, draws on Noel Ignatiev's *How the Irish Became White* in order to question the concept of race and illustrate how, especially in the case of Irish immigrants to the US, race can be read in terms of social status rather than physical difference. Through a review of the circumstances surrounding American Society's initial treatment of Irish immigrants, such as the consistent stereotyping processes that labeled the Irish in the US as unavoidably poor, violent, and papist as well as the mechanisms by which Irish-Americans managed to revert those stereotypes, San José Rico illustrates how the Irish's cultural, religious, and, most especially, social differences earned them the label of racialized Others despite their apparent physical and linguistic similarities with the dominant society.

"Hospitality Rituals and Caribbean Migrants: Tom Wolfe's *Back to Blood*, Ana Lydia Vega's 'Encancaranublado,' and Francisco Goldman's *The Ordinary*

Seaman," by Ana María Manzanas Calvo continues with the notion of hostility towards the racialized migrant Other and its representation in literature by analyzing, in this case, the experience of Caribbean migrants before and after their arrival in the US as portrayed in the two novels and the short story referenced in the title. Navigating between images of land and water, sea and coast, and the boat/ship as a transitional space of *hostipitality*, the chapter brings to the fore the ambivalent relationship between hospitality and hostility, exclusion and inclusion, as well as the double consciousness of being both guest and host and of the host turned guest. Resonating with notions from the previous chapters such as that of the *hosted-host*, or the power relations established as a result of language barriers among hosts and guests, this chapter goes back to the issue of racial and linguistic difference as a marker of otherness in the US and, consequently, as a rationale behind hostility towards the racialized migrant.

If hospitality was mostly theorized on board the ship or the water in the previous chapter, Chapter 11, "Tim Z. Hernandez's *Mañana Means Heaven*: Love on the Road and the Challenge of Multicultural Hospitality" by Maria Antònia Oliver Rotger, focuses on the road as a liminal space where hospitality between cultures and races can ideally take place, insomuch as it comes to be understood as a potentially transgressive force between boundaries. Discourses on race as a marker of otherness return in this chapter as the author compares the apparent forceful racialization of Bea Franco in the fictionalization of her relationship with Jack Kerouac that appears in the second chapter of *On the Road* and in his short story "The Mexican Girl" to the clearly white-looking yet more culturally distinct real Bea Franco as depicted in Tim Z. Hernandez's metafictional retelling of this story: *Mañana Means Heaven*. Again, otherness as a realization of social status rather than physical difference is brought to the fore in Hernandez's problematization of the "stereotyped cultural fantasies of the Other" and the myth of multicultural hospitality present in Kerouac's work.

Finally, to close the discussion of the Other, Chapter 12, "'Parasites in a Host Country': Migrants, Refugees, Asylum Seekers, and other Zombies in *The Walking Dead*" by Ángel Mateos-Aparicio and Jesús Benito Sánchez take up the notion of the parasitic migrant Other again, this time focusing on what we could call 'the new race': the Zombie. The chapter recaptures the previous discussions on conditional and unconditional hospitality in the face of the alien Other through the analysis of the popular TV series *The Walking Dead*. Mateos-Aparicio and Benito Sánchez provide an overview of the different interpretations of the zombie as the "fictional expression of Western anxieties over capitalist exploitation, consumerism, and mass immigration," while at the same time problematizing acts of hospitality and hostility, whether it is among humans or towards zombies and paralleling them to contemporary American society. By drawing parallels between the representation of the zombie in the series with that of the migrant in American culture, the authors place emphasis once more on the issue of the migrant or the otherwise displaced person as the parasitic Other, which is refused hospitality or is met with acts of open hostility and violence in the face of its menacing difference. The zombie is, therefore, regarded as the result of the oppression imposed by the capitalist system on the hordes of cheap laborers, illegal immigrants, or asylum seekers that abound in our contemporary society and to which contemporary discourses of hospitality make reference.

The volume's broad scope, with myriad violent clashes and encounters, represents an exponential shift away from the fundamental and ancient rules of hospitality: the right of the stranger has been stripped from him, and the host has acquired a kind of entitlement that goes against the very nature of the virtue. *The Poetics and Politics of Hospitality in US Literature and Culture* illustrates that hospitality is no longer viewed as a virtue but as a weakness in the texture of national identities. The welcome of difference in Whitman's poem, quoted above, has given way to policies of exclusion. These are but a few of the issues that, through discussions on the image and subjectivity of the Other in a variety of linguistic and cultural representations, are addressed in the following chapters.

References

Barnett, Clive. 2005. "Ways of Relating: Hospitality and the Acknowledgement of Otherness." *Progress in Human Geography* 29 (1): 5–21.

Braidotti, Rosi. 1994. *Nomadic Subjects*. New York: Columbia UP.

Brown, Garrett W. 2010. "The Laws of Hospitality, Asylum Seekers and Cosmopolitan Right. A Kantian Response to Jacques Derrida." *European Journal of Political Theory* 9 (3): 308–327.

Damai, Puspa L. 2005. "Messianic-City: Ruins, Refuge and Hospitality in Derrida." *Discourse* 27 (2/3): 68–94.

Damai, Puspa L. 2012. "Welcoming Strangers: Hospitality in American Literature and Culture." PhD diss., University of Michigan, Ann Arbor.

De las Casas, Bartolomé. 1992. *A Short Account of the Destruction of the Indies*. Translated by Nigel Griffin. London: Penguin.

Derrida, Jaques. (1997) 2000. *Of Hospitality: Anne Duformantelle Invites Jacques Derrida to Respond*. Translated by Rachel Bowlby. Stanford: Stanford UP.

Derrida, Jaques. (1997) 2001. *On Cosmopolitanism and Forgiveness.* Translated by Mark Dooley and Michael Hughes. London and New York: Routledge.
Derrida, Jacques. 1999a. *Adieu to Emmanuel Levinas.* Stanford: Stanford UP.
Derrida, Jacques. 1999b. "Hospitality, Justice and Responsibility: A Dialogue with Jacques Derrida." In *Questioning Ethics: Contemporary Debates in Philosophy*, edited by R. Kearney and M. Dooley, 65–83. London: Routledge.
Derrida, Jacques. 2000. "Hostipitality." *Angelaki* 5 (3): 3–18.
Kandiyoti, Dalia. 2009. *Migrant Sites: America, Place, and Diaspora Literatures.* Hanover, NH: Dartmouth College P.
Kant, Immanuel. (1970) 1991. "Perpetual Peace: A Philosophical Sketch." In *Kant's Political Writings*. 2nd ed., edited by Hans Reiss, 93–130. Cambridge: Cambridge UP.
Kearney, Richard. 2006. "Introduction: Ricoeur's Philosophy of Translation" in Paul Ricoeur *On Translation.* New York and Abingdon: Routledge, pp. vii–xx.
Levinas, Emmanuel. 1969. *Totality and Infinity: An Essay on Exteriority*, translated by Alphonso Lingis. Pittsburgh: Duquesne UP.
Levinas, Emmanuel. 1984. "Ethics of the Infinite." In *Dialogues with Contemporary Continental Thinkers: The Phenomenological Tradition*, edited by R. Kearney. 47–70. Manchester: Manchester UP.
Levinas, Emmanuel. 1987. *Time and the Other and Additional Essays.* Translated by Richard A. Cohen. Pittsburgh: Duquesne UP.
Levinas, Emmanuel. 1998. *Otherwise Than Being or Beyond Essence.* Translated by Alphonso Lingis. Pittsburgh: Duquesne UP.
Lilla, Mark. 2018. *The Once and Future Liberal.* London: Hurst.
Manzanas Calvo, Ana María. 2013. "Junot Díaz's 'Otravida Otravez' and Hospitalia: The Workings of Hostile Hospitality." *Journal of Modern Literature* 37 (1): 107–123.
Manzanas Calvo, Ana María. 2017. "The Line and Limit of Britishness: The Construction of Gibraltarian Identity in M.G. Sanchez's Writing." *ES Review. Spanish Journal of English Studies* 38: 27–45.
Manzanas Calvo, Ana María and Jesús Benito Sánchez. 2017. *Hospitality in American Literature and Culture. Spaces, Bodies, Borders.* New York and London: Routledge.
McCormick, Patrick T. 2004. "The Good Sojourner: Third World Tourism and the Call of Hospitality." *Journal of the Society of Christian Ethics* 24 (1): 89–104.
O'Gorman, Kevin. 2007. "Dimensions of Hospitality: Exploring Ancient and Classical Origins." In *Hospitality: A Social Lens*, edited by Lashley, Conrad, Paul Lynch and Alison J. Morrison, 17–32. Amsterdam: Elsevier.
Plant, Bob. 2003. "Doing Justice to the Derrida-Levinas Connection. A Response to Mark Dooley." *Philosophy and Social Criticism* 29 (4): 427–450.
Ricoeur, Paul. 2006. *On Translation.* New York and Abingdon: Routledge.
Rodríguez Guerrero-Strachan, Santiago. 2008. "Exiliados y refugiados de la lengua." *En torno a los márgenes.* Madrid: Minotauro digital, 77–102.

Rodríguez Guerrero-Strachan, Santiago. 2018. "The Rhetorics of Hospitality in Walt Whitman's Specimen Days." *Miscelánea: a Journal of English and American Studies* 58: 67–82.

Still, Judith. 2005. "Derrida: Guest and Host." *Paragraph* 28 (3): 85–101.

Still, Judith. 2010. *Derrida and Hospitality: Theory and Practice*. Edinburgh: Edinburgh UP.

Treanor, Brian. 2011. "Putting Hospitality in its Place." In *Phenomenologies of the Stranger: Between Hostility and Hospitality*, edited by Richard Kearney and Kascha Semonovitch, 49–66. New York: Fordham UP.

Van Dijk, Teun. 2014. *Discourse and Knowledge: A Sociocognitive Approach*. Cambridge: Cambridge U P.

Vidal Claramonte, M. Carmen África. 2014. "Translating Hybrid Literatures. From Hostipitality to Hospitality." *European Journal of English Studies* 18 (3): 242–262.

Whitman, Walt. 1982. *Complete Poetry and Collected Prose*. Edited by Justin Kaplan. New York: The Library of America.

Winthrop, John. (1637) 2003. "A Declaration in Defense of an Order of Court Made in May, 1637." In *Puritan Political Ideas, 1558–1794*, edited by E. S. Morgan, 145–48. Cambridge: Yale UP.

CHAPTER 2

Hospitality from Below? Native Americans in the Host-Guest Binary

Puspa Damai

Abstract

A non-Western immigrant seeking or receiving hospitality in the metropolitan centers of the West is a paradigm that dominates contemporary discourses on hospitality. Jacques Derrida tweaked this paradigm by adding to the category of the immigrant-guest a variety of new figures including the homeless or stateless asylum seekers, foreigners, exiles, nomads, and refugees. Though Derrida deconstructs the host-guest binary, still the West in his scheme of things occupies the place of the host. Gayatri Spivak traces a different law of hospitality which she calls "hospitality from below" according to which a colonized subject acts as host to a colonizer guest. This postcolonial view on hospitality apotheosizes a figure she calls a resident alien—a figure invisible in the immigrant model of hospitality championed both by the thinkers of multiculturalism and deconstruction.

Using Spivak's notion of hospitality from below as its point of departure, this essay examines the place of Native America in the guest-host binary. It studies three novels dealing with the challenges faced by Native Americans in the nineteenth, twentieth and twenty-first century America: *The Life and Adventure of Joaquin Murieta* (1854); *Ceremony* (1977); and *Flight* (2007).

While this paper follows Spivak in tracing the notion of hospitality from below in these three novels, it also interrogates Spivak's anthropocentric premises that flipping the roles and reinstating the colonized as host would be more hospitable, and it would constitute some form of decolonization. It argues that all three Native American novels mimic the immigrant/refugee model of hospitality. They depict hospitality from below not because Native Americans act as hosts, but because a more immanent form of hospitality of contiguity, cosmopolitanism, and planetarity emerges from these narratives.

Keywords

hospitality – Native American literature – Jacques Derrida – Gayatri Spivak – decolonization

1   From Courteous Host to Dependent Nations

Roger Williams (1603–1683), English colonist and Puritan minister, who founded the colony of Providence, Rhode Island by purchasing or receiving the land from "his Indian friends, Canonicus and Miantinomo" (Mudge 1871, 85), gives a curious title to his 1643 study of a local 'Indian' dialect: *A Key Into the Language of America*. He could have called the book *A Study of Indian Language* or *How to Learn the Narragansett Dialect* or *The Tribal Language of the Bay Colony Indians*. He not only calls the Narragansett dialect 'a language,' he also calls the study 'a key' and the dialect 'language of America,' thereby implying that the continent belongs to Native Americans. In his evaluation of the customs, manners, and religious beliefs of the natives of New England, Williams notes that the Narragansett Indians are "remarkably free and courteous to invite all Strangers in; and if any come to them upon any occasion, they request them to *come in*, if they come not in of themselves" (Williams 1997, 7). Williams was in a unique position to approach and mingle with natives upon his banishment from the Massachusetts Bay Colony after his accusations that King Charles had no right to grant the land to immigrants because Native Americans were the true owners of it. Williams considered it a sin "to take and give away the lands and countries of other men" (Williams 2007, 461).

About two centuries after Williams's study, in 1831, the Supreme Court heard and ruled on a seminal case concerning the fate of Native Americans in the United States: *Cherokee Nation vs. the State of Georgia*. In his majority opinion, Chief Justice John Marshall (1755–1835) acknowledged that Native Americans "have an unquestionable, and heretofore unquestioned, right to the lands they occupy," yet these tribes "which reside within the acknowledged boundaries of the United States" may only "be denominated domestic dependent nations," for "they are in a state of pupilage; their relation to the United States resembles that of a ward to his guardian" (Marshall 2001).

How did the status of Native Americans change from owners of the land to domestic dependent nations? What historical and political events reduced the "free and courteous" hosts to become "the ward[s]" of the United States? One obvious answer to these questions is the fact that between Williams's attribution of host-status to Native Americans and Marshall's reduction of them to that of mere dependence, lies the eventful and paradoxical history of simultaneous colonization and postcolonial nation-building in the United States. What these two textual examples (Williams's study and Marshall's majority opinion) reveal, however, is the role hospitality has played in American history. Hospitality not only helps us gauge the shift in the fortune of Native Americans, it also indicates how, potentially, it could be instrumental in any course correction of history towards what the Bureau of Indian Affairs has clearly identified: Native America's self-governance and self-determination (Indian Affairs n.d.). If the use and abuse of hospitality represent the process of colonization in North America, hospitality also potentially foreshadows Native America's post-colonial condition.

2   Hospitality and Postcolonial Theory

Despite this crucial relevance of hospitality to the analysis of colonization of Native Americans in the United States, the topic apparently suffers a double disavowal: both American literary studies and postcolonial studies overlook hospitality. This chapter intends to examine these denials, particularly within the field of postcolonial theory in congruence with discussions on "the absence of hospitality as a *critical* concept in American studies" (Damai 2012, 9). To welcome hospitality to the discussion of American literature in general, and Native American literature in particular, will not only help us articulate America's unique colonial history but it will also help us theorize the decolonization of Native America.

And yet hospitality marks a space of insightful blindness at the heart of postcolonial theory. The anti-colonialist and anti-imperialist movements of the twentieth-century neither needed nor wanted to think about hospitality. Whether it is Mahatma Gandhi's 'Quit India' or Marcus Garvey's 'Africa for Africans,' hospitality figured as almost irrelevant to most anti-colonialist movements across the globe. Postcolonialism, by contrast, is unthinkable without hospitality insofar as the postcolony calls for a relationship not of resistance or collaboration but of conviviality "fraught by the fact of the commandment and its subjects having to share the same living space" (Mbembe 2001, 104). And yet, none of the *major* postcolonial thinkers engages directly with hospitality. In fact, barring a few exceptions (e.g., Mireille Rosello's *Postcolonial Hospitality* (2001)), postcolonial theory, in general, fails to dwell on hospitality. Even Homi Bhabha's *Our Neighbors, Ourselves* (2011), which represents postcolonial theory's almost solitary treatment of hospitality, dwells only remotely on the topic, for it lumps hospitality as one convenient term with other terms in the now all-too-familiar Bhabhaesque repertoire: liminalities, ambivalence, third-ness (Bhabha 2011, 6).

Why would postcolonial theory deliberately or unwittingly refuse to engage with hospitality even when its very origin and nature imply that it owes its existence and survival to nothing but hospitality? One of the reasons, perhaps, is postcolonial theory's inability to seriously come to terms with settler colonialism. Settler colonialism represents a process of displacing and in certain cases exterminating the indigenous population of a colony in order to claim it as home or mother country for the colonizers. The brutal nature of settler colonialism has led one of its critics to claim that one and only one logic dominates settler colonialism, and that logic is "negative articulation" or "elimination," which "strives to replace indigenous society with that imported by colonizers" (Wolfe 1999, 27). However, other theorists believe that beyond the logic of elimination, settler colonialism "actively produces refugees" (Veracini 2015, 103) so that "that which remained could be subtly absorbed within the dominant culture" (Hixon 2013, 12). Settler colonialism turns indigenous people into refugees whereby colonists appropriate the role of hosts. Thus, any act of decolonization in a settler colonial society would have to imagine a politics of recognizing natives as hosts.

3 Hospitality from Below?

One unique model of such politics can be found in Gayatri Spivak's very short piece "Resident Alien" (2002). Even though Spivak's discussion of hospitality in this piece reads like an after-thought triggered by her encounter with Jacques Derrida's *Of Hospitality*, and even though the map into which Spivak spreads her scattered thoughts on hospitality might not exactly be contiguous with settler colonialism, her model nevertheless is capable of opening up a space quite hospitable to indigeneity. At the center of Spivak's text is her reading of Rabindranath Tagore's novel: *Gora*. Tagore's novel tells the story of the titular character Gora—the White One—who espouses an orthodox ideology of Hindu nationalism as a foil against the British Raj, only to discover that he himself is an outsider—an Irish foundling adopted and raised by a childless Bengali Brahmin couple. Spivak calls this historically unverifiable and fictional figure a "resident alien," (47) who she juxtaposes with immigrants from Third World countries in search of citizenship in the multicultural metropolis of the West.

Perhaps following a cue from Derrida's juxtaposition of conditional and unconditional hospitality (Derrida [1997] 2000, 25), Spivak contrasts her own duplex of hospitality: one revolving around the figure of the immigrant and the other that of the resident alien. If we stretch the parallel a bit further, an immigrant in the metropolitan West belongs to the conditional hospitality of postcolonial diaspora and globalization. A resident alien must then mirror Derrida's concept of unconditional hospitality in the sense that the figure defies conditions of law and citizenship. Spivak places the resident alien beyond the dyad of the immigrant-guest from the Third World and the citizen-host of the First World. However, the parallel between Derrida and Spivak ends right there, for Spivak questions the rigid, stable and therefore conditioned binary of immigrant-guest and citizen-host in Derrida's putatively unconditional hospitality. A resident alien for Spivak proposes a new paradigm which she calls "hospitality from below" in which the colonizer is guest to the colonized host (Spivak 2002, 54).

Spivak's intriguing reading of Tagore's *Gora* yields an illuminating perspective on hospitality vis-à-vis postcoloniality. The fact that her concept of 'hospitality from below' is premised on anagnorisis—the critical discovery of Gora's *outsiderness* at a moment when he felt an unassailable *insiderness*—its resonance with settler colonialism is unmistakable. Settler colonialism institutes the false consciousness of *nativeness* in figures who refuse to recognize their resident *alienness*. The discourse of hospitality to immigrants not only perpetuates this ideology of *nativeness*, it also forestalls the moment of anagnorisis; the task of postcolonial literature and theory is, as Spivak seems to imply, not only to distinguish between a multicultural/immigrant model of hospitality and hospitality from below, but also to precipitate the moment of anagnorisis.

If we summarize Spivak's theorization of 'hospitality from below,' foregrounding of anagnorisis would intimate at least four key movements: (i) a subtle reversal in the host-guest binary in which the native reappropriates the role of host from the colonizer, (ii) the native critiques the law of the father, (iii) anagnorisis reveals a space of intimacy between colonizer and native; and (iv) the possibility of 'a wild justice.' If settler colonialism institutes the colonizer as host thereby turning the colonized into a perpetual resident alien, any attempt at decolonization must reverse the host-guest binary by turning the son against the law of the father even at the cost of endorsing a wild form of justice in which violence becomes necessary and justified. Spivak's notion of wild justice refers to Mahashweta Devi's story "The Hunt" in which Mary, daughter of a tribal woman raped by her white master, decides to kill her pursuer by luring him to a secret ravine, playing a game of love with him, then chopping him up with her machete (Devi 1995, 16). Spivak believes that Mary's solitary wild justice violently redresses the brutalities and injustices of history against subalterns. It seeks to correct the failure of decolonization insofar as Mary's resistance or revolt against her perpetrator goes beyond her personal revenge in order to initiate or institute "a reinscription of aboriginality" (Spivak 2002, 61). Spivak's notion of 'hospitality from below' as its point of departure, this essay examines the place of Native America in the guest-host binary. It studies three texts dealing with the challenges faced by Native Americans in nineteenth-, twentieth-, and twenty-first- century America: *The Life and Adventure of Joaquin Murieta* (1854) by Yellow Bird (1827–1867), a Cherokee; *Ceremony* (1977) by

Leslie Marmon Silko (1948–), a Laguna Pueblo; and *Flight* (2007) by Sherman Alexie (1966–), a Spokane-Coeur d'Alene Indian.

While this chapter follows Spivak in tracing the notion of 'hospitality from below' on these three novels, it also interrogates her anthropocentric and ontological premises that flipping the roles and reinstating the colonized as host would be more hospitable and would constitute some form of decolonization. It shows that all three of Native American novels discussed here mimic the immigrant model of hospitality. In other words, the moment of anagnorisis in these novels is not the critical and ironic discovery of the colonists' *outsiderness* or the imputation of host status to natives; anagnorisis in the novels rather hints at a moment which is potentially bigger than the guest-host binary implied by both 'hospitality from above' and 'below.' If they depict hospitality from 'below', they do so not in order to show Native Americans as hosts, but in order to underscore a more immanent form of hospitality of contiguity, cosmopolitanism, and planetarity.

4 Hospitality in Native American Literature

The novels by Bird, Silko, and Alexie have been selected for discussion here not because they are the *only* texts that effectively represent the field of Native American Literature nor because they cover the entirety of the topics, issues, or debates important to Native American writers. In fact, these novels are less similar to each other than alike in terms of their forms, themes, and even politics. Their singularity in fact may be what makes them more suitable for analysis in relation to hospitality as focusing on what makes them seem similar would necessitate excluding their differences, which is inhospitable. These novels provide a glimpse of the vicissitudes of fortune faced by Native Americans from the mid-nineteenth century to the present; and their singular agendas and approaches capture Native America's cultural, historical, and geographic diversity—a reminder that lumping all First Nations together as 'Indians' only perpetuates the ideology of colonialism—which a study on hospitality and decolonization must avoid at all costs. The only similarity that these novels or their authors may have, is that they foreground difference: if Yellow Bird and his family were accused of supporting the Indian Removal, Silko has been charged with revealing the sacred clan ceremonies of Indians to outsiders. For instance, Paula Gunn Allen in "Special Problems in Teaching Leslie Marmon Silko's 'Ceremony' " concludes that Silko's novel is "a clan story, and is not to be told outside the clan" (Allen 1990, 382). In the same vein, another Native American writer has accused Sherman Alexie of not being ethically responsible and not defending "treaty protected reservation land bases as homelands to the indigenes" (Cook-Lynn 1996, 68).

If these novelists are considered outliers, their novels, discussed here, could be dubbed oddities. The protagonists of these novels are outliers themselves who occupy marginal positions in Native American culture or are on the other side of the fence entirely. These characters exemplify what Spivak would call the resident alien—an intimate Other. Furthermore, these novels help us understand three major concepts from Spivak's theorization of hospitality: critique of the law of the father; access to an intimate space; wild justice through anagnorisis or restitution of native as host.

Individually none of these novels dwells on all three of the concepts above. However, each novel exemplifies one of the three critical steps that constitute Spivak's theory of hospitality. The dominant impulse in Yellow Bird's novel is revenge. It represents the critical and parricidal phase in Spivak's theory of hospitality. Silko's *Ceremony* is driven by the question of recuperation and *re-membering*—a slow ritualistic movement towards an intimate relationship with one's now forgotten self and the world. Alexie's novel represents as well as refutes Spivak's notion of wild justice through anagnorisis. Alexie's protagonist is haunted by the question of his true identity, but at the same time, he also exemplifies the impossibility of anagnorisis. Let's take a closer look at these novels, starting with the first published novel by a Native American writer.

Life and Adventures of Joaquín Murieta, the Celebrated California Bandit is a novel by John Rollin Ridge (1827–1867), who also went by his tribal name Yellow Bird. Considered to be the first novel published by a Native American writer, this text chronicles the 'true story' of a Mexican bandit who spreads, or plans to spread, a reign of terror in California. Yellow Bird was born in Georgia of a Cherokee father and a white mother, just a few years before President Andrew Jackson signed the Indian Removal Act in 1830 to remove Cherokees from Georgia. Yellow Bird's grandfather and father supported the removal, arguing that staying back would be costly and untenable, a view which in turn proved costly to Yellow Bird's family, for his father and grandfather were assassinated in Oklahoma by those Cherokees who were against the removal. These events together with the fact that Yellow Bird happened to kill a person later in his life have led critics to believe that *Joaquín Murieta* "is not only 'autobiographical' but in some spirit 'Indian'" (Allmendiger 1998, 37).

Yellow Bird's readers might have expected him to provide a story about the complex history of Indian removal, which resulted in the Trail of Tears. He chose, instead, to discuss the issue of Mexican immigration in California immediately after the Mexican-American War (1846–1848). Is this novel a plea for justice for Mexican immigrants, or an allegory of the affliction affecting

Native Americans? This question leads us to Spivak's fundamental distinction between the immigrant model of hospitality and the resident alien model of hospitality. The novel seems, on the one hand, to ask us to take a leap of imagination from a Mexican immigrant to a Native American resident alien. On the other hand, it questions our need or desire to have a protagonist identifiable or classifiable by culture, ethnicity, or race. Who is the real protagonist of Bird's novel, an immigrant or a native? A Cherokee or a Mexican? This ambivalence is the foundational anagnorisis on which other forms of anagnorisis are built in the novel.

The problem of recognizing the protagonist replicates three crucial questions of recognition. The first two questions are: "Is Joaquín Murieta a hero, or a bandit?" and "Is America an all-welcoming nation of immigrants, or a country which is not welcoming of immigrants from certain places such as Mexico?" The first of these questions deals with the moral overdetermination imposed on Murieta's character. Yellow Bird neither exonerates Murieta from the carnage the bandit causes nor does he refrain from praising the bandit for "his noble spirit which had been his original nature" (Bird 2003, 52). The second question of anagnorisis—does America welcome all or only some immigrants?—raises another key issue: how to distinguish an immigrant from a native if, in California circa 1850, Mexicans were both simultaneously natives and immigrants? After all, California became a US territory when the war between the United States and Mexico ended in 1848. The "lawless and desperate men who bore the name of Americans but failed to support the dignity of that title" (Bird 2003, 3) and who violently attacked Murieta and sexually assaulted his mistress were themselves 'immigrants' in California.

This uncertainty leads us to the third, and perhaps most important, question pertaining to anagnorisis in the context of settler colonialism: Who is the host and who is the guest in the novel? Once California belongs to the United States, Americans are hosts to all immigrants including Mexicans. However, for the hosts, Mexican immigrants are "infernal Mexican intruder[s]" (Bird 2003, 4), a racially motivated basis for their refusal to receive the guests. The Native American author of the novel at this point metaphorically steps in to defend Murieta's right to settle in California, thereby playing host to this Mexican immigrant; a crucial move that his fellow Native Americans, for whom Yellow Bird has nothing but disdain and disgust in the course of the narrative, have not performed.

If Americans thought of themselves as a "haughtier and superior race" to Mexicans as a way of justifying their tyranny and abuse (Bird 2003, 3), Murieta made revenge his sole objective in life. After chronicling several events of humiliation and violence to which Murieta and his mistress were unfairly subjected, and after referring to the bandit's violent response to those insults and injuries, Yellow Bird's narrator asks:

> Thus far, who can blame him? But the iron had entered too deeply in his soul for him to stop here. He had contracted a hatred of the whole American race, and he was determined to shed their blood whenever and wherever an opportunity occurred. (Bird 2003, 6)

Yellow Bird not only blames Americans for changing the noble Murieta into a monster, he also implies that Murieta's banditry results from the racial and political animus engendered by the Treaty of Guadalupe Hidalgo (1848), which, according to analyst Griswold del Castillo, "established a pattern of inequality between the two countries" and ensured that "Mexico would remain an under-developed country well into the twentieth century" (Castillo 1990, xii). Murieta's patricidal goal of revenge, that is, to shed the blood of his 'hosts'— "the whole American race" in general (Bird 2003, 6)—leads him to utilize his knowledge of the terrain and convert his revenge mission into a full-fledged revolt against America. Bird seems to discern a pattern of colonial subjugation repeated towards Mexico and Mexicans as had been the case with Cherokees and other Native Americans.

Murieta plans "a clean sweep" of the southern counties in California where he wished to kill "the Americans wholesale" (Bird 2003, 60). He wanted to wind up his career with this mission's completion; only then, he said, would his band be avenged of their "wrongs" and of "the wrongs done to [their] poor, bleeding country" (Bird 2003, 60). The readers know that his wish was never fulfilled, and yet this desire to effect a wild justice not only changes him in the eyes of his followers from a petty thief to a 'hero', it also makes him the resident alien (and not an immigrant) of which Spivak speaks, the sole agent of hospitality from 'below', or decolonization. If Spivak prefers a resident alien who is driven to defend herself by executing a wild justice as a reinscription of aboriginality—and if Bird follows the same path of wild justice in his bid to correct the failure of decolonization—then hospitality from below or even wild justice as unconditional hospitality for other Native American writers takes a somewhat different hue. If we fast forward a century and look at a twentieth-century Native American novel such as *Ceremony* (1977), we will notice that hospitality as a correction of the failure of decolonization represents a different kind of wild justice.

Leslie Marmon Silko's widely acclaimed *Ceremony* depicts the state of Native America in the United States during the tumultuous years of World War II. The novel revolves around Tayo, a mixed-blood Laguna Pueblo (like the novelist), who comes back home from the war in the Pacific with "battle fatigue" (Silko 2006, 7). His frail physique was devastated by nausea and fever, and his disoriented mind was haunted and tortured by hallucinogenic visitations of his dead relatives, and their scandalous mixing with the enemy. When doctors at a VA (Veterans Affairs) hospital in Los Angeles failed to ease his pain, Tayo's 'Grandma' referred him to two native medicine men: Old Ku'oosh and Betonie. Thus began Tayo's personal, as well his people's collective, journey towards healing, "re-membering" (Weaver 2003, 216) and self-discovery through ceremonies or rituals derived from ancient Pueblo stories.

Ceremony, according to Peter Beidler, is "a series of discoveries: the discovery in himself [Tayo] of the ability to use words; the discovery that there is life to be derived from an infusian (sic) of Mexican blood; the discovery that evil and witchery can be resisted [...] the discovery that Betonie's ceremony can indeed cure" (Castillo 1990, xii). We must add to Beidler's list of those discoveries initiated and actualized by *Ceremony*'s central anagnorisis Tayo's transition, not just from confusion to clarification but also from the margins of Laguna Pueblo culture and identity to their center. Tayo's recuperation accompanies the reversal of his condition from a refugee or recluse to someone central to the reinvention and transformation of ancient ceremonies. This reversal is instrumental in elevating Tayo from his peripheral position to the center, thereby making him a host. This shift from the margins to the center, however, does not represent 'hospitality from below' in the sense in which Spivak evoked the terms. Spivak's understanding of hospitality wittingly or unwittingly remains anthropocentric and ontological such that a colonized subject reverses role from guest to host and initiates the event of anagnorisis. Ceremonies in Silko epitomizes processes of recuperation and reversal which are larger than an individual.

In his interaction with Betonie, Tayo quickly realizes that "the white doctors" were wrong in advising that "he had to think only of himself" because his "sickness was only part of something larger, and his cure would be found in something great and inclusive of everything" (Silko 2006, 116). Betonie makes him understand that healing and hospitality must converge and that, in order for Tayo to be fully cured, he must locate something larger and all-inclusive. What afflicts him, therefore, is not necessarily the war alone but all the events of the abuse of hospitality of which war is an instance. The fundamental anagnorisis in *Ceremony*, therefore, is Tayo's ability to make this connection between hospitality and healing.

If Tayo's own aunt is ashamed of him for being a "bastard" child, he is despised by his peers on the reservation for being a half-breed (Silko 2006, 39). Emo, for instance, minces no words when he accuses and attacks Tayo: "You drink like an Indian, and you're crazy like one too—but you aren't shit, white trash. You love Japs the way your mother loved to screw white men" (Silko 2006, 58). For his Rez friends, he is white trash and represents the Other; for white Americans, he is an untouchable. Once out of his military uniform, the narrator notes, "the white lady at the bus depot [who might have happily said "God bless you" to Tayo in the uniform] "is careful now not to touch your hand when she counts out your change" (Silko 2006, 39). Another name given to this inter-tribal hatred and alienation is "witchery" responsible for making Native Americans "see only the losses—the land and the lives lost" and "forget the stories of the creation [and] cling to ritual without making new ceremonies" (Silko 2006, 231). In other words, witchery would want Native Americans to reflect and remember what they have lost, not what they can or could create and envision.

To counter the calculative logic of witchery which counts only the losses and gains, Tayo must think in terms of the incalculable—the unconditional or all-inclusive hospitality. Spivak would go to any extent to keep an immigrant apart from an indigene. When the sight of Asian immigrants around Los Angeles triggers in Tayo traumatic memories of war in the Pacific, especially the visions of his uncle Josiah mingling with the Japanese, Tayo's ceremonial hospitality would resort to Betonie's historical perspective: "It isn't surprising you saw him with them. You saw who they were. Thirty thousand years ago they were not strangers" (Silko 2006, 114–15). Joanne Lipson Freed interprets Betonie's assertion as a revelation of "the shared marginalization and state-sponsored violence experienced by those, such as Japanese Americans and Native Americans, whom nationalist discourse defines as outsiders" (Freed 2017, 56). But there is more to it: what brings Native Americans and Japanese Americans together is not only their shared political and historical experiences as two marginalized groups abused by an empire, but also their pre-historical ties as people connected through a common-place of origin and destiny—a speculation which further jeopardizes Spivak's investment in keeping the indigene distinct from the immigrant.

It is no surprise, therefore, that Tayo's ceremony concludes only after he reaches Trinity, the site where the first atomic bomb exploded. It is located only a few miles from the uranium mine and "top-secret laboratories where the bomb had been created" on the land the US "government took from Cochiti Pueblo" (Silko 2006, 228). Tayo's cure lies in his ability to tear through witchery's obfuscation. Tayo feels relieved when he sees the pattern and realizes: "he was not crazy, he had never been crazy. He had only seen and heard the world as it always was: no boundaries, only transitions through all distances and time" (Silko 2006, 229). For Louis Owens, the central issue in American Indians' novels is "a consciousness and worldview defined primarily by a quest for identity: What does it mean to be an Indian or mixed-blood in contemporary America?" (Owens 1992, 20). What we see in Silko is much more than that: not only a realization that "all living things [are] united by a circle of death" (Silko 2006, 228) but also "an awareness of plants, animals and earth being much more of a holistic unit" (Silko and Arnold 1994, 180). This is Silko's idea of wild justice, a reinscription of aboriginality without any machete, a wild justice in which plants, animals, and earth figure as inter-connected entities.

How would a twenty-first-century version of hospitality as wild justice for decolonization look? This is a question we would now like to ask Sherman Alexie's 2007 novel *Flight*. Even though stylistically and thematically *Flight* is a decidedly twenty-first century narrative, it nevertheless continues and incorporates many concerns raised by Bird and Silko in their novels. *Flight*'s rebellious and contentious approach may resemble Silko's *Almanac of the Dead*, while, as in *Ceremony*, Alexie also hints at the witchery driving the US and the world on the path of destruction. In fact, *Flight* dramatizes witchery in a more effective way than does Silko's lyrical treatment of the subject in *Ceremony*. Zits, Alexie's protagonist in *Flight*, who likes "to start fires," (Alexie 2007, 8) and is haunted by a "recurring dream of killing black men and going cannibal" (Alexie 2007, 26), is told that he is "programmed for violence" (27) and confesses that he is "a time-travelling mass murderer" (84), also has much in common with Bird's bandit.

Bird's abusive and antipathetic characterization of Chinese immigrants and Native Americans in *Joaquin Murieta* find an echo in Alexie's dream of cannibalizing African Americans. And yet, Alexie's novel also makes implicit overtures to other anti-colonial and postcolonial narratives. Zits strongly resembles the titular Gora in Tagore's novel inasmuch as both Gora and Zits have Irish blood, and both are closer to their mothers than their fathers. If the figure of the father is absent in Alexie, in Tagore, Gora's foster father is preparing his own last rites. Zits's vison of wild justice through mass murder also brings him closer to Devi's machete queen Mary. Zits's love for music and TV shows, his traumatizing fear of step-fathers or foster-fathers, and his self-confessed involvement with crimes both historical and personal also overlap with the anxieties and traumatic experiences of Salman Rushdie's protagonist in *Fury*. As a result, Zits figures in the novel as a resident alien who must through anagnorisis come to terms with his outsiderness and seek to correct the failures of decolonization for Native Americans.

Sherman Alexie's *Flight* transports us to this world without any boundaries and with the holistic awareness of plants, animals, and earth. Zits is a pyromaniac teenager fleeing from one foster home to another in Seattle, Washington, after the death of his Irish mother and the disappearance of his Indian father. While Zits's escape from his numerous foster parents constitutes the novel's primary flight, there are at least three other 'flights' involved in Alexie's narrative: Zits's flight from the police after he attempts a mass murder at a bank; his time traveling into history, including some of the key moments of US history; and the flight training that he as Jimmy provides to an Islamic terrorist. Each of these begin when, at the instigation of his white cell-mate, Justice, Zits decides to kill everyone at a Seattle bank so that he can perform a Ghost Dance to bring his mother and father back. When the fury of the mass murder ends, he wakes up back in 1975 as Hank, an FBI agent in charge of putting down an IRON (Indigenous Rights Now) insurgency in Red River Idaho. After killing one of the activists, Zits is transported back a century to 1876 and lands as a twelve-years-old voiceless Indian boy in an Indian camp as Crazy Horse and Sitting Bull prepare to take on Colonel Custer, later known as the Battle of the Little Big Horn. As his Indian father exhorts him to kill a white boy during the battle, he loses consciousness again only to wake up as Gus, an old Indian tracker, in a settler camp in Kansas. His next avatar is a pilot named Jimmy who teaches an Ethiopian Muslim named Abbad to fly a plane, who in turn crashes a plane, reminiscent of the events of 9/11, into downtown Chicago during rush hour.

When the guilt of training a terrorist finally kills Jimmy, Zits wakes up as his father—lying half-naked and fully drunk in an alley in Tacoma, staring at a rat:

> The rat stares at me.
>
> It's a huge wharf rat, two feet long, with intelligent eyes. And the rat seems to be thinking, *You're too big to kill, but I'm going to take a bite out of your ass anyway.*
>
> I panic and roll away, thinking that the rat's violent intentions might actually be amorous. What if I've dropped into the body of a rat? What if I'm about to get fucked by another rat?
>
> Shit.
>
> But no, I feel human. I am human. A human who rolls away from a rat. (Alexie 2007, 131)

With this encounter, Zits completes the Ghost Dance by bringing his father back. Zits, who is named after his pimples, must co-coexist with, co-inhabit the alley with, and evolve with a rat. He not only has this intimate relationship with his father, with Indian-killing agents, and with 'real' Indian warriors, but also with animals. His perpetual flight refutes any possibility of a fixed, univocal and stable identity, and his frequent time-traveling, his constant deaths and reappearances alternately as a victim and a victimizer make his existence inseparable from simultaneous revelation and refutation of anagnorisis. Yellow Bird offered hospitality to a mass-murdering bandit, whom he considers worthier of welcome than many Americans of his time. Alexie gives the honor of welcoming a "foster-kid with a history of fire setting, time traveling, body shifting and mass murder contemplation" (Alexie 2007, 173) to Dave, a white cop who eventually finds a home for Zits, who believes that by agreeing to live with Dave's brother and his wife, Zits "can save [Dave] too" (177).

5 Conclusion

Deploying the concept of hospitality in the context of postcolonial theory to study Native American literature enables us to revisit the history of colonialism in the United States. Particularly relevant to this task is Gayatri Spivak's concept of 'hospitality from below' according to which the failure of decolonization for the natives would be corrected only when natives re-appropriate the position of host. Central to Spivak's concept of hospitality is the figure of the resident alien whose identity depends on anagnorisis, an interplay between native and foreigner, and host and guest. While Spivak makes the reversal of the host-guest binary, parricide and wild justice of the machete (in which the hunter is hunted down) indispensable to the reinscription of 'aboriginality,' the three novels by Native American writers we have looked at in this chapter transform the meaning of both resident alien and wild justice by opening these concepts to include non-human animals and the planet as well. By narrating the stories of three eccentric and singular individuals, Yellow Bird, Leslie Marmon Silko and Sherman Alexie question the guest-host binary by demonstrating that hospitality worthy of its name is bigger than the individuals involved in either welcoming or being welcomed. A politics of hospitality, they seem to imply, capable of generating energies powerful enough to precipitate the events of decolonization must come to terms with the land, the environment, and the shared destiny of the human and the non-human together.

References

Alexie, Sherman. 2007. *Flight*. New York: Black Cat.
Allen, Paula Gunn. 1990. "Special Problems in Teaching Leslie Marmon Silko's 'Ceremony'." *American Indian Quarterly* 14 (4): 379–386.
Allmendinger, Blake. 1998. *Ten Most Wanted: The New Western Literature*. New York: Routledge.

Beidler, Peter. 2002. "Animals and Theme in *Ceremony*." In *Leslie Marmon Silko's Ceremony: A Casebook*, 17–22. Oxford: Oxford UP.

Bhabha, Homi K. 2011. *Our Neighbors, Ourselves: Contemporary Reflections on Survival*. Berlin: Walter de Gruyter.

Bird, Yellow. 2003. *The Life and Adventures of Joaquín Murieta, the Celebrated California Bandit*. Grass Valley: Poitin P.

Castillo, Richard Griswold del. 1990. *The Treaty of Guadalupe Hidalgo: A Legacy of Conflict*. Norman: U of Oklahoma P.

Cook-Lynn, Elizabeth. 1996. "American Indian Intellectualism and the New American Story." *American Indian Quarterly* 20 (1): 57–76.

Damai, Puspa. 2012. "Welcoming Strangers: Hospitality in American Literature and Culture." PhD diss., University of Michigan, Ann Arbor.

Derrida, Jaques. (1997) 2000. *Of Hospitality: Anne Duformantelle Invites Jaques Derrida to Respond*. Translated by Rachel Bowlby. Stanford: Stanford UP.

Devi, Mahasweta. 1995. "The Hunt." In *Imaginary Maps*, translated by Gayatri C. Spivak, 1–18. New York: Routledge.

Freed, Joanne Lipson. 2017. *Haunting Encounters: The Ethics of Reading across Boundaries of Difference*. Ithaca: Cornell UP.

Hixon, Walter. 2013. *American Settler Colonialism: A History*. New York: Palgrave.

Indian Affairs, US Department of the Interior. "Programs and Services." [Accessed online on December 16, 2017].

Marshall, John. 2001. "Cherokee Nation vs. Georgia." *PBS: The Archives of the West 1806–1848*. [Accessed online on December 16, 2017].

Mbembe, Achile. 2001. *On the Postcolony*. Berkeley: U of California P.

Mudge, Zacharia Atwell. 1871. *Foot-prints of Roger Williams: A Biography*. New York: Carlton and Lanahan.

Owens, Louis. 1992. Other Destinies: Understanding the American Indian Novels. Norman: U of Oklahoma P.

Rosello, Mireille. 2001. *Postcolonial Hospitality: The Immigrant as Guest*. Stanford: Stanford UP.

Silko, Leslie Mormon. 2006. *Ceremony*. New York: Penguin.

Silko, Leslie Marmon and Ellen L. Arnold. 1994. "Listening to the Spirits: An Interview with Leslie Marmon Silko." In *Conversations with Leslie Marmon Silko*, 162–196. Jackson: UP of Mississippi.

Spivak, Gayatri C. 2002. "Resident Alien." In *Relocating Postcolonialism*, edited by David Theo Goldberg and Ato Quayson, 47–65. London: Blackwell.

Veracini, Lorenzo. 2015. *The Settler Colonial Present*. London: Palgrave.

Weaver, Jace. 2003. "Leslie Marmon Silko." In *Leslie Marmon Silko's Ceremony: A Case Book*, edited by Allan Chavkin, 213–222. Oxford: Oxford UP.

Williams, Roger. 1997. *A Key into the Language of America.* Bedford: Applewood.
Williams, Roger. 2007. *The Complete Writings of Roger Williams.* Eugene: Wipf and Stock.
Wolfe, Patrick. 1999. *Settler Colonialism and the Practice of Colonialism.* London: Cassell.

CHAPTER 3

Language Interaction and Hospitality: Combating the *Hosted-Host* Figure[1]

Amanda Ellen Gerke

Abstract

Notions of hospitality and issues of receiving migrants and refugees have been highlighted in the political rhetoric and various critical and literary approaches. The concept of hospitality is rooted in the interactions, or non-actions between both the host and the guest, and is tied to relational dynamics of knowledge and power. As Michel Foucault states, "there is no power relation without the correlative construction of a field of knowledge, nor any knowledge that does not presuppose and constitute at the same time power relations" (Discipline and Punish: The Birth of the Prison, 27). Power is generated in relation to the Other; one member has power when the other lacks. Therefore, knowledge and lack of knowledge can be considered as actions, since they constitute what pushes and pulls the actors in the host situation.

When this knowledge is linguistic, or takes on characteristics of speech acts, it in turn holds a space of its own and shakes up the rules of engagement between a host and guest, and poses the following questions: How are hospitality roles formed among the migrants, or Others themselves? Are the notions of oppression and control, both physically and ideologically, addressed in terms of an internal code—or code switching—among the guests themselves? Is there a push and pull connected to a 'host of hosts' identity? And can 'hospitable violence' be understood by linguistic means? And finally, how does the maternal *pathos* emerge to be the strongest (linguistic) actor against a patriarchal host-figure? The answers to these questions rest on an analysis at the intersection of Michel Foucault's theories of knowledge and power, Teun van Dijk and Norman Fairclough's developments in critical discourse analysis, as well as De Certeau's concepts of language space.

---

1 This article was made possible thanks to the financial help provided by the Spanish Ministry of Science and Technology through the research project "Critical History of Ethnic American Literature: An Intercultural Approach" (ref. FFI2015-64137-P), directed by Prof. Jesús Benito Sánchez, and by the European Project "Hospitality and European Film 2017-1-ES01-KA203-038181" directed by Prof. Ana María Manzanas Calvo.

In Junot Díaz' *This is How You Lose Her*, and Sandra Cisneros' *The House on Mango Street*, the concept of linguistic space helps demonstrate the interplay of different occupied spaces throughout the stories, at the same time that it uncovers overarching themes of knowledge, power, and oppression. In both collections, migrant families must come to terms with occupying a different type of spatiality; one that is both of the physical and the non-physical, a geographic reality and a verbal reality. In *The House on Mango Street*, those who "No Speak English" are reduced to occupying the bottom rung of society, and in "Invierno," speaking English is seen as the key to gaining access to the outside world. And, in both collections, a mother-figure becomes a prisoner in different apartments because of linguistic barriers. Figures alluding to a 'hosted host' identity permeate both collections, as there are actors among the guest groups that take on a *Gatekeeper* role, and passage through the gate becomes a driving force among the characters. Norman Fairclough (2010) develops this notion of access and power, and assigns a conceptual function to those who control this discoursal access. The powerful enactors, or "Gatekeepers," are the ones that have control over the flux of knowledge and access to discourse (47). The idea of 'power behind discourse' posits that the whole social order of discourse is constructed and maintained as a hidden effect of power in that discourses depend on special knowledge and skills which have to be learned (19-68). Key players in the collections observe that the lack of language creates a powerlessness, but that the ability to pass through planes of linguistic space will give them power.

Keywords

Junot Díaz – Sandra Cisneros – linguistic space – blended spaces – discourse analysis – language and power

∙ ∙ ∙

> The limits of my language are the limits of my world.
> LUDWIG WITTGENSTEIN
> *Tractatus Logico-Philosophicus*

∙ ∙
∙

Against the backdrop of political turmoil surrounding the reception of migrants and refugees, notions of hospitality are at the forefront of political rhetoric and of various critical and literary analyses. The concept of hospitality is tied to the process of constructing dominant and subordinate identities, as well as to relational dynamics of knowledge and power. Furthermore, power is generated in relation to the Other; it creates the field of what is acceptable and what is not, creating a set of knowledge and ethics as well as giving sense to a worldview while, at the same time, building its limits. The action-oriented notion of hospitality is, moreover, anchored in the *access*—and its control. Receiving and being received are practical, social engagements comprising a complex system of roles which are constantly constructed and deconstructed. It is *interactive*, requiring equal participation by both host and guest.

The dynamics of interactive hospitality can also be understood in relation to the concept of language interaction in that discourse itself is intrinsically a social phenomenon requiring the exchange or the withholding of knowledge in a social setting. The key to understanding language interaction is to recognize the power relations involved in social structures through the construction of ideologies and speaker identities. When the knowledge-power tandem in the hospitality relationship is viewed alongside linguistic agency or is recognized in congruence with speech acts, it in turn occupies its own space; it shakes up the rules of engagement between host and guest and poses the following questions: When hospitality roles are formed among migrants, how does the relationship manifest? Is there a push and pull connected to a *hosted-host* identity?

In Junot Díaz's (1968–) "Invierno" from *This is How You Lose Her* (2012) and Sandra Cisneros's (1954–) *The House on Mango Street* (1984), the concept of linguistic space helps demonstrate the interplay of different occupied spaces that uncover overarching themes of knowledge, power, and oppression. In both collections, migrant families must come to terms with occupying a different, simultaneously physical and non-physical, spatiality: a geographic reality and a verbal reality. In *The House on Mango Street*, those who 'No Speak English' are reduced to occupying the bottom rung of society, and, in "Invierno," speaking English is seen as the key to gaining access to the outside world. Norman Fairclough (2010) develops this notion of access and power and assigns a conceptual function to those who control this discursive access. The powerful enactors or "gatekeepers" have control over the flux of knowledge and access to discourse (47). This chapter claims that in both collections, figures alluding to a *hosted-host* identity permeate both physical and linguistic spaces, taking on a *gatekeeper* role, and that the passage through the gate becomes a driving force among the characters: key players in both collections observe that language barriers create powerlessness but, through linguistic and physical agency, they gain power.

1   The *Hosted-Host* Identity

> Thinking about hospitality is not only to think about a generous and cordial welcome. Thinking about hospitality, more importantly, is to think about *openings* and *recognition*. Although boundaries form an inherent part of the notion of hospitality, without which such a notion would perhaps be unnecessary, hospitality, I want to argue, is about opening, without abolishing, these boundaries and *giving spaces* to the stranger where recognition on both sides would be possible.
>
> MUSTAFA DIKEÇ
> "Pera Peras Poros: Longings for Spaces of Hospitality"

The concept of *giving spaces* to the guest is impregnated with the notion that the *recognition* of rights is extended into physical spaces and a mutual understanding of each party's vulnerabilities (Dikeç 2002, 229). However, even in the ideal situation in which the host and guest maintain those boundaries, the (perhaps) primordial need to exercise power does not escape the mind of each party. From this, hospitable violence manifests. When Dikeç speaks of the opening of spaces and recognition, hospitality in its ideal state is achieved. However, the giving or assigning of spaces also may lead to (in)hospitable situations in which control, oppression, and concepts of patriarchy overpower the host-guest relationship and construct a violent space of imprisonment.

Understanding hospitality as a "refusal to conceive the host and guest as pre-constructed identities" and that it is "about a recognition that they are mutually constitutive of each other and thus relational" (Dikeç 2002, 239), conceptualizes the planes of hospitality, then, as deconstructed through actions and interactions and divided into sub-levels of hospitable identities. If the host-guest relationship relates to who is able to conquer or be conquered, the guest attempting to maintain some sort of hierarchical control may assume what I call a *hosted-host* identity and therefore create a subdivision of roles, fulfilling a need to exert power over subaltern figures. The *hosted-host* in "Invierno" and *The House on Mango Street* takes the form of the patriarchal figure. Here, the *hosted-host* is the dominant migrant male who exercises control over the subordinate matriarchal group (migrant women and children). Therefore, the migrant female and children are not only guests in the primary host space (the host country), but also guests in the secondary space (the home) governed by the *hosted-host*.

The conceptual *hosted-host* also finds congruency in notions of power-plays in discourse directly rooted in the construction of social knowledge. Teun van

Dijk, in *Discourse and Knowledge: A Sociocognitive Approach* (2014), states that since knowledge is socially shared and distributed among members of communities, it is through *actions* and *interactions* that the society-cognition interface manifests (142–143). Knowledge is often represented in episodic memory and represents the everyday experiences of social actors, including their own perceptions of their situational environment. Furthermore, this social knowledge is acquired during socialization alongside the acquisition of language thus creating a "semantic memory" representing the knowledge system of the community (van Dijk 2014, 143). In terms of designated 'space' and 'knowledge,' the migrant males in Díaz's and Cisneros's novels have, in a sense, reacted to their own guest-status and have subdivided those within their own community. They must recognize that they are given spaces and must not conquer the primary host. As recompense, and in order to regain conqueror status, they take on the role of the violent host in order to achieve supremacy. The migrant male's *modus operandi* utilizes a set of strategies rooted in the knowledge/power tandem, as well as the control of physical (and sometimes linguistic) spaces to regain control.

The space which the *hosted-host* constructs and controls, takes form in the concept of *community*. This point is crucial in understanding that the primary host, essentially, does not have as much power over the primary guest as one may assume, due to the fact that communities are defined by shared beliefs, knowledge and language and by their characteristic *practices* (Van Dijk 2014, 180), each of these aspects being formed by epistemic knowledge procedures. Even within a space 'designated' (figuratively or not) to a migrant group, it is those within the community who create, define, shape, maintain and govern its spaces and thus, create micro-hegemonies towards which they orient their actions (Blommaert & Varis 2011, 2). I claim that it is the patriarchal group that controls the community and the spaces within, yielding the *hosted-host* as the community's powerful enactor, remaining elusive to the primary host. In the migrants' case, the *hosted-host* relies on the transfer of socialized knowledge and language from the home-country and brings this into the new space in order to maintain dominance.

In Díaz's "Invierno," it is young Yunior's father who assumes the role of *hosted-host* upon bringing his family to the US from the Dominican Republic. Having spent much time already in the host country before bringing his wife and children over, he 'welcomes' his family to the new country only to keep them contained in the family apartment. Here, the *opening* of spaces is rather the assigning of a prison-like space. This act keeps his family in a guest position, even in their own home. His time in the US before his family arrives allowed a special type of access to the host-place, gained through time, experience, and knowledge. This includes seemingly banal knowledge about everyday tasks and acts that, with a deeper understanding, demonstrates the dichotomy of knowledge and ignorance between guest and host. He has gained access not only to the host-world, but also has special access to the subdivision of host spaces, taking full control. When the family first arrives in the apartment, he shows his wife and children how to run the sinks and flush the toilets (Díaz 2012, 122), simple acts that subtly draw attention to the father's dominance. Books and TV are a source of knowledge in the apartment and the father's actions show his integration by his fully taking part in them; "Those first few weeks in the States, Papi spent a great deal of his home time downstairs with his books or in front of the TV. He said little to us that wasn't disciplinary, which didn't surprise us" (125). The seemingly mundane tasks he shows his family and his interaction with artifacts of the host country is a firm reiteration of his knowledge of the host world, of which his family remains ignorant.

Yunior's father constantly sets up situations of power and control by reminding his family of their shortcomings, a psychological tactic that ensures his position:

> Papi had a thing with shoelaces. I didn't know how to tie them properly and when I put together a rather formidable knot, Papi would bend down and pull it apart with one tug. [...] Rafa showed me how [...] but when Papi was breathing down my neck, his hand on a belt, I couldn't perform; I looked at my father like my laces were live wires he wanted me to touch together. (126)

Reflecting on Foucault's statements on the "correlative constriction" of fields of knowledge (1977, 27) and Van Dijk's posit that societal knowledge is interactive (2014, 142–143), knowledge and ignorance are seen as actions that push and pull societal members. In the case of the *hosted-host*, the 'knowledge actions' are what sets them apart from their primary guest status and allows their dominant place. Yunior's father exercises his power over his two sons with punishment and intimidation. He does not allow his family members to leave the apartment and his chastisements are harsh.

> He was free with his smacks and we spent whole afternoons on Punishment Row—our bedroom—where we had to lay on our beds and not get off, because if he burst in and caught us at the window, staring out at the beautiful snow, he would pull our ears and smack us and then we would have to kneel in the corner for a few hours. If we messed that up, joking around or cheating, he would force us to kneel down on the cutting side

of a coconut grater and only when we were bleeding and whimpering would he let us up. (Díaz 2012, 130)

The father's authority is also metaphorically connected to the host environment around the family apartment, to which he also has undeniable access. In "Invierno," winter is a penetrating force that both reminds the family of their status as guests—as the weather in New York is in stark contrast to that of the island home—and is also evidence of the father's access to the host country. That is, while the family is confined deeper into the apartment because of the cold, "the apartment was cold in the morning and leaving the bed was a serious torment" (124), the father seems unaffected by it, even wearing short sleeve shirts. In fact, he is not only immune to the cold but also embraces it and uses it to keep his family contained. Winter, to the father, represents his integration into the host country where, to his family, winter is a threatening reminder of their guest status. After Yunior's head is shaved by his father, Mami is concerned, "the cold is going to make him sick" (129). In response, Papi places his cold hand on Yunior's head to remind his family that the cold is indeed a threat and that he is a part of it.

The host-guest relationship within this family is further highlighted by the shift in behaviors and demeanor of the family members while in their 'prison.' As the family apartment is the space assigned to the family, Dikeç's *recognition* of rights is seen in the father's position of conqueror and the family's position of conquered. The mother, who back in her home enjoyed the freedom of being nobody's guest, is now met with a violent contrast and submits to her husband's control. As Yunior reflects, "Mami, who had been our authority on the Island, was dwindling" (132) and her once fierce nature was subdued: "My mother was not a woman easily cowed, but in the States she let my father roll over her" (138). The father's power as the *hosted-host* impacts Yunior's brother as well. Rafa, like his mother, was spirited back at home, but when it comes to his father, he "obeyed him with a scrupulousness he had never shown anybody" (136). Yunior observes that in their father's house, Rafa "had turned into some kind of muchacho bueno. [...] It was as if the passage to the U.S. had burned out the sharpest part of him" (136). Both for Rafa and Mami, the decomposition from free-spirits to contained guests is quick and sharp. They are prisoners in their own home, assigned a violent space and forced within a knowledge/power tandem that maintains their position.

In *The House on Mango Street* the same attributes of the father in "Invierno" extend from the individual level, to a wide-spread patriarchal control over an entire neighborhood by many 'fathers.' In this novel, many spaces are constructed, occupied and assigned. Like "Invierno" the father-figure(s) fight back against primary host by exercising violent power moves and assigning spaces. As primary guests, the patriarchal group is placed into a sector of Chicago, designated for impoverished migrants, namely Latinos. In *The House on Mango Street* Cisneros presents concepts of 'place,' the space that Latinos occupy, on different planes. The first layer that makes up the conceptual area of the *hosted-hosts'* space is in the contrast between places designated for Latinos and those that are not. On a broader plane, it is the Latino neighborhood itself. As Esperanza reflects, "Those who don't know any better come into our neighborhood scared. They think we're dangerous. They think we will attack them with shiny knives. They are stupid people who got here by mistake" (28). The people outside of Esperanza's space are afraid of those inside; they do not venture into the neighborhood 'allocated' to this Latino group. Similarly, the Latino group finds it difficult to venture into the primary-hosts' space, exemplifying the push and pull of spatial divisions. On the one hand, the people in Esperanza's neighborhood are socially designated an area, impoverished and isolated from the non-Latinos. However, there is an internal pull to keep Esperanza's neighbors inside these boundaries on the part of the male migrant, the *hosted-host*.

The rules of engagement inside the community are kept by gender divisions; "The boys and the girls live in separate worlds. The boys in their universe and we in ours. My brothers for example. They've got plenty to say to me and Nenny inside the house. But outside they can't be seen talking to girls" (8). Esperanza finds herself in a setting designated to her and her Latino neighbors, but even within this space she is delineated by the shame that comes with this assigned space: "You live *there?* The way she said it made me feel like nothing. *There.* I lived *there*" (5). Karen W. Martin (2008), reflects on these layers of space in *The House on Mango Street* and states that these designations "reflect the dynamic nature of urban community buildings and reinforce race, class and gender hierarchies imposed externally by the dominant Anglo culture, as well as those internally imposed upon the inscribed space of Mango Street by Latino patriarchy" (50). Martin also implies, however, that Esperanza is not only aware of her designation, but also attempts to negotiate her way through the spaces:

> Esperanza plays into hegemonic forces' stereotypical notion of poor Latino space, using these tenements to evoke sympathy so that she can gain access to the bounded, privileged space of the canteen. [...] Her temporary negotiation of access to this idealized space points out the hostile, unwelcoming nature of partitioned space for the outsider who attempts to penetrate it. (57)

Esperanza, as representative of the migrant female, understands where she has been situated and, throughout the novel, (figuratively) negotiates her way through and out of it. Notably, the female space designated to Esperanza and her neighbors reflects a female domestic life that mirrors the prison-like experience that Mami is subjected to in "Invierno." The women in *The House on Mango Street* are also secluded in the home in a type of non-space in comparison to the 'outside male world' but with even more subjection than in Díaz's story. On Mango Street, women are placed on the floor of the home: "a woman's place is sleeping so she can wake up early with the tortilla star, the one that appears early just in time to rise and catch the hind legs behind the sink, beneath the four-clawed tub, under the swollen floorboards nobody fixes, in the corner of her eyes" (31).

The nature of the female migrant in Cisneros's novel is inverted in her new space, similar to that seen in "Invierno." Just as Yunior's mother's "once fierce nature is subdued" (138), Esperanza's great-grandmother's spirited nature is also overturned by the Latino patriarch: "My great-grandmother. I would've liked to have known her, a wild horse of a woman, so wild she wouldn't marry. Until my great-grandfather threw a sack over her head and carried her off. Just like that, as if she were a fancy chandelier. That's the way he did it" (10–11). Although this episode presumably occurred in Mexico, it demonstrates the carrying-over of patriarchal control into the new space dominated by the *hosted-host*. The oppressed domestic space that the women in *The House on Mango Street* are assigned is passed on through the generations. It is a symbol of male-domination that pushes the migrant women further into their place on the floor; it is a dreaded and forsaken, yet inevitable inheritance. In the case of Alicia, who has to take her place on the floor because her mother has died, she has to juggle her dreams of studying and also the reality of inheriting "her mama's rolling pin and sleepiness" (31). Alicia represents the woman who, despite her intellect and strength, cannot overcome the oppression that passes through her bloodlines. She who "studies all night and sees the mice, the ones her father says do not exist. Is afraid of nothing except four-legged fur. And fathers" (32). The mice, as a symbol, here embody the oppression that Alicia experiences and tries to reject. However, as her father states that the mice do not exist, that the oppression is not real, her father exerts more control over her by denying there is even a problem. Alicia is afraid of her position (the mice) and also 'Fathers,' the patriarchal system that keeps her there and which her daughters will also inevitably acquire.

Esperanza, like Alicia, fears her inheritance and what she may become. She sees her fate in the experience of her great-grandmother who was reduced to looking, "out her window her whole life, the way so many women sit their sadness on an elbow," (11) and as Esperanza, named after her great-grandmother and therefore tied to a certain plot in life, rejects this: "I have inherited her name, but I don't want to inherit her place by the window" (11).

The window itself is another strong metaphor for the domestic space the *hosted-host* has assigned the female migrant and children. In both *The House on Mango Street* and "Invierno," the window serves as a physical space for the bottom-rung guests, the imprisoned. The window is the door's counterpart; the *hosted-host* has access to the door, symbolizing not only his entry to the outside world that the migrant female is denied, but also the notion that he is the key-holder, warden, or gatekeeper of the cloistered-like experience of the secondary guests. In Díaz's story, the metaphor is more clear-cut. The mother and children in "Invierno" are not allowed outside, they are not even allowed to pass through the front door. Instead, they see the wintry outside world through windows: "Beads of water gathered on the windows like bees and we had to wipe the glass to see outside" (121). It is no surprise that the windows themselves are threatening—wiping the glass to see outside is dangerous—as if they were covered with bees that would sting if the boys attempted to look out. These 'bees' are delineative of the winter weather that seems to aid the father in keeping his family imprisoned.

In *The House on Mango Street*, the despotism that windows and doors represent is subtler, yet reveals a reality even more severe as it is hereditary and unavoidable. The migrant woman is not always kept inside by physical violence like in "Invierno," however, her place by the window represents the invisible violence of patriarchal oppression over the female migrant experiencing various degrees of helplessness. Rafaela, a secondary character, for example, imagines herself throwing her hair out the window like Rapunzel to escape her situation. Instead, she throws out a clothesline which the children use to send up the coconut and papaya juice she asks them to buy. Rafaela "wishes there were sweeter drinks, not bitter like an empty room, but sweet like the island" (79–80). Instead of a magical mane that will lead her to freedom, she remains imprisoned at the window with only a rope, symbolizing her bondage. Esperanza's own house on Mango Street alludes to the prison that holds her hostage: "It's small and red with tight steps in front and the windows so small you'd think they were holding their breath. Bricks are crumbling in places and the front door so swollen you have to push hard to get in," (4) and with the windows barred so the family won't fall out (or get out).

In both "Invierno" and *The House on Mango Street*, the patriarchal figure(s), in an effort to regain some of the power lost as a primary guest in the host country, creates a space for the migrant women and children, maintained by physical violence and psychological strongholds. The matriarchal figures are kept in assigned domesticity, in the kitchen, on the floor, and by the window, but their positions are also maintained by an invisible ideological chain passed from generation to generation of women (and men). There is, however, a different kind of space occupied throughout both story and novel that takes form in a less 'tangible' way; the space of language. It is also keyed by the *hosted-host* figure whose position is strengthened by his control over this domain as well.

2   Language Interaction

> The job of the linguist, like that of the biologist or the botanist, is not to tell us how nature should behave or what its creations should look like, but to describe those creations in all their messy glory and try to figure out what they can teach us about life, the world and, especially in the case of linguistics, the workings of the human mind.
> ARIKA OKRENT
> *In the Land of Invented Languages*

Language as interaction forms a greater part of the terms of hospitality than any other aspect. The rules of engagement between a host and guest are continuously mulled over and reconstructed. The language system surrounding their interaction does not just reveal how each party should behave, but rather it explains the workings of the human mind and the intricacies involved in identity formation and reinforcement. The concept of language interaction mirrors the act of receiving and being received, in that it is a practical and social engagement because it is made up of a complex system of roles that requires actions or movements by both host and guest and also requires the exchange and/or regulation of knowledge. It consists of ideologies formed by power relations and results in the construction of identities which, in turn, are interpreted and continually reinforced by the social participants (van Dijk 1997, 16). In "Invierno" and *The House on Mango Street*, the matriarchal groups are not only confined by the lack of physical agency, but also by limitations of interaction that demonstrate the congruence of language and space; social freedoms fluctuate as much as the female characters' degree of physical agency.

From a sociological perspective, spaces of diaspora can be seen as constitutive and agentive in terms of the multilingual capacity to communicate and interact. As Blommaert et al. suggest (2005), language spaces are connected to a scaling process, "movements across space involve movements across scales of social structure having indexical value and thus providing meaning to individual, situated acts" (200). Meaningful conduct that happens in polycentric environments relies on, not necessarily the individual's ability to navigate the language space, but rather the systematic construction of that language space. The authors assert that "Processes such as diaspora are *structural* processes which develop over long spans of time and result in *lasting* or at least more or less permanent social configurations" (Blommeart et al. 2005, 201). From a discourse analysis perspective, Teun van Dijk describes language interaction as "social action" since meaning-making on the discourse level is situated— discourse is described as taking place or as being accomplished in situations— so speech acts themselves hold a physical space (1997, 10–11). That is to say that the knowledge/power tandem in terms of language use creates a tangible space where illocutionary acts are able to manifest. Norman Fairclough's developments in language interaction also shed light on the type of 'language space' that can be utilized to gain agency. Fairclough states that, in relation to power and discourse, the powerful enactors are those with control over the flux of knowledge and access to discourse (2010, 47). The "Gatekeepers" as he calls them, are not only granted entry into the social space, but also control the information that passes across the knowledge gate. Access, here, is the key term in respect to the matriarchal figures in both "Invierno" and *The House on Mango Street*. These stories present the *hosted-host* identity as not only an entity bred by the need to exercise power, but as a figure who takes the gatekeeper status away from the primary host, as he systematically denies access to his secondary guests. This action transforms him into an even more powerful enactor, as he is the key to both primary and secondary spaces.

Yunior's mother in "Invierno" is never physically abused as her sons are. However, her imprisonment is directly connected to her lack of linguistic knowledge of the host country. The mother's oppression is enacted through a systematic isolation by restricting her language use. Yunior's mother attempts to learn English alongside her two sons by watching TV. However, she is unable to duplicate the words she hears: "Her lips seemed to tug apart even the simplest vowels" (124), and even her sons grew tired of listening to the butchered English from their mother and refused to help her learn (124). In fact, not only are her English attempts thwarted by her sons, but her linguistic engagements even in Spanish are soon cut off as her sons refuse to speak to her after a time: "You should talk to me, she said, but we told her to wait for Papi to get home" (124). The mother's linguistic access is also heavily restricted by her husband. Papi exercises direct abuse of power by belittling his wife and causing muted behavior.

> At dinner she'd try her English out on Papi, but he just poked at his pernil [...].

> I can't understand a word you're saying, he said finally. It's best if I take care of the English.
> How do you expect me to learn?
> You don't have to learn, he said. Besides, the average woman can't learn English.
> Mami didn't say another word. (124)

In this instance, the father uses his preferential access to the host country's language to systematically deny her access, fortifying her status as a secondary guest. She is not only limited to the primary host's world by lack of knowledge, she is not even allowed to come near the gate and her female agency is stripped from her. Her husband takes advantage of her displacement, a movement that affects her ability to navigate the constructed linguistic: he has not only created a psychological prison for his wife, but he has also created a sort of linguistic prison in which he denies her access to the discourse community she strives to reach. As van Dijk states, "Much power in society [...] is not coercive, but rather mental. Instead of controlling the activities of others directly by bodily force, we control the mental basis of all action, namely people's intentions or purposes" (1997, 17) and that this kind of discursive power requires equal participation because "[i]nstead of letting others know what we want through commands [...] we may shape their minds in such a way that they will act as we want out of their own free will" (19). This type of hegemonic power is what the *hosted-host* relies on in order to maintain his position.

The House on Mango Street's female characters also experience the double aggression of a physical prison maintained by a more fundamental linguistic confinement. However, Cisneros's portrayal includes accounts of multiple female voices whose restriction ranges in severity. On the one hand, there is what might be perceived as trivial rejections of the Spanish language against the power language of English, mainly seen in Esperanza's aversions to the patriarchal tongue passed to her against her will:

> In English my name means hope. In Spanish it means too many letters. It means sadness, it means waiting. [...] It is the Mexican records my father plays on Sunday mornings when he's shaving, songs like sobbing. It was my great-grandmother's name and now it is mine. (10)

These reflections are not inconsequential as her name is not only representative of an inherited place of enclosure, the Spanish of her name is directly connected to the *hosted-host* figure, the patriarchal gatekeeper that denies her access to her English-labeled counterpart, which is *hope*. The fact that Esperanza translates her name, marking the Spanish as oppressive and sad and the English as liberating, illustrates her yearning for access to the freedom that comes with the primary host's language. In Esperanza's world, those who do not speak English are doomed to the shame with which the migrant identity is impregnated: "He wasn't her boyfriend or anything like that. Just another *brazer* who didn't speak English. Just another wetback. You know the kind. The ones who always look ashamed" (66).

The muted mother-figure seen in "Invierno," discouraged in her English attempts, has an interesting parallel in Mamacita in *The House on Mango Street*. However, the muting process seems almost an inversion of Díaz's character. Mamacita is brought to the US by her husband, yet instead of forbidding the use of English, he urges her to use the language. In fact, her husband has worked very hard to get her to the US, working two jobs and has "saved and saved because she was alone with the baby boy in that country" (76). When Mamacita, a vibrant figure in her home country, arrives to her new home, the taxi door opens "like a waiter's arm," and "[o]ut stepped a tiny pink shoe, a foot soft as a rabbits ear, then the thick ankle, a flutter of hips, fuchsia roses and green perfume" (76). She is big and beautiful, drawing attention with her pink attire and her regal exit from the car: "All at once she bloomed. Huge, enormous, beautiful to look at, from the salmon-pink feather on the tip of her hat down to the little rosebuds of her toes" (77). She steps into her new world still carrying the full-of-life appearance that she occupied in her country. However, like Mami in "Invierno," Mamacita quickly becomes a recluse, diminished from her colorful dynamics into another woman in Esperanza's neighborhood who takes her place by the window. After Mamacita's grand entrance, Esperanza recalls her swift change:

> Then we didn't see her.
> Somebody said because she's too fat, somebody because of the three flights of stairs, but I believe she doesn't come out because she is afraid to speak English and maybe this is so since she only knows eight words.
> [...] She sits all day by the window and plays the Spanish radio show and sings all the homesick songs about her country in a voice that sounds like a seagull. (77)

Mamacita's self-imposed isolation reflects her immediate decay in the new environment. Just like the roses on her shoes, she is a flower that immediately wilts when cut off from her life source. She laments her position and cries out "¿Cuándo, cuándo, cuándo?" (78), when will we go home? To which her husband replies "*Ay, caray!* We *are* home. This *is* home. Here I am and here we stay. Speak English. Speak English. Christ!" (78). This interaction demonstrates that her female identity is tied to where her husband is. The patriarchal figure, although seemingly compassionate, given his efforts to get his family to the new country, reminds Mamacita that her home is necessarily the space that he allows her; he is her host and she must accept the terms of her position. And, although the fact that he urges her to speak English may seem counter to the linguistic limitation of Mami in "Invierno," it is the same manipulation and construction of language space that Blommaert et al. describe, thus yielding the same incapacitating result.

> What happens [...] is not that the individual is *losing* multilingual resources or skills or that s/he is *having* a lack of capacity to communicate and interact, but that the particular environment *organizes* a particular regime of language, a regime which *incapacitates individuals*. (2005, 198)

Furthermore, just as Mami, in "Invierno," gradually witnesses her sons' own integration by learning English from TV, Mamacita "who does not belong," has her heart broken as her "baby boy, who has begun to talk, starts to sing the Pepsi commercial he heard on T.V." (78). Her heart falls because, with her son's English utterances, she now understands, to her dismay, that her situation is irreversible because her son is now a part of the host-space.

The women in Cisneros's novel represent a range of degrees of integration; however, each of them, despite their level of supposed access to the primary host's environment, has her own shortcomings that keep her in her designated space. Even in the case where the matriarchal figure may have access to the host-language, it is not enough to navigate the primary host's world, as this knowledge has been kept from her as well through a socialization process. Esperanza's own mother laments that she could not gain access to the outside world, despite the fact that she speaks two languages, because "she doesn't know which subway train to take to get downtown" (90). As Karen Martin points out, the women in Cisneros's novel mark an attempt to "give voice to marginalized protagonists and the strategies by which these young women attempt to transgress gendered borders and gain corporeal mobility" (2008, 51). In terms of the range of 'access' of Cisneros's female characters, a key point in Martin's analysis is that "Cisneros's work becomes a restrictive zone of violence, deterritorialization and exclusion whose semi-public nature taunts female characters with the possibility of agency while simultaneously precluding their transgression of externally and internally maintained borders" (2008, 51).

Language agency is the key term in both collections. We have seen parallel themes in both "Invierno" and *The House on Mango Street*; both present characters displaced from their homelands and 'welcomed' to a new country, not by the primary host, but by the *hosted-host* figure. Both Mami and Mamacita are appear diminished in their new space; their only hope for agency is obstructed by forces outside their control. The correlative theme of imprisonment in both collections also carries a parallel resolution directly related to agency through speech. The matriarchal groups, both in "Invierno" and *The House on Mango Street*, create a tandem-theme of 'walking and talking' that leads the female character to her symbolic freedom. Mami, in "Invierno," makes a choice at the end of the story to walk out of her physical prison and take back the agency she once had on the island. Esperanza is prophesied to take a different path that will eventually lead her back to Mango Street. However, the liberation of the female migrant in both collections rests on the figurative overtaking of the *gatekeeper* status that the patriarchal figure enjoys throughout the stories.

3 Walking Free

> What may be lost in the song as it travels from Mumbai to Sydney either linguistically or in terms of semantic moorings may open up other unanticipated venues. [...] [T]here opens up a cultural and temporal space in which all of us are modified and 'translated', where mutations and reconfigurations of travelling songs echo back our strains even as they bring in new notes. Border crossings are all about his. The vulnerable at our borders change us as we change them. Citizenship, then, is *processual* and about becoming.
> VAIDEHI RAMANATHAN
> *Language Policies and (Dis)Citizenship*

Hospitality is rooted in the interactions and non-actions of both the host and the guest. When talking of borders, the idea of citizenship or an authentic belonging is tied to a 'becoming'; a gradual process starting at the access point and involving change. As seen in the previous sections, the patriarchal figure(s) takes on a *hosted-host* identity in order to recuperate a status previously degraded as primary guest and the matriarchal group lacks linguistic and physical agency. The actions—physical intimidation, abuse, and oppression—are strengthened by the non-actions of the matriarchal figure—she remains stagnant and muted. However, in these stories, the vulnerable group transform into the saviors and the free-walkers—their non-actions are overridden by their linguistic actions. Fairclough's *gatekeeper* status yields preferential access to and control over both ideological aspects and linguistic aspects that make up the community.

Access, in both collections, is controlled by the male migrant and father figure while the migrant female and child lack physical and linguistic access to the outside world. In "Invierno," Díaz's characters confront the realities of displacement and experience a conflict of identity. At the same time, they undergo a transformation of self as they work through the systematic process of 'losing oneself' and in turn dynamically shifting their own will with forward momentum. In the case of Mami, it is unclear if she ever experiences the physical abuse that her sons suffer at the hands of their father. However, so oppressive is her language restriction that she becomes a muted and docile figure. As the most severely confined member within the home, it is she who makes the decision to walk out of her prison. "Invierno" ends with a scene in which the father is caught in a snowstorm and is unable to return home. Yunior and his brother are frightened, worried about being snowed in. Despite their fear, the boys, guided by their mother, decidedly walk out of the apartment for the first time together. Mami understands, finally, that she must make a choice to counter her husband; she comes to the realization that her husband is not who she once thought he was. "I went to the porch and watched the first snow begin to fall like finely sifted ash" Yunior recalls, "If we die, Papi's going to feel bad, I said. Mami turned away and laughed" (144). The boys have seen their mother slip out to the front porch a few times, ducking back in, almost with trepidation. However, when her sons—who had previously participated in her muting process—come to her side and take her by the arm so she doesn't fall on the ice, the three of them walk out into the host space together. "Where should we go? Rafa asked. He was blinking a lot to keep the snow out of his eyes. Go straight, Mami said. That way we don't get lost" (145).

With tear-filled eyes, Mami finds her freedom, albeit fleeting. Although throughout the remainder of Díaz's novel the reader finds that the family is not completely free, this instance demonstrates a symbolic freedom in that there is a partial reversion of power dynamics and the stepping outside indicates a new means of movement and a rejection of the *hosted-host*'s omnipresent control. I argue that the act of walking out is analogous to a figurative 'speaking out' against the *hosted-host* and is a propositional act that changes the rules of access, rendering the *gatekeeper* powerless in turn.

Esperanza's experience, while much more dynamic and layered in *The House on Mango Street*, mirrors Mami's repossession of agency. Just as Mami's 'voice' is connected with her choice to move freely, Esperanza's voice is found through a similar parallel of locutionary acts and the physical act of moving one's feet. Throughout the vignettes, themes of language restriction and lack of voice are scattered among images of *walking*. Esperanza is tied down to her neighborhood and her community, not only by patriarchal power-relations, but also by her feet. When Esperanza's mother buys her a new outfit for her cousin's baptism, she forgets to buy her new shoes. Esperanza feels that she can be reinvented by changing her appearance, but then is reminded that she cannot shake the identity that haunts her through her shoes: "I forget that I am wearing only ordinary shoes, brown and white, the kind my mother buys each year for school" (47). Her feet are confined within the ordinary brown shoes that hold the dirt of her life on the soles. These shoes are assigned to her 'place' in the world and although she wants to break free, she hasn't found her feet yet. As much as her mind wants to run free from her confines, she recognizes that her feet keep her grounded in her abysmal reality, the same as the other women around her.

> Sally, do you sometimes wish you didn't have to go home? Do you wish your feet would one day keep walking and take you far away from Mango Street, far away and maybe your feet would stop in front of a house, a nice one with flowers and big windows [...]. You could close your eyes and you wouldn't have to worry what people said because you never belonged here anyway and nobody could make you sad and nobody would think you're strange because you like to dream and dream. (82–83)

Esperanza's feet will take her out of her situation in the end, however, and she does this through her ability to transgress boundaries of language. She uses writing as a means to circumlocute her existing identity and transform or translate her experience into a poetry that moves her outside of her existing condition. As Betz (2012) describes, Cisneros's women are bound to their homes, situations, and neighborhood. Esperanza, however, "cannot follow in her female ancestors' footsteps" (20). She also adds that the "personification of Mango Street symbolizes the entire group of women that hold back from conquering their ambitions" (20), yet Esperanza refuses this. She consciously connects her writing to her world, understanding that if she makes an utterance or writes words on a page, she is somehow in control of her bodily movements as well: "I make a story for my life, for each step my brown shoe takes. I say, 'And so she trudged up the wooden stairs, her sad brown shoes taking her to the house she never liked'" (Cisneros 1984, 109). Earlier she had been encouraged to write: "You just remember to keep writing, Esperanza. You must keep writing. It will keep you free and I said yes, but at the same time I didn't know what she meant" (61) and now she makes the conscious effort to write herself out of her situation, at first only figuratively. Esperanza at this point takes the prophecy to heart that she will indeed one day find her way out of her guest position and repossess her life and identity. She will do this through writing. Her words will help her find her feet. However, Esperanza must remember that her identity cannot change and that part of it is being a voice for those who do not have one, back on Mango Street.

> When you leave you must remember always to come back, she said. [...] A circle, understand? You will always be Esperanza. You will always be Mango Street. You can't erase what you know. You can't forget who you are. [...] You must remember to come back. For the ones who cannot leave as easily as you. (105)

Esperanza agrees to this and makes it her mission; she will write herself out of her prison, but also come back for the ones she left behind, "[f]or the ones who cannot out" (110). The act of writing allows her agency. "I put it down on paper and then the ghost does not ache so much. I write it down and Mango says goodbye sometimes. She does not hold me with both arms. She sets me free" (110).

Esperanza, like Mami, overrules the power of her host, represented in the patriarchal system that carries over into her world. She rewrites her role as guest into that of host.

> One day I'll own my own house, but I won't forget who I am or where I came from. Passing bums will ask, Can I come in? I'll offer them the attic, ask them to stay, because I know how it is to be without a house. Some days after dinner, guests and I will sit in front of a fire. Floorboards will squeak upstairs. The attic grumble. Rat's they'll ask. Bums, I'll say and I'll be happy. (87)

The rats in the attic—much like Alicia's mice who haunt her on the floor, the ones her father denies exist and in essence denies Alicia's oppression—are now replaced with guests in Esperanza's attic. Her dream home will not be filled with evidence of her oppression like the scampering feet of the allegorical mice, but rather will be filled with a marginalized person who finds refuge in Esperanza's home. She becomes a powerful host, gracious, generous, and welcoming. Esperanza's language on the page becomes the movement of her feet and redefines her role as savior and free-walker.

4 Conclusion

The concept of linguistic agency, as a byproduct of the interactive nature of knowledge and power, leads to the understanding that the action that occurs in speech acts gives agency. As we have seen in this analysis, it may manifest in a muting, an utterance, or in an attempt at breaking down linguistic barriers. Or, as Esperanza dreams, a chance to recreate, or rewrite, individual identity from a clean page as white as snow. This agency is precisely what I claim creates a space that has a trifold affect: one, it questions the rules of engagement in the host-guest relationship and reveals a substratum for a complicated host-guest relationship. In turn, it also pushes the patriarchal figure outside of his domain of control and, finally, it allows for the matriarchal *voice* to emerge as the ultimate *mobile* element in the host-guest equation. In "Invierno" and *The House on Mango Street*, the *hosted-host* exercises control over a perceived paltry matriarchal group of migrant women and children swept in to a domestic space that is governed not only by the primary host but also by a secondary, more violent and intrusive host. Women are silenced in both stories. Women are placed on the floor by the window and inherit a dynamic, yet fixed identity, from which they cannot escape. However, linguistic agency turns the tide and its interactive nature leads to a repossession of space, identity, and facility.

Just as Mami's voice consociates movement and freedom, Esperanza's voice is found through an analogous parallel of physical and linguistic agency. Throughout the stories, notions of language restriction and inhibited enunciations are coupled with images of walking. One's feet trace along one's place in the world and although they want to forge a new path, they are bound to a prescribed labyrinth with no semblant exit. However, the matriarchal figures in both "Invierno" and *The House on Mango Street* break out of the *hosted-host's* control by overthrowing their *gatekeepers* and, in turn, utilize linguistic movement to gain power and agency and allude to the power of the authors themselves in their diasporic context. Both Cisneros and Díaz give voice and freedom to the Other through their work. Both authors allocate space on their pages, rejecting a community's assigned place, and act as a vessel of language that frees 'the ones who cannot out.'

References

Betz, Regina M. 2012. "Chicana 'Belonging' in Sandra Cisneros' *The House on Mango Street*." *Rocky Mountain Review. Special Issue*: 18–33.

Blommaert, Jan and Piia Varis. 2011. "Enough is enough: The heuristics of authenticity in superdiversity." *Tilburg Papers in Culture Studies* 2: 1–13.

Blommaert, Jan, James Collins and Stef Slembrouck. 2005. "Spaces of Multilingualism." *Language and Communication* 23 (3): 197–216.

Cisneros, Sandra. 1984. *The House on Mango Street*. New York: Vintage.

Derrida, Jacques. (1996) 1998. *Monolingualism of the Other; or, the Prosthesis of Origin*. Translated by Patrick Mensah. Stanford: Stanford UP.

Derrida, Jaques. (1997) 2000. *Of Hospitality: Anne Duformantelle Invites Jaques Derrida to Respond*. Translated by Rachel Bowlby. Stanford: Stanford UP.

Diaz, Junot. 2012. *This is How You Lose Her*. London: Faber.

Dikeç, Mustafa. 2002. "Pera Peras Poros: Longings for Spaces of Hospitality." *Theory, Culture & Society* 19 (1–2): 227–247.

Dikeç, Mustafa, Nigel Clark and Clive Barnett. 2009. "Extending Hospitality: Giving Space, Taking Time." *Paragraph* 32 (1): 1–14.

Fairclough, Norman. 1989. *Language and Power*. London and New York: Longman.

Fairclough, Norman. 2010. *Critical Discourse Analysis: The Critical Study of Language*. 2nd ed. New York: Routlege.

Foucault, Michel. 1972. *The Archaeology of Knowledge*. Translated by AM Sheridan Smith. New York: Harper.

Foucault, Michel. 1977. *Discipline and Punish: the Birth of the Prison*. Translated by Alan Sheridan. New York: Pantheon.

Gumperz, John. J., ed. 1982a. *Discourse Strategies*, vol. 1. Cambridge: Cambridge UP.

Gumperz, John. J., ed. 1982b. *Language and Social Identity*. Cambridge: Cambridge UP.

Manzanas Calvo, Ana María. 2013. "Junot Díaz's 'Otravida, Otravez' and *Hospitalia*: The Workings of Hostile Hospitality." *Journal of Modern Literature* 37 (1): 107–123.

Martin, Karen. 2008. "The House (of Memory) on Mango Street: Sandra Cisneros's Counter-Poetics of Space." *South Atlantic Review* 73 (1): 50–67.

Okrent, Arika. 2009. *In the Land of Invented Languages*. New York: Spiegel and Grau.

Ramanathan, Vaidehi, ed. 2013. *Language Policies and (Dis) Citizenship: Rights, Access, Pedagogies*. New York: Multilingual Matters.

Van Dijk, Teun A. 1993. "Principles of critical discourse analysis." *Discourse & Society* 4 (2): 249–283.

Van Dijk, Teun A. 1996. "Discourse, Power and Access." In *Texts and Practices: Readings in Critical Discourse Analysis*, edited by Carmen Rosa Caldas-Coulthard and Malcolm Coulthard, 84–104. London and New York: Routledge.

Van Dijk, Teun A., ed. 1997. *Discourse as Social Interaction*, vol. 2. London: Sage.

Van Dijk, Teun A. 2014. *Discourse and Knowledge: A Sociocognitive Approach*. Cambridge: Cambridge UP.

Wittegenstein, Ludwig. 2013. *The Project Gutenberg EBook of Tractatus Logico-Philosophicus by Ludwig Wittgenstein*. London: Routlege.

Wodak, Ruth and Norman Fairclough. 2004. *Critical Discourse Analysis*. London: Sage.

CHAPTER 4

Latino Immigrants at the Threshold: a Sociolinguistic Approach to Hospitality in US *Barriocentric* Narratives[1]

Luisa María González Rodríguez

Abstract

Drawing on Levinas's contention that language is inextricably connected to hospitality because it allows us to share the world with the Other, this article explores controversial issues related to language exchanges and linguistic tensions that spring when power, hospitality, and space are being questioned and contested. US barriocentric novels vividly portray how linguistic barricades separate outsiders from insiders by delimiting a psychical and linguistic territory where the immigrant is at a disadvantage in a decidedly monolingual host country. This article examines the metaphor of hospitality in Sandra Cisneros's *The House on Mango Street* and Piri Thomas's *Down these Mean Streets* through the magnifying lens of language use and code switching in order to gain a deeper insight into the ways in which ethnolinguistic identities are constructed and power relationships negotiated and challenged. In these novels, the use of the home language versus the host language brings to the fore other concerns connected to displacement and unstable resettlement as well as identity issues that reflect a fractured mode of belonging. In Cisneros's novel, the main issues posed by the dichotomy of the use of homeland versus host-country language create a breach between immigrants who are willing to accept assimilation and sameness as a sign of empowerment, and those who prefer to protect their linguistic space in order to maintain the link that connects them to their homeland's culture and values, as well as to delimit identitarian borders. In Thomas's *Down These Mean Streets* (1997) the linguistic enactment of identity becomes even more complex since the characters are forced to either resort to their homeland language or to code switching to challenge stereotypical social and ethnic categories. Most of the characters of Piri's novel have hybrid sociolects and, therefore, use linguistic forms from different language varieties of Spanish and English

---

1 This study is part of a larger research project entitled "Las fronteras de la hospitalidad en los estudios culturales de Estados Unidos y Europa" funded by a grant from the Regional Ministry of Culture of the Autonomous Government of Castile and Leon (ref. number SA342U14) and directed by Prof. Ana Mª Manzanas Calvo.

to display multifaceted identities that undermine the negative clichés attached to the immigrants living in depressed and impoverished inner cities. These characters, by challenging the power expressed though language, are also questioning the possibility of experiencing these migrant sites as habitable places. Their refusal to use Standard English clearly proves they know that the spatial limitations are also linguistic barricades. Furthermore, as Smith (2013) aptly points out, by refraining from crossing the linguistic threshold, the viability of experiencing hospitable encounters and the host country's capacity to open up spaces of hospitality are seriously questioned. A further aim is to explore how the language is used in these two autobiographical novels to establish sociocultural boundaries and activate different social roles or multiple facets of their shattered identities.

Keywords

Sandra Cisneros – Piri Thomas – sociocultural boundaries – hospitality – codeswitching – language and identity – ethnolinguistic identity – linguistic threshold – barriocentric narratives

In a globalized world where large masses of people from poor or unsafe countries have been forced to migrate, the governments of First-World countries have adopted protective measures to contain massive displacement. The restrictive policies implemented by rich countries have contributed to reinforcing socioeconomic and spatial boundaries that become a demonstration of the host's power over the guest (Pheng 2013) and unveil the oppressive side of hospitality by redefining it as hostility and racism (Ben Jelloun 1999; Dikeç 2002). The physical walls erected to stop immigrants at the borders of each country have not only promoted the construction of the Other as a threat or an enemy, but they have also resulted in the provocation of the threshold, where the collision of cultural values and different languages comes to the foreground. Within cities, psychic inner walls separate neighborhoods by using subtle barriers such as socioeconomic, ethno-racial, cultural, or linguistic parameters that stigmatize whole urban ghettos and widen the gap between privileged and marginalized populations (Watkins 2007). As a result, inner cities emerge where language is used by the host country as an exclusionary weapon that hinders hospitality and challenges the notion of the *barrio* as a habitable place. Therefore, an analysis of the verbal interactions in these ghettoized neighborhoods will raise questions of identity, hospitality/hostility issues, and power relationships related to the ownership of both physical and linguistic spaces.

Drawing on Emmanuel Levinas's ([1961] 1979, 254) pronouncement that language is inextricably connected to hospitality because it allows us to share the world with the Other, this chapter explores controversial issues related to language exchanges and linguistic tensions that spring up when power, hospitality, and space are being questioned and contested. US *barriocentric* novels vividly portray how linguistic barricades separate outsiders from insiders by delimiting a psychical and linguistic territory where the immigrant is at a disadvantage in a decidedly monolingual host country. This article examines the metaphor of hospitality in Sandra Cisneros's *The House on Mango Street* and Piri Thomas's *Down these Mean Streets* through the magnifying lens of language use and code-switching in order to gain a deeper insight into the ways in which ethnolinguistic identities are constructed and power relationships are negotiated and challenged within US marginalized neighborhoods. In these novels, the use of the home language versus the host language brings to the fore other concerns connected to displacement and unstable resettlement as well as identity issues that reflect a fractured mode of belonging. Moreover, the use of Spanish, or Spanish interference in English, in an essentially English monolingual society separates individuals on the basis of race or social class and, thus, language becomes a weapon of exclusion used by the host society to negatively stereotype lower-class immigrants. A further aim is to explore how language is used in these two autobiographical novels to establish sociocultural boundaries and activate different social roles or multiple facets of their shattered identities.

1 Language as a Weapon of Sociospatial Exclusion

The House on Mango Street ([1984] 1991), an autobiographical novel written by the Chicano writer Sandra Cisneros (1954–), subtly depicts how language can be used to delimit the boundaries between majority and minority society, and also serves to construct negative sociolinguistic stereotypes that are tinged with xenophobia. In fact, the novel addresses the notion that language divergence becomes a symbolic strategy for maintaining spatial, social, and ethnic hierarchies. The Latinos living within the ghettoized community of Mango Street become conscious of the fact that mastering the English language might entail prestige and acceptance while speaking Spanish, the lower status language, might provoke xenophobic reactions in the host society. When language is racialized in this way it is usually perceived as a hindrance to "the natural progress of social mobility" and "as an insurmountable barrier to such progress" (Urciuoli 2013, 18).

As this novel clearly emphasizes, the notion of hospitality is closely connected to issues of language and identity. The immigrant is forced to adhere to the host's cultural patterns in order not to be perceived as a stranger or an ungrateful person who refuses to accept the cultural values that will grant him protection. The insider-outsider dynamic reveals the mechanisms whereby language divergence contributes to strengthening the host-society's systems of exclusion. Forcing the immigrant to speak the host's language is the first sign of hostility as he is not only stigmatized but also situated at a disadvantage, particularly regarding social interaction. In *The House on Mango Street*, Esperanza, the narrator-protagonist, sheds light on American society's indifference and hostility towards immigrants by narrating her father's experience: "My father says when he came to this country he ate hamandeggs for three months. Breakfast, lunch and dinner. Hamandeggs. That was the only word he knew. He doesn't eat hamandeggs anymore" (77). This experience illustrates the ways in which linguistic discrimination gives rise to the establishment of different hierarchies of belonging in which the immigrant is relegated to the lowest position. By disallowing the guest to use his heritage language, the host is also dispossessing him of his identity. Thus, minority members who do not master the English language become invisible to the mainstream society. An example of this is Geraldo, the main character of the vignette "Geraldo No Last name," who, after being killed by a car that hit him and drove away without stopping, is described as "[j]ust another *brazer* who didn't speak English. Just another wetback. You know the kind. The ones who always look ashamed" (66). Geraldo, a Mexican who is unable to speak English, embodies the social figure of the stranger who is relegated to a position below the threshold of social recognition. Pierre Bordieu in *Language and Symbolic Power* contends that "[s]peakers lacking the legitimate competence are *de facto* excluded from the social domains in which this competence is required, or are condemned to silence" (1991, 55). Furthermore, the language politics imposed by the monolingual, hegemonic society also serves to construct negative stereotypes, thus generating low self-esteem issues and feelings of self-hatred among immigrants once those prejudices are internalized by them.

As this novel clearly illustrates, language divergence often gives rise to segregation and prejudice since the majority group relies on norms of language choice to exert their power and manage foreigners. This creates two spheres of relations among immigrants that, as some sociolinguists have pointed out, are established along lines that connect social hierarchy or prestige and language (Bailey 2001). In diglossic communities, a rigid distinction is established between the low-prestige language spoken in the inner sphere among friends, neighbors, and family and the high-prestige variety spoken in the outer-sphere

(Montes-Granado 2012; Urciuoli 2013). In the Chicano neighborhood depicted in *The House on Mango Street*, Spanish-speaking dwellers seem to be used to interacting in a mixture of English and Spanish and code-switching is considered a natural part of daily communication within this inner sphere. Although Cisneros uses Spanish sparingly in this novel, her heritage language looms steadily throughout her stories as an identity marker. The English-dominant narrator-protagonist intersperses Mexican cultural words like *"frijoles"* (37, 38), *"tamales"* (47), *"tembleque"* (51), *"las comadres"* (91, 103) or *"los espíritus"* (63) to describe the simple daily life of the barrio. Spanish is the language used to express emotions in intimate domestic spaces; therefore, when Esperanza's father has to tell her that her grandfather has died he resorts to Spanish: "Your *abuelito* is dead, Papa says early one morning in my room. *Está muerto*" (56). Within the private space of the household and neighborhood, both languages are mixed because there are no clear boundaries between the two languages, as can be inferred from Cisneros's vignettes. In fact, it could be argued that "in everyday speech, code-switching adds extra layers of meaning, defines situations and expresses ethnic identity simply through the chosen language" (Martin 2005, 408). Moreover, code-switching practices allow Latinos to overcome the English versus Spanish dichotomy, as well as reaffirm their hybrid cultural and linguistic identities.

Yet, the Chicano characters are painfully aware that Spanish and Spanglish are only allowed at home or within the marginal spaces of the *barrio*, whereas English is required in outer-sphere interactions. Unfortunately, the "language that works for bilingual at home and around the neighborhood is disallowed by outsiders who take to themselves the power to judge language difference in moral terms" (Urciuoli 2013, 35). Interactions in Spanish or interference of Spanish into English are usually equated with marginalized, impoverished inner cities. These prejudices enacted through language induce a feeling of shame among minority members that force them to abandon their mother tongue for fear of being discriminated against by the majority society. Moreover, the forced choice between their native language and the host language also gives rise to identity issues both among immigrants who feel more attached to their home country as well as among those with a hyphenated identity.

2 Language, Identity, and Power Relations

In Cisneros's novel, the main issues posed by the dichotomy of the use of homeland versus host country language create a breach between immigrants who are willing to accept assimilation and sameness as a sign of empowerment and those who prefer to protect their linguistic space in order to maintain the link that connects them to their native culture and values, as well as to delimit identitarian borders. Whereas some of the Mexicans depicted in the novel perceive language as a tool to express and preserve their identity and, therefore, they cling to Spanish; others, like Esperanza, her family, and Mamacita's husband, think that they need to master the English language to achieve new levels of empowerment in terms of economic and political participation. The latter consider that being competent in English is crucial for overcoming the barriers erected by the receiving country and that it is the first step towards becoming full citizens. In so far as language, "dictates expectations others have of us and opportunities we are afforded, expectations and opportunities that help us rise or constrain us to remain where we are" (Domínguez-Rosado 2015, xiii), immigrants will be forced to admit that in order to be recognized they will have to yield to conditional hospitality and accept the rules imposed on them. Language racialization results in negative group identity, with some members seeking membership into the mainstream society by speaking the high-status language.

However, Mamacita, the main character of the vignette "No Speak English," a chapter entirely devoted to the theme of language and hospitality, refuses to accept both the language and culture of the host country. Language is crucial for preserving an individual's social identity and, therefore, she refuses to lose her identity by yielding to the dominant English-speaking community. This character feels homesick; she is a foreigner in a monolingual country with a language "that sounds like tin" (78). She never goes out and Esperanza wonders why: "Somebody said because she's too fat, somebody because of the three flights of stairs, but I believe she does not come out because she is afraid to speak English" (77). Mamacita does not want to be assimilated by the host country and she decides to remain a stranger. She belongs to the groups of immigrants who do not feel they belong to the new country and, therefore, they cling to the country they left behind. This country is not her home, she perceives the new place as hostile territory, a foreign place, which makes her long for her home:

> Home. Home. Home is a house in a photograph, a pink house, pink as hollyhocks with lots of startled light. The man paints the walls of the apartment pink, but it's not the same, you know. She still sighs for her pink house, and then I think she cries. I would. (77)

Her behavior brings her into direct confrontation with her husband, who has a completely different opinion about the host country. Thus, when Mamacita manifests her sadness and wants to know when they are going back to Mexico by asking "¿*Cuándo, cuándo, cuándo*?" (78), her husband replies: "¡*Ay, caray*! We are home. This *is* home. Here I am and here I stay. Speak English. Speak English. Christ!" (78). The use of Spanish versus the use of English clearly illustrates the underlying divergence between them. Both characters enact their identities in divergent ways and language choice helps us visualize those differences. Mamacita clings tightly to Spanish as a way of reclaiming her Mexican subjectivity. By contrast, her husband, inasmuch as he is striving for sameness, has decided to conform to the host country's ways and language in order not to suffer rejection and exclusion because of being a foreigner. This only serves to further aggravate the conflict between them as does Mamacita's sense of alienation and non-belonging: "¡Ay! *Mamacita*, who does not belong, every once in a while lets out a cry, hysterical, high, as if he had torn the only skinny thread that kept her alive, the only road out to that country" (78).

As the narrator suggests in this chapter, some characters like Mamacita perceive the English language not as a tool for empowerment, but as a barrier separating them from their own culture. She considers that speaking the language of the oppressor means absorbing all of his values and habits. For her, language is intrinsically linked to identity and, by adamantly refusing to speak English, she is resisting the idea of being dispossessed of her identity, which results in alienation and estrangement. From a sociolinguistic perspective, this is an example of how "language becomes a marker of displacement and reclamation, a marker of self-identity and self-empowerment" and of how "every Spanish word represents a refusal to capitulate to English ethnocentricity" (Pérez-Torres 1995, 227). Therefore, she has decided to stay at home and create her own safe space, a refuge which recreates a Mexican atmosphere and protects her against a hostile language and culture, and this is the reason why she "sits all day by the window and plays the Spanish radio show and sings all the homesick songs about her country in a voice that sounds like a seagull" (77). For Mamacita moving from Mexico to the United States has led to 'spatial dislocation' and estrangement. As a result, she refuses to cut the umbilical cord that connects her to Mexican tradition, language, and culture. She clearly clings to the hope of returning to her country and the language is the only way of maintaining that link. As Betz cogently explains, "rather than assimilating or accepting her newfound double-identity, *Mamacita* denies the English language and views America as the distant road away from the home where she belongs" (2012, 24). It is clear that for some individuals within these marginalized communities rejecting the dominant language is a way of preserving their identities and avoiding the sense of not belonging, which causes alienation and unhappiness. However, as Erber aptly points out, "it is not just language as an instance of power that is being questioned; it is the very notion of hospitality, refuge and a habitable place that is being contested" (2015, 100).

Another interesting issue that this vignette brings to the fore is the common scenario that children and grandchildren of Spanish-speaking immigrants will probably not develop proficiency in their family's mother tongue. Kim Potowski, after analyzing the sociolinguistic dimensions of immigration in the United States, concludes that "immigrants abandon their heritage languages for a variety of reasons including peer pressure, lack of opportunity to use the language, or fear that it will interfere with their ability to learn English or get ahead in American society" (2013, 37). As language divergence becomes racialized and foreign or non-standard linguistic codes are perceived as a constraint for social mobility, many second-generation immigrants decide to speak the prestige language and adopt American values. This creates a cultural and communicative breach between parents and children, which results in a weakening of family ties and the loss of parental authority. Thus, when Mamacita's son begins to use English, she feels he is committing an act of betrayal against his Mexican linguistic heritage and identity:

> And then to break her heart forever, the baby boy, who has begun to talk, starts to sing the Pepsi commercial he heard on T.V.
> No speak English, she says to the child who is singing in the language that sounds like tin. No speak English, no speak English, and bubbles into tears. No, no, no, as if she can't believe her ears. (78)

Her words not only anticipate some of the aforementioned conflicts between parents and children, but also the possibility that her child may become an English-dominant bilingual whose heritage language and cultural values will be contaminated by those imposed by the host society. This prospect is very painful for Mamacita who foresees that her son's words in English separate her even further from her beloved homeland.

3 The Racialization of Language Difference or the Metaphor of the Threshold

Piri Thomas's (1928–2011) *Down These Mean Streets* ([1967] 1997) is another *barriocentric* novel that vividly epitomizes the signs of language prejudice within urban ghettos. By underlining the sociopolitical context to which ethno-racialized populations are relegated this novel renders itself ripe for anthropolitical linguistic analysis. This perspective provides a revealing insight as to how the members of stigmatized groups are assigned to "static and disparaged ethnic, racial and class identities, and that identifies them with static and disparaged linguistic codes" (Zentella 1997, 13). As this autobiographical novel reveals, language boundaries are inextricably linked to the way in which Puerto Rican immigrants construct their identities and are allowed to socialize in the host country. These boundaries give the host a sense of superiority and control over the guest that turns hospitality into hostility. Thus, the power assumed by mainstream society in the US to judge language differences in moral and racialized terms reveals not only the oppressive side of hospitality, but also the impossibility for immigrants to cross the linguistic threshold set by the host. According to Smith,

> [t]he metaphor of the threshold allows issues to be raised concerning the use of home and host language, including the quite frequent instances of code-switching within single utterances, when speakers return to their native language: the almost complete rejection of complete threshold-crossing, which throws doubt on the viability of a hospitality-based model for migrant meetings: and the relevance of these issues outside the central relationship, concerning the ambient language and the capacity for welcome of the host country as a whole. (2013, 82)

The host country's need to reaffirm its sovereignty over the place has a ghettoization effect, whereby spatial, ethnic, and linguistic boundaries are drawn to separate insiders from outsiders, natives from foreigners. In this context, whole speech communities associated with ethnic minorities are stigmatized and discriminated against for not abandoning their heritage languages or not speaking standard English, thus precluding contact and integration. For, as Jane H. Hill contends, "[w]hite public space is constructed through intense monitoring of the speech of racialized populations such as Chicanos and Latinos and African Americans for signs of linguistic disorder" (1998, 680). Language difference is, therefore, perceived as a barrier hindering access to socio-institutional spaces as well as a boundary for establishing categories of social inclusion or exclusion.

Down These Mean Streets vividly depicts how Puerto Ricans settle into New York City Spanish Harlem, an underprivileged neighborhood they call *el Barrio*, where they create close-knit communities that are "an important mechanism of language maintenance" (Milroy 1987, 182) due to the strong cultural links they maintain with the green island. Their knowledge of *Barrio* Spanish qualifies Puerto Rican immigrants as members of the community and yields them a positive social identity. Most of these immigrants naturally juxtapose or alternate between English and Spanish, thus their blurring of the linguistic boundaries imposed by the host becomes an in-group marker among the members of the Puerto Rican community living in el Barrio. In the inner sphere, when they are interacting with friends, family, and neighbors, they feel comfortable code-switching from one language to another. Spanish is usually chosen to interact with parents and other elder members of the community and that is the reason Piri addresses his father's friends, who are first-generation immigrants, in Spanish:

> '*Cómo está, Mr. Rivera?*'
> '*Muy bien, Piri. Y tú?*'
> '*Muy bien, gracias. Cómo está, Mr. González?*'
> '*Bien, gracias. Y tú?*'
> '*Bien, gracias. Cómo está*, Mr. Rod—excuse me— er, Mr. López?'
> 'Fine, *hijo*. You are up late, eh?' (6)

This dialogue brings to the fore interesting sociolinguistic aspects regarding the use of Spanish and the negotiation of identity within this speech community. First, it could be argued that Spanish is preferred among first-generation, middle-aged immigrants. This means that they are not fully integrated into American mainstream society and that most of their interactions take place within the Puerto Rican community, where they have built a close-knit network structure. Second, Spanish is used by the younger generation in deference towards the elder members of the community as well as to show respect for their ancestors' language and cultural heritage. Finally, Piri uses the Spanish language as a symbol of identity in so far as he wants to demonstrate his involvement and attachment to the community.

The family is the first socializing sphere and, as this novel reveals, it is where Puerto Rican linguistic, ethnic, and cultural heritage is transmitted. The narrator-protagonist and his siblings like to lovingly gather around their mother to listen to her stories about Puerto Rico: "Tell us, tell us about Porto Rico," says one of Piri's sisters, to which her mother replies that "It's not Porto Rico, it's *Puerto* Rico" (9). The mother, who speaks English with a heavy Puerto Rican accent, here takes the role of the gatekeeper to the Spanish language, thus putting special emphasis on correcting her children's pronunciation. In the chapter entitled "Puerto Rican Paradise," Piri's mother enjoys conveying an idealized view of their home country, which makes her feel homesick: "Moms copped that wet-eyed look and began to talk about her *isla verde*, Moses' land of milk and honey" (9). In her description of the island, the narrator's mother code-switches into Spanish, thus revealing that Spanish is the language of intimacy, the code they use to express emotions: "When I was a little girl [...] I remember the getting up in the morning [...] and the quiet of the greenlands and the golden color of the morning sky, the grass wet from the *lluvia ... Ai, Dios*, the *coquís* and the *pajaritos* making all the *música*" (9). But code-switching also becomes a marker of their heteroglossic identity, which is connected to the family members' sense of linguistic and cultural in-between-ness. As Benjamin Bailey observes, "[t]he juxtaposition of diverse linguistic elements in single utterances [...] reflects social negotiations and a social reality in which neither linguistic practices nor social identities fit into static, unitary categories of language and identity" (2007, 270). Furthermore, in the intimate sphere of the household, all the family members constantly codeswitch into Spanish not only to erase the linguistic barriers imposed by the host society between English and Spanish, but also to recreate the comfort and racial tolerance of their Puerto Rican Paradise. At home, Piri feels that he can reconcile his two identities, black and Puerto Rican, for he is "a funny *morenito*" (18) or a "*negrito*" (19), as his mother lovingly calls him.

However, with his Puerto Rican friends, Piri uses a hybrid sociolect that combines non-standard varieties of English and Spanish to negotiate his social identity. Puerto Rican teenagers switch from one language to the other almost unconsciously, which reveals their hybrid, in-between identity as Nuyoricans. For example, the narrator asks Carlito, one of his Puerto Rican friends: "What's *nuevo*?" and he answers: "*Nada* new, 'side's being strung out" (328). Even if they are English-dominant bilinguals, these youngsters constantly use Spanish swear words and insults, such as "*coño*" (3) or "*estúpido*" (18), as a way of reinforcing their social identity as stigmatized members of a marginal group. Despite the low prestige associated with their Puerto Rican Spanglish, young members of these segregated communities use these sociolects as enactments of their ethnicized identities and as a way of restoring pride in their heritage language. Moreover, in order to reinforce the solidarity of the in-group, these teenagers' interactions reveal speech patterns that "are challenging the dominant class definition of what is a legitimate and illegitimate language and defining their hybrid, heteroglossic and borderless language" (Casielles-Suárez 2017, 160). Within the comfortable space of the inner sphere language choice serves to nurture their identitarian solidarity as well as to give these teenagers a sense of empowerment; however, the refusal to speak the dominant code in outer-sphere interactions leads to further stigmatization as their ethnolinguistic identity becomes explicit through language choice.

In the United States standard English is the only variety with overt social prestige and the use of other languages is scrutinized and employed as a marker of exclusion. As Bailey cogently points out, "[s]tereotypical language-based judgements of social class status often overlap with stereotypical language-based judgements of race and ethnicity, and ways of speaking that are popularly understood as 'African American' or 'Latino' are generally associated with lower socioeconomic status" (2010, 77). For the Puerto Rican community depicted in Thomas's novel, linguistic boundaries prove to be social barriers that limit access to socioinstitutional spaces. In outer-sphere interactions speaking a low-status language may result in unbalanced power relationships that create feelings of shame and insecurity. The chapter entitled "Home Relief" illustrates the asymmetrical relationship between host and guest. When Piri's father loses his job, his mother tells him: "*Hijo*, today you no go to school. I want you to go to the Home Relief Office and help me explain about your father losing his job with the WPA" (41). There he observes that most of the people are Puerto Ricans and blacks and that "it seemed that every mother had brought a kid to interpret for her" (42). The pressure of linguistic boundaries is so powerful in outer-sphere interactions that it condemns these immigrants to silence. This episode clearly epitomizes how dominant groups establish language as a mechanism for social control and symbolic domination. By stigmatizing certain language varieties as low-prestige codes associated with underprivileged inner cities, the dominant group engenders the minority's feelings of inferiority for, as Urciuoli contends,

> Accents, 'broken' English, and 'mixing' become signs of illiteracy and laziness, which people are morally obliged to control through education. Not controlling language results in 'bilingual confusion.' Bilingual neighborhoods are equated with slums, an equation familiar to people who live in them [...] Language, like physical features or a person's name, is metacommunicative, contributing to an interpretive frame in which anything one says or does is assessed in terms of the category suggested, for example, 'Spanish,' 'white,' 'black.' One's words and actions are read as 'typical of people like that' and one's worth judged accordingly. (2013, 26)

4 Enacting a Bilingual Identity to Counteract a Racial Identity

This autobiographical novel also provides interesting insights into how racial discrimination has been redefined from biology to language and how language divergence has contributed to reinforcing the barriers to social integration. For Piri Thomas, being himself a dark-skinned Puerto Rican, US racial categorization and language-based stereotypes confront him with racial prejudices that in Puerto Rican society are non-existent. Considering that Puerto Ricans view themselves as outside the binary black/white system (Bailey 2001), the protagonist seeks to resist being deprived of his multicultural ethnicity. The American binary division makes racial identity particularly problematic for dark-skinned Puerto Ricans who, as Piri depicts, have to face language prejudice and social exclusion from institutional spaces and structures. When Piri and his family moved from the Spanish Harlem to Babylon, a suburb on Long Island, in search of better opportunities, he was confronted with negative stereotypes based on language differences and the racialization of discourse. This is illustrated by the episode he narrates at the lunchtime swing session in the school gym where he meets a girl called Marcia and is faced with the dogmatic US racial dichotomy during his conversation with her. Marcia tells him that his accent sounds like Jerry's, another dark-skinned student, thus revealing that language difference determines the class/race category to which individuals are assigned. Her words not only reveal the underlying stigmatization of certain non-standard varieties, they also hide the host's need to highlight socioeconomic boundaries. For, as Ferreira aptly remarks,

> Judgements concerning the correctness and purity of linguistic varieties are social rather than linguistic. There is nothing whatsoever intrinsic in non-standard varieties that could make them inferior. Any evident inferiority is due only to their association with speakers who are considered to be from under-privileged, low-status groups. (2011, 237)

The girl has automatically assumed that a black skin and the use of African-American vernacular English entail a black identity, while Piri decides to challenge hegemonic assumptions that misrepresent and denigrate him. Thus, the protagonist resorts to Spanglish in order to resist Marcia's static connections between phenotype and ethnic identity. Conscious as he is that a Puerto Rican identity grants him a better status, he speaks Spanish as a resource to dissociate himself from African Americans. In this threatening context, Piri tries to reaffirm his language-based identity as a Puerto Rican and, therefore, code-switching is also used to enact a hybrid identity that could subvert language boundaries:

'I also was at the field when you smashed that ball a mile'
'That was *suerte*,' I said
'What's that' she asked.
'What?'
'What you said—"swer-tay."'
I laughed. 'Man, that's Spanish.'

'Are you Spanish? I didn't know. I mean you don't look like what I thought a Spaniard looks like.'
'I ain't a Spaniard from Spain,' I explained. 'I'm a Puerto Rican from Harlem.'
'Oh—you talk English very well,' she said.
'I told you I was born in Harlem. That's why I ain't got no Spanish accent.'
'No-o, your accent is more like Jerry's.'
[...]
'Did you know Jerry?' she asked. [...]
'Yeah, I know Jerry,' I said softly. 'He moved away because he got some girl in trouble. I know Jerry is colored and I know I got his accent. Most of us in Harlem steal from each other's language or style of living. And it's *suerte*, s-u-e-r-t-e. It means "luck".' (83–84)

As this dialogue demonstrates, language difference is used by the host society to establish categories and hierarchies that bring to the fore the ways in which hospitality is restricted and made conditional. For Urciuoli, "[r]acializing discourses equate language difference with disorder, with images of illiterate foreigners flooding the United States and refusing to speak English or hordes of the underclass speaking an accented English with 'broken' grammar and 'mixed' vocabulary" (2013, 18). It could be stated that the asymmetrical interaction between Marcia and the narrator-protagonist clearly relegates the latter to a vulnerable position where the hegemonic majority group maintains a dominant position by restricting membership of the minority community. In fact, this episode confronts Piri with the paradox of being an American citizen who is treated as an unwelcome foreigner.

Throughout his conversation with the girl, Piri adamantly proclaims his Puerto-Ricanness by challenging a white American community that denies his multicultural identity and insists on categorizing him as black. Thomas code-switches to Spanish in order to label and differentiate himself from African American speakers and to reinforce the idea that for him being Puerto Rican includes cultural and linguistic subtleties that question the categorical distinction between being black or white. For him speaking Spanish is a crucial aspect of his identity as a Puerto Rican. Nevertheless, when he explains that "[m]ost of us in Harlem steal from each other's language or style of living" (84), he wants his interlocutor to understand that Puerto Ricans in Harlem use English language varieties in ways that disclose the complex and inextricable relationship between identity and socioeconomic conditions. For Puerto Ricans adopting African-American vernacular English means that they identify with the black community, with whom they share a segregated and inhospitable space. Furthermore, by acknowledging that language helps to construct a sense of community among the inhabitants of some neighborhoods marginalized by the sociolinguistic construction of difference, Piri's words bring to the fore the notion that marginality also produces counter-hegemonic discourses that challenge simplistic ethnic divisions based on language use.

But, conscious as Marcia is that she belongs to the dominant group, she decides to use her power to draw the boundaries of ethnic, moral, and social divisions based on her own assumptions of language difference. These walls represent, as Smith observes, "an assertion of the power of linguistic exclusion on the part of one who temporarily no longer wishes to offer even the prospect of hospitality" (2013, 85). When Piri leaves the place, he overhears the girl and her friends talking about him and their conversation makes it clear that for most of them Piri is black according to their white/black classification system. As this dialogue clearly demonstrates, conflicts over language usually mask racial hostility and xenophobic attitudes. The narrator's efforts to challenge the negative stereotypes produced by the majority society are doomed to fail once he finally becomes conscious that the host still has a monopoly on insider/outsider designations:

> 'Christ, first that Jerry bastard and now him. We're getting invaded by niggers,' said a thin voice.
> 'You said it,' said another guy. 'They got some nerve. My dad says that you give them an inch them apes want to take a yard.'
> 'He's not so bad,' said a shy, timid voice. 'He's a polite guy and seems to be a good athlete. And besides, I hear he's a Puerto Rican.'
> 'Ha—he's probably passing for Puerto Rican because he can't make it for white,' said the thin voice. 'Ha, ha, ha.' (85–6)

This brief conversation reveals how language divergence is managed by the majority group to classify the minority group according to its own rules and how these boundary ideologies result in the production of the stranger. As the language code spoken by the ethnic group is scrutinized and stigmatized, the members of the minority group are relegated to remaining below the threshold of social acceptance and visibility. As a result, Piri ends up internalizing these language prejudices and decides to return to Spanish Harlem:

> This Long Island was a foreign country. It looked so pretty and clean but it spoke a language you couldn't dig. The paddy boys talked about things you couldn't dig, or maybe better, they couldn't dig you. Yeah, that was it; they didn't dig your smooth talk, and you always felt like on the rim of

belonging. No matter how much you busted your hump trying to be one of them, you'd never belong, they wouldn't let you. (88)

Another example of language exclusion associated with the racialization of language difference is an episode the protagonist narrates in the section entitled "How to Be a Negro Without Really Trying." In this section, the narrator describes how language difference functions as a marker for exclusion and as an insurmountable obstacle to job market access. Piri has a job interview to work as a door-to-door salesman only to find out that blacks are not hired. The attitude of his potential employer, a representative of the white hegemonic system whose excessive politeness is tinged with xenophobia, clearly illustrates that language difference is usually associated with race, ethnicity, or social class: "Oh, I see. But you're not Puerto Rican, are you? You speak fairly good English even though once in a while you use some slang—of course, it's sort of picturesque" (100). These words shed light on the mechanisms whereby ethnic minorities and their linguistic practices are socially excluded through institutionally produced moral categories. As Jane H. Hill cogently remarks, "Puerto Ricans experience the 'outer sphere' as an important site of racialization, since they are always found wanting by this sphere's standards of linguistic orderliness" (1998, 682).

An analysis of the interaction between Piri and his white interviewer also provides interesting information as to how the protagonist tries to construct his personal and social identities in institutional settings: "My parents are Puerto Ricans" (100), Piri says, trying to convince the man that he is not an African American. When the interviewer asks him if Thomas is a Puerto Rican name, he answers that his "mother's family name is Montañez" (100) in an effort to counteract the man's racial prejudices. Moreover, he not only uses Spanish words to avoid being taken for African American, but also tries to differentiate himself from the black community by separating the spaces both ethnic communities inhabit within the same marginal neighborhood. Thus, when the man suggests that Piri's address is in Harlem, the narrator answers: "Yes, sir, it's split up in different sections, like the Italian section and Irish and Negro and the Puerto Rican section. I live in the Puerto Rican section. It's called the *Barrio*" (100). The narrator-protagonist is once again confronted with the assumptions of uniformity held by US mainstream society that understands racialized identities in binary terms. For, as Denton observes,

> For Nuyoricans who find themselves between two languages and two social contexts, language can take on an especially prominent role in defining their identity, both in personal processes of identity formation and

in externally imposed aspects. What often occurs is a double process of Othering, where the knowledge of a non-dominant language becomes the boundary of membership in two different contexts. (2014, 71)

In this episode, the oppressive side of hospitality materializes when language difference is used to reinforce hierarchical differences between host and guest. The host has delimited the linguistic boundaries that give rise to a network of power relations where non-standard varieties are scrutinized so as to become indicators for exclusion. For Piri, this unpleasant encounter persuades him of the impossibility of crossing ethnic and social boundaries. Being considered an outsider not only leads him to a life of drugs and crime but also causes him to fall into an identity crisis. "Fuck Mr. Christian. I didn't need his job anyway. I was selling pot—and smoking it, too—regularly" (p. 105), Piri exclaims, after finding out that he is denied full citizenship and banned from social mobility by those who have the power to set the boundaries between insiders and outsiders. This incident, in so far as it brings into his consciousness the fact that US mainstream society categorizes him as a black man, also forces him to accept and negotiate his blackness. Brew, one of his African American friends, cleverly summarizes Piri's ambivalent feelings when forced to accept that he has been redefined as a racialized Other:

> Sure he's a Porty Rican, but his skin makes him a member of the black man's race an' hit don't make no difference he can talk that Porty Rican talk. His skin is dark an' that makes him ju' anudder rock right along wif the res' of us, an' tha' goes for all the rest of them foreign-talkin' black ovah tha' world. When you're born a shoe, yuh stays a shoe. (159)

Once confronted with the sharp white/black dichotomization and with the painful fact of being taken for "*un Negrito*" (148), the protagonist tries to resolve his Puerto Rican racial ambiguity. In the chapter entitled "Funeral for a Prodigal Son" Piri expresses his resentment at being deprived of his multicultural identity and decides to break with his family who seem unable to admit their mixed-racial heritage. His father admits having suffered social ostracism due to his skin color and that is the reason he proclaims his Puerto-Ricanness: "I noticed how a cold rejection turned into indifferent acceptance when they heard my exaggerated accent. I can remember the time when I made my accent heavier, to make me more of a Puerto Rican than the most Puerto Rican there ever was" (153). Piri, however, decides to leave the safe environment of the Puerto Rican community and go to the South of the United States with his black friend Brew in an attempt to articulate his blackness. The narrator-protagonist thus enters a hostile territory where he becomes aware of the mechanisms of exclusion used by hegemonic white America. His experience proves to be traumatic and sparks within him a deep-seated hatred towards white people. He therefore goes to a brothel where blacks are banned from entering and uses his heritage language to challenge binary racial stereotypes. His Mexican friend tells Piri, "If you do not speak a word of English, you may pass for Puerto Rican" (187). As McGill cogently points out,

> Language is the tool by which he mediates the enunciation of a black Caribbean self. Spanish and English are used in the brothel as dismantling tools: Spanish is used at the point of entry, English as the means of deconstructing the sexual, racial, and cultural politics of his stay in the South [...] his words to the prostitute in English are like weapons. They are a means of lashing out at the white world, if only through words, in a way that momentarily lets him feel his strength and regain his power.
> (2005, 187)

5 Conclusion

These two autobiographical novels vividly epitomize the signs of language prejudice as experienced by Mexican and Puerto Rican communities in marginalized urban enclosures. A sociolinguistic approach to the racialization of language provides a revealing insight into the ways in which language divergence is used by the host country not only to stigmatize ethnic groups but also to draw the boundaries delimiting spaces and marking social inclusion or exclusion. By scrutinizing the linguistic practices of minority groups, the hegemonic majority group creates hostile linguistic landscapes where language is used as a powerful weapon of exclusion. Language politics gives rise to asymmetrical power relationships that bring to the fore serious shortcomings in the ethics of hospitality. As Cisneros and Thomas evince in their autobiographical narrations, language stigmatization generates negative self-esteem and identity issues that will have a devastating impact on how these minority groups interact in both the inner and outer spheres. They show their characters fluctuating between two languages, Spanish and English, and struggling to express their hybrid identities and their sense of in-between-ness. In fact, these hybrid sociolects are used to display multifaceted identities that undermine the negative clichés attached to the immigrants living in depressed and impoverished inner cities. However, while resisting the adoption of the prestige language variety helps strengthen group solidarity, maintaining these non-standard varieties may in the long term hinder their socioeconomic mobility, thus trapping them in cycles of discrimination, vulnerability, and socioeconomic subjugation. These characters, by challenging the power expressed through language, are also questioning the possibility of experiencing these migrant sites as habitable places. Their refusal to use standard English clearly proves they know that the spatial limitations are also linguistic barricades. Furthermore, by prohibiting ethnic minorities from crossing the linguistic threshold, the viability of experiencing hospitable encounters and the host country's capacity to open up spaces of hospitality are seriously questioned.

References

Bailey, Benjamin. 2001. "The Language of Multiple Identities among Dominican Americans." *Journal of Linguistic Anthropology* 10 (2): 190–223.
Bailey, Benjamin. 2007. "Heteroglossia and Boundaries." In *Bilingualism: Social and Political Approaches*, edited by Monica Heller, 257–274. New York: Palgrave MacMillan.
Bailey, Benjamin. 2010. "Language, Power, and the Performance of Race and Class." In *Multiracial Americans and Social Class: The Influence of Social Class on Social Identity*, edited by Kathleen Korgen, 72–86. New York: Routledge.
Ben Jelloun, Tahar. 1999. *French Hospitality: Racism and North African Immigrants*. New York: Columbia UP.
Betz, Regina M. 2012. "Chicana 'Belonging' in Sandra Cisneros' *The House on Mango Street*." *Rocky Mountain Review. Special Issue*: 18–33.
Bordieu, Pierre. 1991. *Language and Symbolic Power*. Cambridge, MA: Harvard UP.
Casielles-Suárez, Eugenia. 2017. "Spanglish: The Hybrid Voice of Latinos in the United States." *ATLANTIS* 29 (2): 147–168.
Cisneros, Sandra. (1984) 1991. *The House on Mango Street*. New York: Vintage Contemporaries.
Denton, Rachel Ann. 2014. *Hablo español, You Know? Language and Identity in the Puerto Rican Diaspora*. Master's Thesis, University of Tenessee.
Derrida, Jacques. (1997) 2000. *Of Hospitality: Anne Duformantelle Invites Jaques Derrida to Respond*. Translated by Rachel Bowlby. Stanford: Stanford UP.
Dikeç, Mustafa. 2002. "Pera, Peras, Poros: Longing for Spaces of Hospitality." *Theory, Culture and Society* 19 (1–2): 227–247.
Domínguez-Rosado, Brenda. 2015. *The Unlinking of Language and Puerto Rican Identity: New Trends in Sight*. Newcastle upon Tyne: Cambridge Scholars.
Erber, Laura. 2015. "No Man's Langue: Rethinking Language with Ghérasim Luca." In *Socioaesthetics: Ambience-Imaginary*, edited by Michelsen, Anders and Frederik Tygstrup, 96–116. Copenhagen: University of Copenhagen.

Ferreira Veras, Adriane. 2011. "Language and Identity in Sandra Cisneros' The House on Mango Street." *Antares. Letras y Humanidades* 5: 228–242.

Hill, Jane H. 1998. "Language, Race, and White Public Space." *American Anthropologist* 100 (3): 680–689.

Levinas, Emmanuel. (1961) 1979. *Totality and Infinity: An Essay on Exteriority*. Translated by Alphonso Lingis. The Hague, Boston and London: Martinus Nijhoff.

Martin, Holly E. 2005. "Code-switching in US Ethnic Literature: Multiple Perspectives Presented through Multiples Languages." *Changing English* 12 (3): 403–415.

McGill, Lisa Diane. 2005. *Constructing Black Selves: Caribbean American Narratives and the Second Generation*. New York: New York University Press.

Milroy, Leslie. 1987. *Language and Social Networks*. Oxford: Blackwell.

Montes-Granado, Consuelo. 2012. "Code-Switching as a Strategy of Brevity in Sandra Cisneros' *Woman Hollering Creek and Other Stories*." In *Short Story Theories: A Twenty-First-Century Perspective*, edited by Viorica Patea, 125–138. Amsterdam & New York: Rodopi.

Pérez-Torres, R. 1995. *Movements in Chicano Poetry: Against Myths, against Margins. Cambridge Studies in American Literature and Culture, 88*. New York: Cambridge UP.

Pheng, Cheah. 2013. "To Open Hospitality and Alienation." In *The Conditions of Hospitality: Ethics, Politics, and Aesthetics on the Threshold of the Possible*, edited by Thomas Claviez, 57–80. New York: Fordham UP.

Potowski, Kim. 2013. "Sociolinguistic Dimensions of Immigration to the United States." *Lengua y Migración* 5 (2): 29–50.

Smith, Alison. 2013. "Crossing the linguistic Threshold: Language, Hospitality and Linguistic Exchange in Philippe Lioret's Welcome and Rachid Bouchareb's London River." *Studies in French Cinema* 13 (1): 75–90.

Thomas, Piri. (1967) 1997. *Down These Mean Streets*. New York: Vintage.

Urciuoli, Bonnie. 2013. *Exposing Prejudice: Puerto Rican Experiences of Language, Race, and Class*. Long Grove, Ill.: Waveland.

Watkins, Mary. 2007. "Psyches and Cities of Hospitality in an Era of Forced Migration: The Shadows of Slavery and Conquest on the 'Immigration' Debate." *Spring* 78: 1–25.

Zentella, Ana Celia. 1997. *Growing up Bilingual: Puerto Rican Children in New York*. Malden, M.A.: Blackwell.

CHAPTER 5

(In)Hospitable Languages and Linguistic Hospitality in Hyphenated American Literature: the Case of Ha Jin[1]

José R. Ibáñez

Abstract

In *Adieu to Emmanuelle Levinas*, Jacques Derrida observed that the author of *Totality and Infinity* privileged the term 'dwelling' over that of 'hospitality' although this work "bequeaths to us an immense treatise of hospitality" (Derrida [1997] 1999, 21). As interpreter of the concept of hospitality in the philosophy of Emmanuel Levinas, Derrida also reminded us of the conditions of the host, as the one that gives asylum, while, at the same time, the law of hospitality, the law of the place (house, hotel, hospital, hospice, family, city, nation, language, etc.) become the delimitation where that host maintains his/her authority (Derrida 2000b, 4). More recently, Abi Doukhan has accounted for a dimension of the Levinassian hospitality, the *exilic* structure, which has been disregarded by many commentators of the Lithuanian-born philosopher (Doukhan 2010, 235).

In this paper, I intend to examine Ha Jin's (a Chinese-born American migrant writer and one of the most successful Asian-American authors in current American fiction) exilic condition. Forced to remain in the United States after viewing on television the response of Chinese authorities to the demonstrations at Tiannamen Square in June 1989, Ha Jin has developed his entire literary career in English, a language that he learned after the end of Mao Zedong's Cultural Revolution. Writing in this language thus became "a matter of survival" (Weinberger 2006, 46), a safe haven to which this author retreated in an attempt to exile himself from Chinese, a language loaded with "a lot of political jargon" (Fay 2009, 122) and unsuitable for the representation of his fictional worlds.

I will be paying close attention to some of Ha Jin's best known essays: "In Defence of Foreignness" and *The Writer as Migrant*. In this latter book, this Chinese-American writer delves into the Manichean relationship that Aleksandr Solzhenitsyn, Lin

[1] The research on this paper was supported by the project CEIPatrimonio, University of Almeria.

Yutang, Vladimir Nabokov, V. S. Naipaul, among other foreign authors, had with the English language so as to justify his own decision to write in English. Having accepted being an outcast from his native language (Chinese), Ha Jin's adopted language (English) became, metaphorically speaking, a hospitable space in which he could secure a successful literary career at the expense of being accused of betrayal by both Chinese intellectuals and authorities.

Keywords

Bilingual creativity – hospitable vs inhospitable languages – hospitality – *hostipitality* – migrant writer – translation literature

∴

> The question of language is critical—forcing the other to speak my language even as they ask for asylum is hardly hospitable.
> JUDITH STILL
> *Derrida and Hospitality*

∴

1 Introduction

Chinese immigration to Gam Saan ('Gold Mountain,' used broadly in Chinese to refer to the western regions of North America) dates back to 1849, the year after James W. Marshall found gold at Sutter's Mill in Coloma, California. In subsequent years, hundreds of Chinese arrived in America to work in the gold mines or to lay tracks for the Central Pacific Railroad's transcontinental line. Chinese women in California were almost totally absent at the time, and it is said that San Francisco became, for the Chinese community, "a colony of 'bachelors'" (Takaki [1993] 2008, 195). A natural disaster, nonetheless, changed the fate of Chinese immigrants in America. On April 18, 1906, an earthquake shook San Francisco, the ensuing fires destroying almost all municipal records. This disaster served as an excellent opportunity for many Chinese immigrants to bring their wives and children to the United States. According to US law, the children of American citizens were automatically considered US citizens, no matter where they were born (Takaki [1993] 2008, 202). Many of those Chinese children came to America as 'paper sons' and 'paper daughters' as they forged—or purchased—birth certificates to be used as their 'passport' to America. However, matters were not as easy for these new immigrants as it might have seemed. Thousands of Chinese entering San Francisco were compelled to disembark on Angel Island and were placed in barracks at the immigration station there. One of these immigrants later recalled how "they locked us up like criminals in compartments like the cages in the zoo" (qtd. in Takaki [1993] 2008, 202). After their long journey from China, they sailed beneath the Golden Gate Bridge but were not in fact allowed to enter the country. Their forged papers, which should have afforded them a simple means of entering the US, became their worst nightmare. To be sure, inmates on Angel Island Immigration Station were not released unless they could convince the American customs authorities that their papers were legitimate. It is estimated that ten percent of those 'paper sons' and 'paper daughters' who landed on Angel Island were forced to return to China. For those who were detained, Gam Saan turned out to be a great deal less hospitable than the 'Gold Mountain' they had dreamed of back in China. The optimism invested in those forged papers by the Chinese immigrants turned out to be misplaced, and the documents themselves did not become passports, but rather a means of turning them into hostages in the new country.

Angel Island Immigration Center, also known as "The Ellis Island of the West," was in operation for thirty years until its closure in November 1940. The United States Congress repealed the Chinese Exclusion Act in 1942 and the detention center was never reopened as an immigration station. Decades after this infamous episode of Chinese immigration in America, Angel Island was scheduled for demolition in 1970 until a park ranger who was touring the building with a flashlight in his hand noticed the Chinese calligraphy on the walls. Inmates had carved angry and bitter poems onto the cell walls and floors. Other poems by those detainees expressed their fear and shame at being sent back to China, or their hopes of being released and thus finding new opportunities in America (Su *et al.* 1997, n.p.). The barracks where the inmates had been locked up for weeks or months were eventually restored, becoming a *memoria passionis* of the suffering of those Chinese immigrants.

Asian immigration to the US came in waves after the Second World War, and in the final decades of the twentieth century, many Chinese students were afforded the opportunity to continue their graduate education in American universities. One of those students, Ha Jin (1956-), arrived in 1985 to pursue his doctorate in American literature, having promised to return to China upon completion of his studies. Like many other Chinese immigrants, Ha Jin sought refugee status in the United States following the violent response of Chinese authorities to the student protests at Tiananmen Square in June 1989. His decision to become a writer would be a difficult and painful one in that he had to abandon his native language and produce his works in English, the language of his adopted country. Alongside that decision came charges of treason for having renounced the Chinese language. As a migrant writer, as he views himself, Ha Jin has been a controversial figure, with his work both praised and attacked because of his particular use of English. On the one hand, the Chinese language for Ha Jin becomes a sort of *inhospitable* dwelling, in that he associates it with the Chinese repressive regime. On the other hand, English becomes both a *hospitable* and an *inhospitable* place for him, in that he has been confronted by the wrath of certain monolingual English readers who have reacted negatively to the hybrid nature of his fiction.

This chapter examines issues of hospitality and *hostipitality* in Ha Jin's literary production within a Derridean framework, paying close attention to Jin's distinctive use of language. As a migrant writer in the United States, he felt compelled to write in a foreign language, English, bringing about a kind of hybrid literature characterized by conspicuous linguistic features coming from his own cultural background. Following Paul Ricoeur's concept of linguistic hospitality, I intend to gain a better understanding of the hybrid nature of Ha Jin's fiction which may be labeled as "linguistic creativity" (Ibáñez 2016; 2017; 2019), a concept devised by Indian linguist Braj B. Kachru (1932–2016). The singular nature of his literature has enabled Ha Jin to carve out a niche for himself in current literary America. Bearing in mind how the politics of hospitality have emerged as a crucial element in political debate aimed at providing an appropriate response to the refugee crisis, and how Derrida, in *Monolingualism of the Other*, also pointed out that making a guest conform to the norms of the language of the host could be considered an act of violence—a point reiterated by Judith Still when she observed that imposing the host's language on the guest is hardly hospitable (Still 2010, 19)—one might well understand Ha Jin's exilic condition and his fiction's distinctive use of the English language. The ambivalent nature of his writing and the mixed reviews garnered by some early works may account for analysis that could be articulated within the framework of Derrida's notion of *hostipitality*, an approach which helps us to elucidate Ha Jin's own existence in the current American literary scenario.

2   Ha Jin, or the Linguistic Dilemmas of a Migrant Writer in the US

"As a fortunate one I speak for those unfortunate people who suffered, endured or perished at the bottom of life and who created the history and at the same time were fooled or ruined by it" (Jin 1990, 2). Penned by a young Chinese Ph.D. student, these lofty words appear in the introduction to *Between Silences* (1990), Ha Jin's first published book of verse. Who was the designated recipient of these words? Was Ha Jin addressing all those downtrodden Chinese who had left their motherland behind, or else, was he referring to those who, like him, had ventured to come to America in search of a new life? Did he have in mind the sufferings and misadventures of previous generations of Chinese immigrants who became naturalized via Angel Island?

Born in 1956 in Liaoning, in Northern China, Jīn Xuěfēi, who uses Ha Jin as his pen name, suffered the upheaval of Mao's Cultural Revolution (1966–76), during which high schools and universities were closed down and professors accused of spreading bourgeois and capitalist ideas among their students. When universities eventually reopened in 1976, Ha Jin, who had been educating himself in the army, enrolled as a student in the Department of English at Heilongjiang University. After graduating from Shandong University, he arrived in the United States in 1985 to pursue a doctorate in American Literature at Brandeis University. His initial intention to return to China after the completion of his graduate studies was frustrated by the violent response of the Chinese authorities to the peaceful student demonstrations at Tiananmen Square in June 1989. This episode, which Jin has always referred to as "the source of all the trouble" (Fay 2009, 118), compelled him to seek asylum in the United States, where he has remained ever since. He had neither considered living permanently in the US nor becoming a writer originally, and he began writing seriously in English only after the Tiananmen Square massacre. Today he is a renowned author, with a number of literary prizes under his belt, including the 1999 National Book Award for Fiction for his second novel, *Waiting* (1999).

His concerns about being a writer who uses the language of his adopted country has been expressed in *The Writer as Migrant* (2008a) as well as in the essay, "In Defence of Foreignness" (2010). The former is a volume composed of a series of lectures delivered by Ha Jin at Rice University in 2006. In it, he explores identity issues, his exilic condition as a foreign writer who writes in English, and themes that in part resemble those explored by Salman Rushdie in "Imaginary Homelands" (Cheung 2012, 2).

The first dilemma that an exile writer confronts is to determine the language in which he is going to work. In this regard, Stanisław Baranczak notes that "the exiled writer tries to write in the language of his adopted country" because of "his desire [...] to get his message across to a broader audience" (1989, 437). However, other reasons emerged beyond Ha Jin's immediate horizon. Firstly, the impossibility of having a substantial and sustainable Chinese readership in the United States; secondly, the banning of his work by the authorities in mainland China[2]; and thirdly, the need to draw a psychological and linguistic border between himself and Chinese state power which, in his own words, became a matter of survival. In this vein, he has frequently said in interviews that he sees the Chinese language as full of complex jargon, with such linguistic items acting like formulas for public speech (Fay 2009, 122). "The Chinese language is very literary and highbrow," he said in another interview, a language "detached from the spoken word" (Gardner 2000, n.p.). Conversely, "English has more flexiblility. It's very plastic, very shapeable, very expressive language. In that sense, it feels quite natural" (Fay 2009, 122). In a sense, this seems to express something about the hospitable condition of his adopted language, and also hints at his own estrangement from his mother tongue and its inhospitality.

In what follows, I will explore the issue of how languages—both first and second languages—become a migrant writer's homeland (Jin 2008a, 61). I will also examine the Derridean dichotomy between hospitable and inhospitable language in Ha Jin's *oeuvre*. I will then discuss Paul Ricoeur's concept of linguistic hospitality, which he devised as a term to be applied to the field of translation, and that, in the words of Richard Kearney, "asks us to respect that the semantic and syntactic fields of two languages are not the same, or exactly reducible the one to the other" (2006, xvii). Ricoeur's articulation of linguistic hospitality allows us to get a better understanding of the hybrid nature of Ha Jin's work.

Based on these ideas, it is necessary to articulate the following notions within the field of hospitality.

- As a paradigm, we can say that any language potentially becomes an abode, a *dwelling*, a sort of shelter, as anticipated by Derrida.[3]
- As with any home, language is inhabited by *dwellers*, that is to say, speakers who may determine whether a *home* is hospitable or inhospitable. Bearing this principle in mind, it follows that Ha Jin determines the inhospitable character of his mother tongue as a result of its stiffness, and that it is "polluted by revolutionary movements and political jargon" (Jin 2009, WK9)
- Native speakers who inhabit a language can claim themselves to be *hosts* in that *dwelling* on account of their having been born within its confines. By

---

[2] Indeed, with the exception of his award-winning novel *Waiting* (1999) and also *The Nanjing Requiem* (2011), a fictional narrative based on a historical episode set during the Japanese invasion of China, none of his works have been published in China. In spite of governmental censorship, Ha Jin has remained critical of the kind of self-censorship that a writer can impose on himself (Jin 2008b).

[3] "I am monolingual. My monolingualism dwells, and I call it my dwelling; it feels like one to me, and I remain in it and inhabit it. It inhabits me" (Derrida [1996] 1998, 1).

the same token, non-native speakers are regarded as *guests* in that home, and they can merely aspire to receiving a welcome in the *dwelling*.
- Lastly, following Derrida's articulation of hospitality, the final inclusion of the *guest* in the *dwelling* is contingent on the acceptance of the *host*, who has the right of admission into his home. As Tahar Ben Jelloun observes, the *guest* usually "makes me confront myself" while he or she also "teaches me what I am" (qtd. in Manzanas Calvo 2013, 108). Thus, the *host* may decide to welcome the newcomer as a guest, or else to impose a set of rules as a prerequisite for guaranteed hospitality. One of the most frequent rules the guest has to abide by is that of language. Judith Still has noted that "the question of language is critical—forcing the other to speak my language even as they ask for asylum is hardly hospitable" (2010, 19). In this sense, such an imposition, which may include overt violence, entails stripping the guest of his or her own identity, what becomes, in the words of French philosopher Jean Baudrillard, an act of "cannibalism" (Rosello 2001, 31). Once the imposition is established, the *guest* may be forced to obey those rules, or else carve out a niche for himself or herself within that *dwelling*.

In his articulation of the theory of hospitality, Derrida is concerned with those who become absolute strangers in a foreign land: displaced persons, exiles, rootless, nomads, or deportees. Such people always experience two types of nostalgia: for the dead and for their own language. In this respect, Derrida argues that exiles have in their mother tongue their ultimate homeland, their final resting place (Derrida [1997] 2000a, 87–89). I argue that Ha Jin is a member of this group, in that, in his exilic condition, he wrestles with the idea of whether or not English is the appropriate vehicle for his literary production. Having decided to become a *guest* in a new home, he becomes aware of his condition and the implications: the acceptance of the host's rules.

The initial decision to abandon his mother tongue, so as to embrace the seeming hospitality of his adopted language, generated hostile sentiments from many speakers of Chinese. Hosts of the writer's native language accused him of betraying his own country, language, and people. In this regard, Ha Jin explains:

> Yet the ultimate betrayal [for a writer] is to choose to write in another language. No matter how the writer attempts to rationalize and justify adopting a foreign language, it is an act of betrayal that alienates him from his mother tongue and directs his creative energy to another language. (Jin 2008a, 31)

At the outset of his literary career, Ha Jin was faced by a moral choice which would eventually seal his fate as a writer in America: either to remain close to his own cultural and linguistic background or else to adapt his writing to be more 'digestible' to those in the new home. In order to support his claim, Ha Jin reminds us of other writers who, just like himself, suffered Derrida's condition of *hostipitality* in the English language dwelling. One of the best-known cases is that of Joseph Conrad (1857–1924), the Polish writer cited by Ha Jin as the founding father of the migrant-writer literary tradition (2010, 461). Conrad, who saw himself as a foreigner taking refuge in England, faced overt criticism by both hosts of his mother language and those of his adopted home, English speakers. Eliza Orzeszkowa (1841–1910), a Polish novelist and leading writer of the Positivism movement, lambasted Conrad's literary production, accusing him of the desertion of both country and mother tongue:

> And since we talked about books, I must say that the gentleman who in English is writing novels which are widely read and bring good profit almost caused me a nervous attack. When reading about him, I felt something slippery and unpleasant, something mounting to my throat...Over the novels of Mr. Conrad Korzeniowski no Polish girl will shed an altruistic tear or take a noble decision. (qtd. in Jin 2008, 36–7)

Orzeszkowa's accusations were basically threefold: firstly, she accused Conrad of deserting his native country, Poland, when he emigrated to England. "He should have remained in Poland," quotes Ha Jin from Orzeszkowa, "and let his creative talent serve the Polish national cause" (2008a, 37). Secondly, she considered that writing in English instead of doing it in his native language was an act of betrayal to the Polish people. Finally, Orzeszkowa believed that making money out of it reduced Conrad to the level of a peddler, "which in turn will make the writer's work insignificant to his own people" (2008a, 37).

Vladimir Nabokov (1899–1977) is another example of this sentiment of *hostipitality*. Prior to his determination to switch to English, Nabokov had written extensively in Russian, a language that he considered to be in the process of extinction. When he eventually determined to switch from Russian to English, he found the process to be "extremely painful," just "like learning anew to handle things after losing seven or eight fingers in an explosion" (qtd. in Jin 2008a, 48). Though recognized as a genuine writer in American literature, Nabokov was nevertheless admonished in *The New Yorker* by Edmund Wilson, the American literary critic, for the abundance of solecism in Nabokov's translation of *Eugene Onegin* and his excessive use of literary puns, which Wilson regarded as "awful" (Jin 2010, 462).

As Judith Still reminds us, hospitality is about letting the Other into oneself. This assertion brings about a sort of apprehension or invasive attitude on the guest's part which affects the host's self. As a result, the host's response to this occupation of the home could be to 'turn' against the guest, while his/her generosity may depend on a series of duties to be fulfilled by the newcomer (Still 2010, 13). Abiding by those (language) norms and rules imposed by the host may impair the foreign writer's capacity. In this respect, Ha Jin contends that the writer's creativity may be affected and his linguistic abilities crippled. As might be expected, in his exilic condition, the migrant writer can never aspire to match his literature to that produced by a native speaker. Ha Jin recalls that when he began to study English at university in 1977, he, just like many of his classmates, found it difficult to recite phrases that "twisted your tongue, your muscles" and that made those students go to the clinic regularly to get painkillers (Gardner 2000). Later on, when he decided to become a writer in his adopted language, he was aware of the difficulty and of the great tradition of non-native writers producing their works in English:

> At the time, I thought about this and realized it would be very hard, but in the English language, there is a great tradition where nonnative writers became essential writers. I was aware of that tradition and thought my success would depend on whether I had the ability and the luck. (Varsava 2010, 8)

When non-native speakers arrive as *guests* in a language, and are thereafter forced to obey the rules imposed by the *hosts*, they must accommodate themselves to the dwelling, find a shelter in their new home, and strive to sidestep unwelcoming rules as best they can. Being aware of his linguistic prowess, the exiled writer who has adopted a literary language has a particular goal: to reach the wide readership denied to him at home. In many cases, success may be achieved by means of cultural nativization and an adaptation of the author's linguistic traits into the new home.

Ha Jin affirms that it took him almost a year to decide to follow in the footsteps of Conrad and Nabokov (Jin 2009, WK9) and adopt English as the language of his literary production. Having taken this decision, however, he laid claim to hybrid forms of writing within the newly monolingual home. "Hybrid authors are torn by a complicated dilemma," argues Vidal Claramonte, "whether to use the strong language or that of their minor culture as a creative weapon" (2014, 246). Ha Jin thus embarked on a process of readjustment in the English dwelling which enabled him to carve out a niche for himself in the language, to found a new abode without asking permission from the host.

As might be expected, Ha Jin's claims garnered hostile reactions from hosts of his mother tongue and also from hosts of his adopted language. King-Kog

Cheung reveals how Ha Jin's *Waiting* was upbraided by Yiqing Liu, a prominent Professor of English at Peking University, for its content and its Orientalist appeal (Cheung 2012, 5). Furthermore, despite the visions of freedom and self-realization that Ha Jin might have projected for himself after his decision to write in English, reviewers of his literature have objected to its hybridity. Just as Edmund Wilson had previously admonished Nabokov for his fondness for word games, Nancy Tsai disparages Ha Jin's *Chineseness* and his tendency to include Chinese proverbs and idioms as well as to provide translations from his mother tongue for the sake of adding an exotic touch to his fiction. In her view, the pages of Ha Jin's novel *Waiting* "abound with Chinese expressions, idioms, and clichés translated into English and hammered into the sentences like nails" (Tsai 2005, 58). As a defender of the monolingual use of the English language, Tsai accuses Ha Jin of the transgression of language rules, and she painstakingly singles out a number of (mis)translations in his award-winning novel. As I have pointed out elsewhere, Tsai's position is highly questionable in terms of her penchant for correctness in the use of grammatical rules, in that they leave no room for other (un)grammatical varieties of English (Ibáñez 2016, 203).[4]

Hence, a question arises within the hospitality framework: are we entitled, as native speakers of a language, to possess the 'home' and impose *our* rules on newcomers? A negative answer to this question might indeed lead us to reconsider our position as hosts. In *Monolingualism of the Other*, Derrida had already wondered about the relationship between a language and its speakers: "But who exactly possesses it [a language]? And whom does it possess? Is language in possession, ever a possessing or possessed possession?" (Derrida [1996] 1998, 17). If Derrida was right in his claim, we must also admit that the host does not *own* a language as he himself or herself is first and foremost a guest *within* the language, and the home itself does not belong to him or her.

3 Finding a Middle Position: Paul Ricoeur's Linguistic Hospitality

In their study of Junot Díaz's short story "Invierno," Ana María Manzanas and Jesús Benito turn to Paul Ricoeur's concept of 'linguistic hospitality' which they see as "an apt term that reminds us that the Other does not come alone, but has verbal and narrative baggage" (2017, 134). Although Ricoeur did not

---

4 On similar lines, John Updike reviewed Ha Jin's novel *A Free Life* and established that this novel, held in the United States, contains "more small solecisms than in his Chinese novels" (Updike 2007, n.p.).

fully expand this concept in his philosophical works, he defined linguistic hospitality in the following terms:

> Just as in a narration it is always possible to tell the story in a different way, likewise in translation it is always possible to translate otherwise, without ever hoping to bridge the gap between equivalence and perfect adhesion. Linguistic hospitality, therefore, is the act of inhabiting the word of the Other paralleled by the act of receiving the word of the Other into one's own home, one's own dwelling. (qtd. in Kearney 2006, 16)

Linguistic hospitality permits the cordial exchange between the guest and the host, thus allowing the creation of a sort of interwoven fabric of language. Furthermore, the articulation of this concept may also account for the hybrid nature of translation, language or literature. Following Ricoeur, Scott Davidson reminds us that the translator becomes an intermediary between two masters, the author and the reader, as he or she is always caught up between the dialectics of fidelity and betrayal (2012, 3). Along the same lines, the migrant writer has to strive to incorporate into the host language what he brought along with him from his mother tongue. "As the host welcomes the guest," Manzanas and Benito argue, "a parallel process unfolds where the dominant language assumes the mastery over the immigrant language transformed into a precarious guest language" (2017, 135).

The concept of linguistic hospitality, therefore, can be borrowed in this study as it may help us elucidate Ha Jin's adaptation to this new abode. Just like those writers who are in a liminal linguistic and cultural situation in America (Chicanos) or in Africa (writers in Nigeria who use English as a second language), Ha Jin found himself adjusting his language and literature to his new dwelling, the English language. He does not assume his role as that of being a hostage in the new dwelling, but claims that he deserves a 'room' within the 'home' of the English language (Jin 2010, 465–67). This process of adaptation, however, takes its toll. One of the consequences is Jin's willingness to sacrifice accuracy in order to make his work accessible to his (Western) readership (Oh 2006, 422). "The writer living in exile," claims Stanisław Baranczak, "has no choice but to make this work lose some of its original flavor—that seems an obvious price to pay" (1989, 431).

Just as Conrad and Nabokov had previously struggled to find a place in the literature of their adopted language, Ha Jin, as a migrant writer, aims to carve out a niche for himself in his newly-adopted dwelling. In his determination to write in a foreign language, and as a result of his diffidence with English, he favors a literature with conspicuous cultural elements from China and salient linguistic features of Chinese that make us reassess linguistic and mental boundaries. However, unlike practitioners of hybrid literature, such as the cases of Latino writers who either incorporate *ad hoc* untranslated expressions or render literal translations from their mother tongues, Ha Jin exhibits a bilingual creativity that enables him to produce a new type of writing that some critics have called "translation literature" (Gong 2014; Ibáñez 2016, 2019). Indeed, what monolingual reviewers of his work regard as linguistic flaws or literal renditions from the writer's mother tongue may be considered conscious linguistic literary recreations aiming to maintain the characters' linguistic difficulties in their new habitat as well as to present a reflection of the ideological transition from one culture to another (Gong 2014, 158). To be sure, Haomin Gong affirms that although some unfortunate misuses of English have been singled out by reviewers, "the author's intentional use of non-idiomatic English that characterizes his translational style is unique" (2014, 148).

In Ha Jin's literary production, examples of this accommodation to his new home abound. His bilingual creativity manifests itself through different linguistic processes, namely, the nativization of cultural aspects and contexts, the nativization of rhetorical strategies, such as similes and metaphors, and the transcreation of curses, proverbs, and idioms.[5] Regarding the nativization of those elements in his fiction, Ha Jin has argued that they are not literal translations from Chinese but adaptations of his Mandarin-speaking characters: "in most cases," he explains, "I altered the idioms some, at times drastically, to suit the context, the drama and the narrative flow" (2010, 466).

There are many examples in Ha Jin's fiction which reveal conspicuous traits of the exclusive use of the English language and that confirm this accommodation into his new home. Indeed, I would like to highlight some of the most noticeable from two short stories. The first is "Winds and Clouds over a Funeral," a narrative included in his second collection of short stories, *Under the Red Flag* (1997), and "probably the best rendering of a faithful representation of Chinese tradition, language and culture" (Ibáñez 2016, 206). It explores the struggle between the millenary tradition of Confucianism and the new tradition that Maoism introduced into China. Linguistic and cultural elements alien to Western readers proliferate throughout the entire story and Ha Jin takes pains to tailor this tradition to his new cultural abode.

Set in a small commune in rural China during the years of Mao's Cultural Revolution, "Winds and Clouds over a Funeral" is the story of the death and burial of the mother of Ding Liang, the chairman of the commune. On her

---

5 I am indebted to the taxonomy established by Braj B. Kachru in *The Alchemy of English* (1990) which I also borrowed for an article on Ha Jin's bilingual creativity (Ibáñez 2016).

deathbed, Ding had promised his mother that he will never allow her body to be cremated, even though, as a politician, he knows that authorities forbid the burial of the dead in the ground, this as a way to preserve the land for the future generations. Cultural contexts and concepts are nativized by both narrators and characters in the story. The whole commune is divided into two factions, those who support Ding and those who want to see him fall. At one point, Ding is suspicious of the loyalty of those men who support him. Feng, one of his closest friends, tells Ding: "Loyal words jar on your ears—[like] bitter medicine is good for your illness" (Jin [1994] 1997, 53). This simile is a homely adaptation from a Chinese expression which can be interpreted as "frank criticism is hard to swallow, though it may come from your own comrades."[6] As mentioned above, the author saw fit to adjust this simile to his Western readership since the expression has no suitable counterpart in English.

Another example of the nativization of rhetorical strategies can be found in the following metaphor: "from now on *all the guns must have the same caliber*" [my italics] (Jin [1994] 1997, 61). This metaphor is used by Ding to exhort his comrades to adopt a unified approach so as to make their story credible. The original saying may carry a historical reference dating back to the Second Sino-Japanese War (1937–1945). At that time, China imported ammunition from different European countries, which made it impossible to have a unified system of weaponry, and the metaphor indicates that the use of different calibers prevented the Chinese armies from sharing ammunition stocks (Ibáñez 2016, 213).

In the same story, Sheng, one of the protagonists, is referred to as being a prudent man. The narrator comments that "[h]is experience in the army had taught him that *disasters always come from the tongue*" [my italics] (Jin [1994] 1997, 64). The italicized expression is Ha Jin's personal rendition into English of the Chinese idiom, "illness enters by the mouth,"[7] a proverb that warns against the danger of having a loose tongue and the trouble it may cause. Being one of the oldest and richest languages in the world, Chinese has an ample stock of proverbs and idioms the majority of which cannot be translated directly into English. However, through these peculiar homely adaptations into the English language, Ha Jin accommodates what the linguist Braj B. Kachru describes

---

6 The Chinese expression is "zhōng yán nì ěr, liáng yào kǔ kǒu" [忠言逆耳，良药苦口] which translates as "truthful words sound bad to your ears, just as the good medicine tastes bitter." All translations from this point on have been provided by the author with the help of an online dictionary (*chinese.yabla.com*).

7 The Chinese expression is "bìng cóng kǒu rù, huò cóng kǒu chū" [病从口入，祸从口出] and can be literally translated as "illness enters by the mouth, trouble comes out by the mouth."

as "the wit and wisdom of the ancestors [...] passed on to new generations" (Kachru 1990, 168).

The final example that I would like to examine here is from "The Bridegroom," a short story included in the eponymous collection published in 2000. This is a tragicomic tale about Beina, an extremely unprepossessing young girl to whom Baowen, a very good-looking young man, proposes; she ultimately marries him. A few months after the wedding, Beina finds out that her husband is homosexual, a crime seen as a bourgeois issue and, as such, one that is punished severely by the Chinese authorities. When Baowen proposed to Beina, villagers could not help but gossip about how lucky the girl was. One of those villagers uses an idiomatic expression to refer to the situation: "a fool always lands in the arms of fortune" (Jin [1999] 2000, 92), conveying the idea that such an ugly girl had found the best match she was ever likely to have. This phrase is simply an adaptation of a Chinese expression which may be rendered more directly into English as "the fool's luck."[8] The narrator has adapted it for Western ears by attributing god-like connotations to the concept of 'fortune.' In this sense, Ha Jin is almost equating a concept taken from his Chinese background with another one found in the Greek and Latin traditions, as Fortuna was a Latin goddess, corresponding to the Greek goddess Τύχη. The protagonist, thus, falls in the arms of the goddess of Fortune.

These are just a few examples of how Ha Jin's fiction supports the idea that hybridity challenges monolingual views of language while, at the same time, calling into question the rules that the host imposes on the guest. The foreign writer takes possession of the home by adding new features she or he brings along, a step that might be regarded by many home dwellers as both an invasion of *their* language as well as a threat to the monolingual character of the home. The hybrid nature of such writers' literary production seems to confirm one of the main ideas expressed by Derrida in *Monolingualism of the Other*—that we, as speakers, do not *own* a native language. Indeed, bearing this principle in mind, it follows that, as home dwellers, our habitat is not ours: "My language, the only one I hear myself speak," affirms Derrida, "is the language of the other" (Derrida [1996] 1998, 25). Since we never speak only one language, monolingualism never does exist, and Derrida wonders if there is nothing but plurilingualism ([1996] 1998, 21).

"As hospitality evolves into hostility," Manzanas and Benito remind us, "the guests metamorphose into hostages" (2017, 134). Chinese immigrants who

---

8   The Chinese expression is "shǎ rén yǒu shǎ fú" [傻人有傻福] and can be translated as "fortune favors fools."

came to the United States as 'paper sons' and 'paper daughters' arrived in California in the hope that they would be welcomed into a hospitable land, yet they found that their forged documents rendered them hostages. The passing of the Magnuson Act, signed in December 1943, permitted Chinese nationals already residing in the US to become naturalized citizens for the first time since the Chinese exclusion act of 1882. It also marked the end of decades of discrimination against and segregation of Asian Americans in the United States. The Tiananmen Square incident in June 1989, still shrouded in mystery after three decades thanks in part to the government's efforts to obliterate the disaster and its consequences, also marked the lives of many Chinese students who refused to return to their country. Ha Jin was forced to remain in the US and ended up becoming a prolific and successful writer in his own right. Like many other hyphenated writers in America, Ha Jin challenges monolingualism. According to Vidal Claramonte, these hyphenated authors, "understand language as a political instrument, as part of a cultural representation process in which the construction of meanings demands the participation of the reader and forces him or her to make an interactive textual transcoding and to rethink his or her own identity as cross-cultural" (2014, 250). Alongside the creation of a hybrid language, Vidal Claramonte affirms that these writers cultivate linguistic difference while, at the same time, refuse to "live in" one language and to embrace only one identity. Ha Jin's *oeuvre* is characterized by his bilingual creativity and is paving the way for new forms of literature in the United States.

References

Baranczak, Stanisław. 1989. "Tongue-Tied Eloquence: Notes on Language, Exile and Writing." *The University of Toronto Quarterly* 58 (4): 429–438.

Cheung, King-Kok. 2012. "The Chinese American Writer as Migrant: Ha Jin's Restive Manifesto." *Amerasia Journal* 38 (2): 2–12.

Chinese.yabla.com. Online dictionary. [Accessed online on June 28, 2018].

Davidson, Scott. 2012. "Linguistic Hospitality: The Task of Translation in Ricoeur and Levinas." *Analecta Hermeneutica* 4: 1–14.

Derrida, Jacques. (1996) 1998. *Monolingualism of the Other; or the Prosthesis of Origin*. Translated by Patrick Mensah. Stanford, CA: Stanford UP.

Derrida, Jacques. (1997) 1999. *Adieu to Emmanuel Levinas*. Translated by Pascale-Anne Brault and Michael Naas. Stanford, CA: Stanford UP.

Derrida, Jacques. (1997) 2000a. *Of Hospitality, Anne Dufourmantelle invites Jacques Derrida to respond*. Translated by Rachel Bowlby. Stanford, CA: Stanford UP.

Derrida, Jacques. 2000b. "Hostipitality." Translated by Barry Stocker with Forbes Morlock. *Angelaki. Journal of the Theoretical Humanities* 5 (3): 3–18.

Doukhan, Abi. 2010. "From Exile to Hospitality. A Key to the Philosophy of Emmanuel Levinas". *Philosophy Today* 54.3 (Fall): 235–246.

Fay, Sarah. 2009. "Ha Jin: The Art of Fiction No. 202." *The Paris Review* 191 (Winter): 117–145.

Gardner, Dwight. 2000. "Ha Jin's Cultural Revolution." *The New York Times*. 6 February. [Accessed online on January 7, 2018].

Gong, Haomin. 2014. "Language, Migrancy, and the Literal: Ha Jin's Translation Literature." *Concentric: Literary and Cultural Studies* 40 (1): 147–167.

Ibáñez, José R. 2016. " 'All the guns must have the same caliber:' A Kachruvian Study of Ha Jin's *Chineseness* in 'Winds and Clouds over a Funeral.' " *Concentric: Literary and Cultural Studies* 42 (2): 195–220.

Ibáñez, José R. 2017. "Márgenes en la 'literatura de traducción': La creatividad bilingüe en la narrativa breve de Ha Jin. In *Superando límites en traducción e interpretación*, edited by Carmen Valero Garcés and Carmen Pena Díaz, 120–127. Geneva: Editions Tradulex.

Ibáñez, José R. 2019. " 'Although the sparrow is small, it has a complete set of organs'. Literatura de contacto y creatividad bilingüe en los relatos cortos de Ha Jin." In *La traducción literaria a finales del siglo XX y principios del siglo XXI: hacia la disolución de fronteras*, edited by Ingrid Cáceres Würsig and María Jesús Fernández-Gil. *Vertere*, 21, 173–193.

Jin, Ha. 1990. *Between Silences. A Voice from China*. Chicago & London: The U of Chicago P.

Jin, Ha. (1994) 1997. "Winds and Clouds over a Funeral." *Under the Red Flag*, by Ha Jin, 44–67. Athens, GA: U. of Georgia P.

Jin, Ha. 1999. *Waiting*. New York: Pantheon.

Jin, Ha. (1999) 2000. "The Bridegroom." In *The Bridegroom*, by Ha Jin, 91–115. New York: Pantheon.

Jin, Ha. 2008a. *The Writer as Migrant*. Chicago & London: U of Chicago P.

Jin, Ha. 2008b. "The Censor in the Mirror." *American Scholar* 77 (4): 26–32.

Jin, Ha. 2009. "Exiled to English." *The New York Times*. May 31. WK9.

Jin, Ha. 2010. "In Defence of Foreignness." In *The Routledge Handbook of World Englishes,* edited by Andy Kirkpatrick, 461–470. London & New York: Routledge.

Jin, Ha. 2011. *The Nanjing Requiem*. New York: Vintage.

Kachru, Braj B. 1990. *The Alchemy of English: The Spread, Functions, and Models of Non-Native Englishes*. Urbana: U of Illinois P.

Kearney, Richard. 2006. "Introduction: Ricoeur's philosophy of translation." In *On Translation,* by Paul Ricoeur and translated by Eileen Brennan, vii-xx. London and New York: Routledge.

Manzanas Calvo, Ana María. 2013. "Junot Díaz's 'Otravida, Otravez' and *Hospitalia*: The Workings of Hostile Hospitality." *Journal of Modern Literature* 37 (1): 107–123.

Manzanas Calvo, Ana María and Jesús Benito Sánchez. 2017. *Hospitality in American Literature and Culture. Spaces, Bodies, Borders.* New York and London: Routledge.

Oh, Seiwoong. 2006. "Cultural Translation in Ha Jin's *Waiting*." In *Querying the Genealogy: Comparative and Transnational Studies in Chinese American Literature*, edited and introduced by Jennie Wang, 420–427. Shanghai: Shanghai Yiwen.

Rosello, Mireille. 2001. *Postcolonial Hospitality: The Immigrant as Guest.* Stanford, CA: Stanford UP.

Still, Judith. 2010. *Derrida and Hospitality: Theory and Practice.* Edinburgh: Edinburgh UP.

Su, John, et al. 1997. "About Angel Island." *Modern American Poetry*. [Accessed online on January 4, 2017].

Takaki, Ronald. (1993) 2008. *A Different Mirror. A History of Multicultural America.* New York: Back Bay Books.

Tsai, Nancy. 2005. "Waiting for a Better Translation." *Translation Review* 70: 58–67.

Updike, John. 2007. "Nan, American Man." Review: *A Free Life* by Ha Jin. *The New Yorker*. [Accessed online on December 4, 2017].

Varsava, Jerry A. 2010. "An Interview with Ha Jin." *Contemporary Literature* 51 (1): 1–26.

Vidal Claramonte, M. Carmen África. 2014. "Translating Hybrid Literatures from Hostipitality to Hospitality." *European Journal of English Studies* 18 (3): 242–262.

Weinberger, Eliot. 2008. "Enormous Changes." *PEN America: A Journal for Writers and Readers* 7: 38–49.

CHAPTER 6

The Contention for Jollity and Gloom: Hospitality in Nathaniel Hawthorne's Historical Short Fiction[1]

Santiago Rodríguez Guerrero-Strachan

Abstract

Nathaniel Hawthorne deals with inhospitable places in several of his short stories. His use of history in his fiction always problematizes the role of British during the Colonial Period, as can be seen in "Endicott and the Red Cross," "The Gentle Boy," and "The May-Pole of Merry Mount." It is my intention to explore the role that places play in these stories. Though they have been variously analyzed, most of the times in symbolic terms, I want to investigate how these places become inhospitable for some characters.

In "Endicott and the Red Cross," Endicott becomes Levinas's displaced host; in "The May-Pole of Merry Mount" the native inhabitants have to suffer the Puritan rule and abandon their pagan traditions. Finally, "The Gentle Boy" deals with the way in which Puritans tried to forbid the Quakers settling in New England. It is my view that Hawthorne wanted to deal with the issue of religion in Salem and the consequences that religious bigotry had in the inhabitants of the town, both native and colonists. With that intention in mind, he created fictional places that would suit his purpose.

Keywords

hospitality – Nathaniel Hawthorne – "Endicott and the Red Cross" – "The Gentle Boy" – "The May-Pole of Merry Mount"

Nathaniel Hawthorne (1804–1864) used his fiction to explore political issues. However, it is interesting to note that although he wrote historical fiction, his underlying aim, as Terence Martin has suggested, was to discuss contemporary issues (1983, 99). His historical fiction was a way of creating a national narrative

[1] This chapter is part of research project "Historia Crítica de la Literatura Étnica Norteamericana: Una Aproximación Intercultural" (FFI2015-64137-P) directed by Prof. Jesús Benito Sánchez and funded by the Spanish Ministerio de Economía y Competitividad.

of the period, but it was also a means of talking about politics. Among the political issues that he was concerned with was that of the creation of a nation that was politically diverse. This is directly related to the question of hospitality as the welcome of strangers. Whether a nation is hospitable in terms of politics and religion or sternly inhospitable affects the character of living together, the limits of liberty, and the scope of democracy. It is my contention that a study of the way strangers are welcomed in Hawthorne's historical short fiction may shed light on his politics of identity. It was the identity of American society that concerned him and that he explored in these, among others, narratives. By writing on political communities, Hawthorne dealt with the actual configuration of American society. In particular, he was concerned with the issue of freedom, both religious and political, and of conscience, in society.

The aim of this chapter is to explore concepts of hospitality in Hawthorne's fiction, arguing that he deals with this topic in ambiguous ways in order to create an alternative foundational narrative. In order to do so, I will analyze "The May-Pole of Merry Mount" (1836), "The Gentle Boy" (1833), and "Endicott and the Red Cross" (1838). I posit that these three stories show the breadth of Hawthorne's interest in American history, religious intolerance, and hospitality. I intend to analyze how hospitality is described and in what instances it is possible. I will explore the ways Hawthorne uses Levinas's concept of the displaced host in his fiction to explore the limits of hospitality as Kant theorized it in *Perpetual Peace*. Throughout the discussion, I will also briefly make use of notions about place and regionalism in New England because I believe that the regionalist view of Hawthorne's poetics is likened to his understanding of hospitality.

The question of hospitality, which Jacques Derrida discusses in "Hostipitality," is the question of self-identity, or *ipseity* as he terms it (2000, 15). Though it is much said that hospitality is primarily a right and an obligation, as Immanuel Kant defined it in *Perpetual Peace* (Derrida 2000, 4), I would emphasize that hospitality is instead related to the conditions of national identity. By greeting conditionally or unconditionally the Other, the citizens of any nation are shaping an image of the national subject that is, to a large extent, a counter-reflection of that Other. The Other reflects both the national subject in itself and the limits of that subject. That is why hospitality is very rarely unconditional and, instead, is conditioned by the keeping of the national identity, as it has reached the present despite its many transformations in the past. Derrida realizes that unconditional welcoming is a desideratum rather than a reality and proposes the term *hostipitality*, which he defines as an aporetic hospitality that deconstructs itself (2000, 5). It can never be achieved completely as it risks the dissolution of national identities. Neither can it ever be totally negated since that would go against the humanist ideals of Western civilization, that is, democracy, equality, and tolerance.

Judith Still argues that hospitality is letting the Other into oneself, to one's own space (2010, 13). This understanding of hospitality, which is not far from Derrida's, is pertinent in an analysis of Hawthorne's hospitality. Letting the Other enter one's place risks colonization, both territorial and of manners. Fear of the Other is expressed as fear of the loss of traditions and manners and of ethnic purity. It is, in short, fear of becoming the Other, which is an issue that in a period of nation-building may easily be exacerbated.

Welcoming cannot be separated from the notion of place. This is defined as "a centre of action and intention [...] 'a focus where we experience the meaningful events of our existence'" (Relph 1976, 42). While people welcome the Other in places that already have an experiential sense, the Other may threaten a possible change of paradigm of the place, that is, by making the place unintelligible due to the change of manners, traditions, language, or religion. It comes as no surprise then that Hawthorne dealt with hospitality in his regional short fiction.

1   The Poetics of Provincial and Historical Narratives

As Lawrence Buell argues, "New England writing codified the regional sense of place" (1986, 283), and, for that purpose, New England writers used Puritanism as a means of articulating New England culture (283). Puritanism and historical writing were part of the creation of New England regional literature to which Hawthorne made an important contribution. By the spring of 1829, Hawthorne "intended to write fiction steeped, as he said, in 'the superstition of this part of the country'" (Wineapple 2003, 74). Although that part of the country was New England generally, Robert Milder has appropriately pointed out that Hawthorne uses Salem synecdochically for New England (2013, 116). There are multiple reasons that explain why Hawthorne chose Salem as the main setting of his stories. It might be that Salem's history haunted him, as Margaret B. Moore has argued (1998, 2). And Michael Colacurcio has pointed out that Hawthorne might want to explore the lives of those who lived in the past due to the different affective quality of the lives they lived (1986, 19). This explains Hawthorne's preference for the historical narrative, but sheds little light on the provinciality of his stories. Hawthorne as cultural anthropologist, as Milder terms him (2013, 116), does not fully explain his interest in Salem. Not even the frustration of living and writing in a society that did not at all care for literature, a fact that Henry James acutely observed (1984, 347–349), explains

Hawthorne's concern with Salem. It was the town where he lived but it also seems to have inhabited him, as Milder has asserted (2013, 117). Hawthorne thought of Salem as the legendary place where a writer can set his fiction, and I would add that the reason is not merely a matter of Romantic poetics and the long shadow that Walter Scott may have cast over American writers of the late eighteenth and early to mid-nineteenth century. Not even nationalism may satisfactorily explain Salem as the setting of Hawthorne's fiction.

I propose that we look towards the concept of provincialism. Provincialism implies restriction to a particular locale away from the center, but also "narrowness, ignorance, immaturity, bias one-sidedness" as G.R. Thompson points out (1993, 6), while Roy Harvey Pearce argues that provincialism opened up a world of creative possibilities for Hawthorne and was the source of his best works (1969, 169ff). Hawthorne's problem is the same that Henry James or Wallace Stevens suffered. The American experience is too thin to nurture culture. While James and Stevens offered different solutions—James naturalizing himself as an English citizen, and Stevens struggling against that experiential thinness with the writing of, for instance, "Anecdote of a Jar"—Hawthorne accepted his provincialism not as a point of departure but as the focal point of his literary career, which, to a certain extent, may explain the paucity of his work. In this sense, Salem is the place where the conditions for fiction are possible. In this chapter, I will make use of Thompson's explanation, particularly the moral connotation of provincialism, as it is my contention that it helps explain hospitality in Hawthorne's stories.

My analysis will be devoted to those stories written in the early period of his career and that were included in one of his early unpublished collections: *Seven Tales of my Native Land* (c. 1827), *Provincial Tales* (ante 1832) and *The Story Teller* (c. 1832–34) (Thompson 1993, 4; Adkins 1945, 119–155), two of which allude to provincialism in the title. Despite the disagreement among critics regarding the issue of the stories that were included in each collection (Adams 1957, 39–57; Adkins 1945, 119–155; Baym 1976, 30; Chandler 1925–26, 1–63; Thompson 1993, 25; Weber 1989, 14–19) it is my view that, in any case, the same impulse guided these three unfinished collections as Hawthorne sketched them out. It is thus secondary to my thesis that "Endicott and the Red Cross" was not included in any collection insofar as it is provincial and deals with the issue of hospitality.

The stories of these projected collections were later subsumed into *Twice-Told Tales* (1837; 1842) and *Mosses from an Old Manse* (1846). These two collections do not maintain the original schema that Hawthorne devised when he first wrote them. Though publication in magazines also decontextualized the meaning of the narratives, there was a design in the original collections as their framing indicates. The early design—which he later disregarded due to problems in publication—together with his comments about the collections suggest that Hawthorne was concerned with the issue of American identity (Bell 1971, 6–17; Cagidemetrio 1992, 35–46; Colacurcio 1986, 18), though more in particular with New England locale as Thompson has pointed out (1993, 24). Most of the tales are either historical, sometimes in a legendary guise, or gothic, quite frequently of the supernatural type. The blending of the historical and the gothic helps create a particular provincial narrative that deals with identity and hospitality with ironic detachment.

2 Jollity and Gloom in "The May-Pole of Merry Mount"

"The May-Pole of Merry Mount" (henceforth, "Merry Mount") was published in *The Token* in 1836 and collected in *Twice-Told Tales* in 1837. Some critics agree that "Merry Mount" deals with the future of the national character (Deamer 1979, 327–339; Drinnon 1980, 385; McWilliams 1977, 3; Sterne 1970, 846–858). This is one of the reasons why the events taking place at Merry Mount have been rewritten in different periods of American history (Drinnon 1980; McWilliams 1977; Sterne 1970). Merry Mount represented an array of possibilities that were finally suppressed in favor of the Puritan worldview.

The narrative poses some challenges to the critic such as the role of the few native inhabitants who appear in the story, the part played by the first settlers in the narrative, and the tone of the narrative voice. This is a story about two groups of colonists. A first group, identified as British, seems to be closer to a pagan worldview as shown in the ritual of the maypole, while the other, the Puritan group of Endicott, is clearly associated with the colonists that would later become American. Moreover, there is a group of Native inhabitants with a minor role in the narrative. The story, roughly divided into an introduction and two sections, each dealing with the first and second group of settlers respectively, revolves around the issues of American identity and tolerance. This reading, however, is complicated by the allegorical mode that informs the narrative and by the ironic narrative voice.

The story is based on the opposition between the days of the early inhabitants of the colony and the period after the Puritans arrived in it. In general terms, the opposition between the past and the present generally creates a feeling of nostalgia. This is not the case in "Merry Mount." Quite interestingly this narrative does not lead to that nostalgic stance that is so common in American literature. The reason for this is that Hawthorne is not concerned with the 'good old days' but with the creation of a nation and with the transition from the state of nature to the social state. For some critics "Merry Mount" is the story of paganism vs. Puritanism or of the opposition between pleasure and culture (Colacurccio 1986; Milder 2013). My reading is informed by political philosophy. It is well known that Thomas Hobbes's (1588–1679) theorization on the state and the government in *Leviathan* (1651) has been interpreted as an explanation of the shift from the state of nature where social institutions did not exist to the social state in which a government is instituted (Hampsher-Monk 1996, 19–20). As such, jollity and gloom in Hawthorne's story can be interpreted as the state of nature and of society respectively. The exact sentence reads: "Jollity and gloom were contending for an empire" (*T&S* 360).[2] There the term empire sounds problematic since it relates the colonial enterprise to the British empire. However, the reader must take into account that Hawthorne is writing the story after the 1812 War that brought about a flood of nationalistic feeling and during a period of continental expansion (J. Gerald Kennedy 2016; Wood 2009, 697). Hawthorne, though he was writing of the past, was describing the present as well. His concern was to write a national narrative that, in the guise of historical fiction, symbolized both the foundation of America as a nation and its development during the nineteenth century when the issue of hospitality was unresolved, as the cases of native inhabitants and Irish immigrants prove. His interest in that present helps explain the absence of nostalgia in the story.

In any case, jollity and gloom have their referents in the text. Jollity is associated with the inhabitants of the colony prior to the arrival of Endicott and the Puritans while gloom is linked to Endicott. The first dwellers are described as a "wild throng" (*T&S* 361), an image which continues with a more minute description of its components. They are not fauns or nymphs, although of Greek ancestry, but rather Gothic monsters. Hawthorne gives them the visages, outlooks, and attributes of beasts with the aim of distancing them from the human complexion. The depersonalization of these inhabitants leads to the negation of human characteristics. It is thus not surprising that a few lines later Hawthorne wrote "Here might be seen the Salvage Man [...] By his side, a nobler figure, but still a counterfeit, appeared an Indian hunter" (*T&S* 361) going on to add "some already transformed to brutes, some midway between man and beast" (*T&S* 362). Hawthorne is pointing to the widespread notion that the British held that the Native Americans lacked human characteristics such as culture.

---

2 Reference to Hawthorne's texts will be parenthetically indicated as *T&S* followed by the number of the page. The reference is to the following edition *Tales and Sketches*. Ed. Roy Harvey Pearce. New York: The Library of America, 1982.

The first element that deserves analysis is the contrast between the early inhabitants and the Puritans. There is a passing allusion to the Puritans: "but a band of Puritans [...] compared the masques to those devils and ruined souls, with whom their superstition peopled the black wilderness" (*T&S* 362). This sentence deserves some comment. In the first place, the reader finds that the 'wild throng' of colonists is using masques in the maypole festivities. Hawthorne makes the reader believe that these early inhabitants are brutes only to show that they simply appear as such as a result of living in the wilderness. Secondly, the narrator mentions the Puritan prejudice of associating wilderness and evil, an idea that is also present in "Young Goodman Brown," for instance. Entering the forest implies the risk of losing the moral attributes that people are supposed to be born with. "The May-Pole of Merry Mount" gives a twist to this prejudice when the narrator acknowledges that this is simply a Puritan superstition. Nonetheless, this superstition is present in Hawthorne's stories. Both in "Merry Mount" and in "The Gentle Boy," the wilderness plays an important role. It is not a coincidence that it is in the wilderness that the main characters face the moral challenge that hospitality offers. In the opposition between the social state and the state of nature, hospitality is an element inherent in nature, while in society hospitality has to be accomplished, even negotiated, an idea that goes against the grain of common notion of both states.

The second contrast comes with the presentation of the two main characters of the early colonists, "the two airiest forms," as the narrator describes them (*T&S* 362). Literally, Hawthorne writes: "Within the ring of monsters, appeared the two airiest forms" (*T&S* 362). The contrast is sharpened by putting both groups, the 'ring of monsters' and the 'two airiest forms,' in the same sentence one after the other. These two characters are a young man and a maiden. The scenario that surrounds them resembles Botticelli's *Primavera: Allegory of Spring* and functions as the setting for the wedding of the two young characters. This is described as a pagan ritual: "All ye that love the May-Pole, lend your voices to the nuptial song of the Lord and the Lady of the May" (*T&S* 362). This ceremony is linked to the ritual that the narrator describes in the opening of the story. The difference lies in the absence of history in the first two paragraphs of the narrative and in the writing in terms that makes the reader think time stands still in Merry Mount while the wedding ritual is already part of history. There has been a passage from paradisiacal timelessness to the historical colony that the narrator interprets in terms that are not philosophical but vital: "From the moment that they truly loved, they had subjected themselves to earth's doom of care, and sorrow, and troubled joy, and had no more a home at Merry Mount" (*T&S* 363). The narrator suggests that love triggers the entrance into history, or, for our purpose, into the social state.

Coherently, Hawthorne makes a survey of the colonization of the New World. The widespread assumption, as Hawthorne puts it, is that people went to America "some to conquer virgin empires; and one stern band to pray" (*T&S* 364). The colonists of Merry Mount, however, do not enter into any of these groups. They "imagined a wild philosophy of pleasure" (*T&S* 364). They have transplanted English customs and manners from England, though what characterizes them is their "veneration for the May-Pole" (*T&S* 364–365). The presence of these colonists offers a new approach to an interpretation of the colonization. There were three groups, not two, that went to America: the merchants to buy and sell the natural resources, the Puritans who had left England due to religious intolerance and, finally, those who went to have a better life but were not concerned with religion or the development of commerce. This last group is represented by the early colonists who, it is implied, went to America in search of religious freedom, since religious tolerance was absent in Great Britain. There arises the question of whether, as immigrants, they expected hospitable hosts in the colonies on their arrival or they thought the newly discovered land was not yet inhabited. The answer to this question offers new views on the question of colonization and hospitality that I will discuss below.

The second group the narrator describes in "Merry Mount" is that of the Puritans. As he says:

> there were men in the new world, of a sterner faith than these May-Pole worshippers [...] a settlement of Puritans, most dismal wretches, who said their prayers before daylight, and then wrought in the forest or the cornfield, till evening made it prayer time again. Their weapons were always at hand, to shoot down the straggling savage. When they met in conclave, it was never to keep up the old English mirth, but to hear sermons three hours long, or to proclaim bounties on the heads of wolves and the scalps of Indians. Their festivals were fast-days, and their chief pastime the singing of psalms. (*T&S* 365)

The whole paragraph is the reverse of the scene of the Merry Mounters. The Puritans are led by the principle *ora et labora* (pray and toil), as opposed to the gay carnivalesque life of the other colonists. They are also characterized by the conquering drive symbolized in the weapons. These two main characteristics are the points around which the Puritans' lives revolve as opposed to the other inhabitants of New England. The final sentence of the paragraph is an appropriate conclusion to the dark image of the colonists: "the whipping-post, which might be termed the Puritan May-Pole" (*T&S* 365). The narrator has been paralleling Merry Mounters and Puritans: "the wild throng" vs. the "most dismal wretches," the festivities vs. the life of praying and toiling, the coexistence with Native Inhabitants vs. the conquest of the territory, the maypole vs. the whipping post to conclude that the Puritans are the dark image of the Merry Mounters.

Initially, the coexistence of both groups is characterized by mutual ignorance though gradually the Puritans become aware of the Merry Mounters' way of living which they consider a threat to their saintly lives: "Who but the fiend, and his bond-slaves, the crew of Merry Mount, had thus disturbed them!" In the end, the conflict is a political one as the narrator says: "The future complexion of New England was involved in this important quarrel" (*T&S* 366).

This coexistence, with degrees of tolerance, ends the moment Endicott appears on stage. The scene resembles a Sabbath: "The leader of the hostile party stood in the center of the circle, while the rout of monsters cowered around him like evil spirits in the presence of a dread magician" (*T&S* 367). This scene provokes the attack of the 'hostile party' and shows that any possibility of coexistence is impossible. Consequently, hospitality becomes impossible as well. The closure of the story is also revealing: "Endicott, the severest Puritan of all who laid the rock foundation of New England" (*T&S* 370). Endicott acts as a function of inhospitality. The story ends with the victory of gloom over jollity, of which Endicott himself is an instigator. Hawthorne suggests that Puritanism is the moral and political foundation of New England. The final words of the narrator regarding the fate of the Lord and Lady of the May evoke Adam and Eve's exit from Paradise, though in this case they are not leaving the paradise but hell as they are going "heavenward" (*T&S* 370). Hawthorne suggests that hell is New England under Puritan rule, that is, an inhospitable community.

It may also be read as a counterexample of Kantian hospitality. For Kant the guest cannot do any harm to the host, as Garret Brown has argued (2010). There is a law of reciprocity that obliges both the host and the guest, and that cannot be violated by any of them. In "Merry Mount," Endicott contravenes the law and abuses the colonists and the Native Inhabitants without any regard to the fact that he is simply a guest.

The brief preface that Hawthorne places before the narrative plays an important role in the meaning of the story. Hawthorne acknowledges that, while the narrative is based on historical facts, it is an allegory. The question one may pose is why he is not writing a realist historical narrative or, at least, a historical romance, but rather chooses the allegorical mode. Hawthorne seemed more interested in the allegory than in the historical romance, despite the five romances that he wrote in later years starting with *The Scarlett Letter*. While allegory might distort the aim that underlies the writing of provincial narratives, the preface attempts to circumvent this objection when Hawthorne asserts "[t]he masques, mummeries, and festive customs, described in the text, are in accordance with the manners of the age" (*T&S* 360).

The allegory may have served him in the creation of characters that are not fully rounded, or even verisimilar or else too candid. It may have served him to give an apocalyptical tone to the political struggle of Puritans against other colonists. This apocalyptic and mythological hue would have helped Hawthorne create a book on provincial customs that dated back to a legendary past, much in Walter Scott's manner. It would have avoided any possible parallelism with the confrontation between conservatives and liberals in Hawthorne's age. One might think that the use of allegory would present the meaning in a universalist style which, considering the religious overtones of the narrative, would not be problematical for Hawthorne's contemporaries. Still, the emphasis on provincialism makes universalism problematic in the story.

3   Inhospitable Religious Communities

"Endicott and the Red Cross" was published in *The Token* in 1838 and in the expanded edition of *Twice-Told Tales* in 1842. This is another piece of short historical fiction intended to reflect on the ideological foundations of America, or as Bell puts it: it portrays "the symbolic birth of the American character" (1971, 57). The main character, John Endicott, was a person whose religious sternness was well known in the colonies. What is at stake in this historical narrative is what Bell has described as "the conflict within Puritanism itself between the forces of tyranny and the forces of liberty" (34). This opposition explains the struggle between the two religious factions.

The narrator provides the reader with a brief historical frame that introduces both the character and the main topic of the story. Religious tolerance stands at the forefront of the story with the mention of religious exiles (*T&S* 542). The war of religion that took place in England during the reign of Charles I, the Republic of Cromwell, and the reign of Charles II forced many Puritans to flee to America and settle in the colonies. Among these were Endicott and other people represented in the story by the Wanton Gospeller and the woman who supported him, as well as Roger Williams, the minister of Salem. He is described as "an elderly gentleman, wearing a black cloak and band, and a high-crowned hat, beneath which was a velvet skull-cap, the whole being the garb of a Puritan minister" (*T&S* 545). The crowd includes a few "stately savages" (*T&S* 544) and the Governor, who is "a wise man,—a wise man, and a meek and moderate," in Endicott's words (*T&S* 546). They conform to a representation of colonial society in which religious compromise rules. Hawthorne deals with the way in which tolerance and compromise are finally replaced by a stern practice of religion that leaves no room for tolerance. This intolerance was already present in the Colonial Period. Both the Wanton Gospeller and the woman who encourages him have been sentenced, and in the crowd there are others who have been condemned to suffer more severe punishments than the gospeller and the woman.

Endicott is the main character and the narrator's description of him is tremendously rich for our analysis. Endicott is the narrow Puritan that Bell analyzes in the second chapter of *Hawthorne and the Historical Romance of New England* (1971, 85-ff).[3] The first description of Endicott focuses on what is mirrored in the breastplate of his armor: the house of prayer (*T&S* 542). Immediately after that, the narrator goes on to describe other elements of the town. Now he focuses on the whipping-post (*T&S* 543). The juxtaposition of the two architectural elements is intended to reflect both the ambivalence of the political foundations of the colony and the union of politics and religion that Endicott sought. While Endicott supports a view of a society in which religion and politics are blended, for Roger Williams, the "elderly gentleman" whose aspect was "that of a pilgrim" (*T&S* 545), politics and religion occupy different spaces in a society. This is one of the ironic reversals Hawthorne uses to undermine any stable interpretation of history and Puritanism in his stories. Though Endicott has not severed the ties of the colony with Britain, and consequently the stern law of Puritanism is not yet complete, the narrator mentions the punishments that some colonists have already suffered: "the whipping-post,—with the soil around it well trodden by the feet of evil-doers, who had there been disciplined" (*T&S*543) or "among the crowd were several, whose punishment would be life-long" (*T&S*542). Any straight explanation of a shift in the politics of the Puritans on the basis of Endicott's severance of British rule is thus mistaken. Even before Endicott "rent the Red Cross completely out of the banner" (*T&S* 548), Puritanism ruled in the colony in both religious and political affairs. Endicott gives voice to this idea when he shouts: "liberty to worship God, not license to profane and ridicule him" (*T&S* 547) as an answer to the Wanton Gospeller. Before that moment he had rhetorically asked the crowd why they had come to America and his answer, in the form of a rhetorical question, is: "Was it not for the enjoyment of our civil rights? Was it not for liberty to worship God according to our conscience?" (*T&S* 546).

---

3   Frederick C. Crews (1989, 33), Michael Colacurcio (1986, 24), and Robert Milder (2013, 123) offer biographical explanations of the Puritan type that Endicott symbolizes which, to my view, do not add anything substantial to a discussion of Endicott as a fictional character.

Though it was political and religious freedom that moved the Puritans to settle in America, curiously enough the latter is not granted to other settlers, as the description of punishments in the first pages of the story shows. The hospitality that Endicott expects from other settlers he does not grant to those who profess a different religious denomination. Endicott appropriates for himself and his fellow Puritans the status of religious exiles, thus making the Others dissenters. This is another of the ironical reverses in the story. While in Britain the Puritans are the dissenters, in America they become the enemies of religious tolerance. This leads them to a rejection of hospitality as Derrida theorizes. While he claims religious freedom for himself—a claim which will be completely established only when the ties with Britain have been severed—he does not allow such freedom to the others, who might have come to America even before he had. Hospitality, for him, means the total acceptance of the religious creed that he professes. He becomes the patron of the household in Derridean terms (Derrida 2000, 4). However, it must be noted that the presence of Puritans on American soil was recent and that, properly speaking, they had the same right to the title of patrons than any other person or religious denomination. Endicott's behavior does not become an example of Kantian hospitality either, as I pointed out earlier.

More importantly, Endicott must be analyzed as the displaced host that Levinas theorizes (Treanor 2011). It might commonly be thought that hospitality during the colonial period refers to the behavior of the Native Inhabitants towards the colonists. However, Hawthorne's view is radically different. For him, the Indians do not have an existence of their own, at least in narrative terms. They are always part of the crowd of people who lived in the colonies before Endicott and the Puritans arrived. In fact, in "Merry Mount" the colonists are not so different from the Native Americans for Hawthorne. He creates a misunderstanding when he writes about the "wild throng" which is composed of the "Fauns and Nymphs" (*T&S* 361) who, in reality, were those who had been persecuted. While describing the attitude, countenance, and costumes of these exiles, Hawthorne mentions "the Salvage Man" only to add that there was also a "nobler figure, but still a counterfeit [...] an Indian hunter" (*T&S* 361). Hawthorne makes the distinction between the salvage man and the Indian since, according to the narrator, the latter is not a fake. Native Inhabitants have no other narrative presence in the story nor are they or their customs described. All descriptions of manners and traditions are related to the early settlers as a group in which British settlers and Native Inhabitants are included. In "Endicott and The Red Cross" the Native Inhabitants play the role of spectators. Still noble, they are described as "stately savages, in all the pomp and dignity of the primeval Indian," the narrator also adds: "Their flint-headed arrows were but childish weapons" (*T&S* 544). Hawthorne equates the imagined state of nature in which the Indians lived with childhood, as if cultures developed as people do. The Native Inhabitants are human beings who live in a less developed, or more childlike, culture. The opposition is established in religious and political terms, British and Indians being included in the same group of early colonists, while the Puritans belong to the other group. I propose to read the tale in terms of the colonists in the role of displaced hosts. This approach sheds light on "Merry Mount" and "Endicott and the Red Cross." By moving themselves from Europe to America, the colonists lose their place in society and have to find a new one. Endicott prefers to acquire the role of the owner of the house in Derridean terms as a prefiguration of the imperialistic attitude the United States would hold later on. His placing as a host (while he is a displaced host in fact) creates a reversal of the roles of guest and host that in Hawthorne's fiction is signaled by the ironical reflections of his fiction, of which the gest in the role of displaced host and the host proper characterized as guest are the two central reversals of these two stories. Besides, this displaced host is the embodiment of the guest that Kant harshly criticized in his essay *Perpetual Peace*. The guest (as a displaced host in this case) cannot act against the host's interests and welfare.

4 The Gentle Hospitality

"The Gentle Boy," first published in *The Token* in 1833 (dated 1832) and then collected in *Twice-Told Tales*, is a model example of hospitality. The narrative has been read variously by Colacurcio (1986) and by Bell (1971), among others. For Colacurcio, it is a story about New England morality (1986, 160). Bell argues that the transformation of the English character in the American wilderness is Hawthorne's main historical theme (117). For Thompson, the tales, together with *The Scarlet Letter*, provide a classic example "of the pervasive theme of sadomasochism" (1993, 118). It is an example of the way characters may be trapped between two worlds (Crews 1989, 65; Folsom 1963, 123–125; Newberry 1987, 48–49). Most critics agree that "The Gentle Boy" is one of the most sentimental stories Hawthorne wrote. Feelings are explicitly present from the beginning of the story. Pearson's sympathy is "fully excited" when he meets the boy (*T&S* 112). A few paragraphs later, the narrator adds: "in the awakened warmth of his feelings" (*T&S* 112). As Abram van Engen argues "[t]he concept of fellow feeling [...] pervaded New England Puritanism and affected the shape of literature" (2010, 533). The expression of affection in literature would help to develop communal affection, van Engen points out, that latter would "b[i] nd political and religious bodies" (533). Putting an emphasis on feelings helped develop a human fabric that would be immune to religious intolerance. As such, sentimentalism would favor hospitality.

The story opens with a brief historical introduction that contextualizes the narrative. Against this context, the narrative will offer insights into hospitality and tolerance. It is a story about religious intolerance and the way in which roles are easily reversed. If Puritans were persecuted in England and migrated to America in order to find a place where they could freely preach and practice their religion, once they arrived in New England they started to exert their religious intolerance over Quakers, a denomination associated with England.

Tobias Pearson is the opposite characterization of the narrow Puritan Bell discusses in other stories (1971). Instead of a stern convinced Puritan, Tobias represents the man who desires to live in a tolerant society where people from various religious denominations may coexist. He converts from Puritanism to Quakerism in a shift that is intended to symbolize the tolerance of a society in which individuals are more important than abstract ideas. For Tobias, religion is not a fixed set of dogmatic rules that people must follow blindly. Rather it is a personal experience that serves the individual as a guide to living morally. Ilbrahim is the actantial object that unleashes Tobias's hospitable feelings and his subsequent conversion to Quakerism. Catharine is Ilbrahim's mother who accepts her son being raised by Puritans without being educated in the principles of Quakerism. This is a central moment in the story as it opposes Tobias's initial hospitality. Catharine regrets that neither Tobias nor his wife, Dorothy, are Quakers (*T&S* 122) and asks them if they will bring him up as a Quaker. To that question Dorothy answers:

> if your child become our child, we must breed him up in the instruction which Heaven has imparted to us; we must pray for him the prayers of our own faith; we must do towards him according to the dictates of our own consciences, and not of yours (*T&S* 123).

As Derrida has argued in discussions of Kantian hospitality (2000, 4), this is the act of kindness that the host makes to the guest, but it is never complete or unconditional. To a large extent, though a right of the guest, hospitality is still marked by the host's preferences, or as Dorothy says in the story, "our own consciences." Hawthorne is subtly opposing feelings to conscience—sentiments and morality. If Tobias acts in a way that conforms to what Derrida defines as total hospitality: "an intentional experience that proceeds beyond knowledge toward the other as absolute stranger, as unknown, where

I know that I know nothing of him" (2000, 8), Dorothy is the representative of a restrained hospitality that has marked politics in Western civilization. Hawthorne, nonetheless, introduces a series of ironic reversals in the story. Tobias the Puritan becomes Tobias the Quaker, while Catharine the fanatic Quaker adopts a milder version of Quakerism at the end of the story. Hospitality in its most radical version is the cause of Tobias's conversion as well as of Catharine's acceptance of Dorothy's comments on Ilbrahim's education. Catharine's acceptance must be understood as the guest's acceptance of limited hospitality. Rather than rebel against this kind of hospitality that limits her rights, she agrees to it in order to save her son from the life of an outcast in the wilderness.

While nature plays an important role in Hawthorne's fictions—not uncoincidentally it is the chronotope of both "The May-Pole of Merry Mount" and "The Gentle Boy"—the wilderness has a meaningful function in the ideological characterization of America as either a hospitable or inhospitable place. There are significant differences between both stories as regards the location. In "Merry Mount" the wilderness plays a minor role in the story and is only part of it in the sense that there is no divide between the colony and the wilderness. The narrator describes it as a "melancholy forest" (T&S 361) where roses grow: "bringing deep verdure to the forest, and roses in her lap, of a more vivid hue than the tender buds of Spring" (T&S 360). The dwellers in the colony live in harmony with that nature which, because of this harmony, ceases to be a wilderness and becomes a paradise. In "The Gentle Boy" the wilderness poses a threat to the inhabitants of the colonies. To begin with, the colony has been established quite recently: "The low, straw-thatched houses were scattered at considerable intervals along the road, and the country having been settled but about thirty years, the tracts of original forest still bore no small proportion to the cultivated ground" (T&S 109–110). The comment suggests that the colony creates a point of disruption in the center of that nature uncultivated until recent times. A couple of paragraphs later the narrator introduces another disruption. The murder of the Quakers in the forest creates an identification of death with the wilderness that is absent in "Merry Mount." While the nature that is part of Merry Mount is vital and paradisiacal until the arrival of the Puritans, the nature that surrounds the colony in "The Gentle Boy" is tinged with the darkness of death from its beginning.

This may be read as the complexion of nature before and after the Puritan colonization. To a certain extent, Hawthorne is dealing with the issue of a paradisiacal America colonized by Puritans after the fall of the first settlers. The story of Merry Mount is the first stage of this sketch of the history of humankind in America. "The Gentle Boy" is the second stage, that of Puritans as rulers and the transformation of nature from paradise to earth (if not hell). This shift in nature can help explain the role of hospitality. While living in a bountiful nature in which death does not make any appearance, hospitality is not necessary at all, as the Law of Necessity has not entered paradise. In contrast, living in an earthly nature ruled by mortality, necessity, and dissension makes hospitality absolutely necessary for a society founded on the principles of political and religious tolerance.

George Bancroft provides another interpretation. In *History of the United States from the Discovery of the American Continent*, originally published in 1834, he argues that the wilderness would serve as an asylum for the purity of religion or the liberty of conscience (1842, 322). The wilderness is a haven or a place of revelation rather than a dangerous site. For him, the colonists were a church in the wilderness. This view of the wilderness makes it function as a heterotopia in Foucaultian terms. Heterotopias are countersites, "a kind of effectively enacted utopia in which the real sites, all the other real sites that can be found within culture, are simultaneously represented, contested, and inverted. Places of this kind are outside of all places" (Foucault 1986, 24). The wilderness functions as such a place in which colonial society is contested and inverted, albeit for a limited period of time. This inversion is enacted by the ironical reversals that Hawthorne places in his stories, among which the displaced host stands at the forefront. By making the guest a host, he would point out the inhumanity of colonization and would also challenge the national view of the shaping of America that was prevalent in his age and embodied in Bancroft's *History*.

5 Conclusion

Hospitality deals with the welcome of strangers as an interrogation of identity. By focusing on religion while discussing hospitality, Hawthorne is challenging the religious tolerance that was the prevalent discourse of the age. Contrary to the generally accepted idea of this religious tolerance, Nathaniel Hawthorne deals with the issue of hospitality in these historical narratives as a means to present religious tolerance in an ironic way. While he establishes two parties, the resolution of the story reveals that there is not always a clearly-cut answer to hospitality. In "The May-Pole of Merry Mount" and "Endicott and the Red Cross" Hawthorne shows, through a series of ironic reversals in the stories, that tolerance is disqualified or given a sense different to the original. Among these ironic reversals stands the shift from exile to patron of the household, in

Derridean terms, that Endicott undergoes in both stories and his becoming the Levinasian displaced host that breaks the Kantian law of hospitality. "The Gentle Boy" shows a change in the behavior of both the Puritan and the Quaker families. Yet the ironic elements embedded in the story make the meaning of the story ambivalent and subject to partisan interpretations. This ambivalence goes against the commonplace view of the colonization of America as a progressive, teleologically-driven event that would end in the creation of America as a nation. Hawthorne scrutinizes the critical breaches in the common history of America that includes historical characters such as Endicott and common people, such as Tobias Pearson and his wife, to contest the prevalent interpretation of such a history.

References

Adams, Richard P. 1957. "Hawthorne's Provincial Tales" *New England Quarterly* 30: 39–57.

Adkins, Nelson F. 1945. "The Early Projected Works of Nathaniel Hawthorne" *The Papers of the Bibliographical Society of America* 39 (2): 119–155.

Bancroft, George. 1842. *History of the United States, from the Discovery of the American Continent*, vol. I. Boston: Charles C. Little and James Brown.

Baym, Nina. 1976. *The Shape of Hawthorne's Career*. Ithaca: New York; Cornell UP.

Bell, Michael D. 1971. *Hawthorne and the Historical Romance of New England*. Princeton, Mass: Princeton UP.

Brown, Garrett W. 2010. "The Laws of Hospitality, Asylum Seekers and Cosmopolitan Right. A Kantian Response to Jacques Derrida." *European Journal of Political Theory* 9(3): 308–327.

Buell, Lawrence. 1986. *New England Literary Culture. From Revolution through Renaissance*. Cambridge: Cambridge UP.

Cagidemetrio, Alide. 1992. *Fictions of the Past: Hawthorne and Melville*. Amherst, Mass.: Institute for Advanced Study in the Humanities.

Chandler, Elizabeth. 1925–26. "A Study of the Sources of the Tales and Romances Written by Nathaniel Hawthorne Before 1853." *Smith College Studies in Modern Languages* 7: 1–63.

Colacurcio, Michael J. 1986. *The Province of Piety: Moral History in Hawthorne's Early Tales*. Cambridge, Mass: Harvard UP.

Crews, Frederick C. 1989. *The Sins of the Fathers: Hawthorne's Psychological Themes*. Berkeley: U of California P.

Damai, Puspa L. 2012. *Welcoming Strangers: Hospitality in American Literature and Culture*. PhD diss., University of Michigan.

Deamer, Robert Glen. 1979. "Hawthorne's Dream in the Forest." *Western American Literature* 13 (4): 37–339.
Derrida, Jacques. 2000. "Hostipitality." *Angelaki* 5 (3): 3–18.
Drinnon, Richard. 1980. "The Maypole of Merry Mount: Thomas Morton & the Puritan Patriarchs." *The Massachusetts Review* 21 (2): 382–410.
Folsom, James K. 1963. *Man's Accidents and God's Purposes: Multiplicity in Hawthorne's Fiction*. New Haven, Conn.: College and UP.
Foucault, Michel. 1986. "Of Other Spaces." *Diacritics* 16 (1): 22–27.
Hampsher-Monk, Iain. 1996. *Historia del pensamiento político moderno*. Translated by Ferran Meler. Barcelona: Ariel.
Hawthorne, Nathaniel. 1982. *Tales and Sketches*. Edited by Roy Harvey Pearce. New York: The Library of America.
James, Henry. 1984. "Hawthorne." In *Literary Criticism, vol 1*, edited by Leon Edel and Mark Wilson, 313–457. New York: The Library of America.
Kennedy, J. Gerald. 2016. *Strange Nation: Literary Nationalism and Cultural Conflict in the Age of Poe*. Oxford: Oxford UP.
Manzanas, Ana M. and Jesús Benito. 2017. *Hospitality in American Literature and Culture. Spaces, Bodies, Borders*. London: Routledge.
Martin, Terence. 1983. *Nathaniel Hawthorne*. Revised edition. Boston: Twayne.
McWilliams, John P., Jr. 1977. "Fictions of Merry Mount." *American Quarterly* 29 (1): 3–30.
Milder, Robert. 2013. *Hawthorne's Habitations. A Literary Life*. Oxford: Oxford UP.
Moore, Margaret B. 1998. *The Salem World of Nathaniel Hawthorne*. Columbia: U of Missouri P.
Newberry, Frederick. 1987. *Hawthorne's Divided Loyalties: England and America in his Works*. Rutherford, NJ: Fairleigh Dickinson UP.
Pearce, Roy Harvey. 1969. *Historicism Once More: Problems and Occasions for the American Scholar*. Princeton, N.J.: Princeton UP.
Relph, Edward. 1976. *Place and Placelessness*. London: Pion.
Sterne, Richard Clarke. 1970. "Puritans at Merry Mount: Variations on a Theme." *American Quarterly* 22 (4): 846–858.
Still, Judith. 2010. *Derrida and Hospitality: Theory and Practice*. Edinburgh: Edinburgh UP.
Thompson, G.R. 1993. *The Art of Authorial Presence. Hawthorne's Provincial Tales*. Durham: Duke UP.
Treanor, Brian. 2011. "Putting Hospitality in its Place." In *Phenomenologies of the Stranger: Between Hostility and Hospitality*, edited by Richard Kearney and Kascha Semonovitch, 49–66. New York: Fordham UP.
Van Engen, Abram. 2010. "Puritanism and the Power of Sympathy." *Early American Literature* 45 (3): 533–564.

Weber, Alfred. 1989. "The Outlines of 'The Story Teller,' the Major Work of Hawthorne's Early Years." *Nathaniel Hawthorne Review* 15: 14–19.

Wineapple, Brenda. 2003. *Hawthorne. A Life*. New York: Random House.

Wood, Gordon S. 2009. *Empire of Liberty. A History of the Early Republic, 1789–1815*. Oxford: Oxford UP.

CHAPTER 7

(In)Hospitable Encounters in Herman Melville's *Clarel*

Laura López Peña

Abstract

Herman Melville's literary production articulates a global consciousness which transcends notions of identitarianism, community, even nationalism, in the midst of an agitated nineteenth centurywhen the United States was redefining itself as 'nation' and constructing its ideals of nationhood at a time of inter-personal hatreds, violence, and eventually civil war. Those inter-personal hatreds—against those considered 'different' inside the nation (African Americans, southerners, Native Americans), but also against those coming from outside with hopes of becoming part of the nation (migrants arriving to the US)—are not only echoed but also explored already in Melville's early novels.

Focusing particularly on Melville's long epic poem *Clarel: A Poem and Pilgrimage in the Holy Land*, written over the postbellum years and published in 1876 (the year the US was celebrating its centennial), yet without forgetting Melville's earlier works in prose, the present chapter aims to analyze in Melville the concept of hospitality as articulated by Jacques Derrida, together with notions of interpersonal ethics and togetherness developed by philosophers such as Emmanuel Levinas, Martin Buber, Hannah Arendt, or Judith Butler. The chapter's objective, therefore, is to focus on moments of 'togetherness'—principally in *Clarel*, but also in Melville's previous novels—in order to show how Melville's works confront readers with hospitable encounters which, however, turn out to eventually reflect on the incapacity to fully embrace the alterity that the Other represents. On a more positive note, the chapter will also present an example of successful hospitality in the *Clarel* character Rolfe, a Melvillean prototype of a successful capacity to embrace alterity and polyphony in what the poem names *manysidedness*.

Keywords

Herman Melville – *Clarel* – Holy Land – United States – otherness – (un)conditional hospitality – empathy – Derrida – Hannah Arendt – Emmanuel Levinas – interhuman encounters – Civil War

∴

> When the host says to the guest, 'Make yourself at home,' this is a self-limiting invitation. 'Make yourself at home' means: please feel at home, act as if you were at home, but, remember, that is not true, this is not your home but mine, and you are expected to respect my property.
>
> JOHN CAPUTO
> *Deconstruction in a Nutshell*

∴

"Are not men built into communities just like bricks into a wall?" (*Israel Potter* 1984, 601). This is one of the final images in *Israel Potter: His Fifty Years of Exile*, published in 1855 by Herman Melville (1819–1891). While this ending expresses the concern that individual differences can be lost to the immensity of a homogeneous whole, the novel constructs a narrative rescuing from oblivion and commemorating the neglected ex-revolutionary hero with the same name. As Melville demonstrates throughout the novel, Israel's subjectivity as character is inseparable from the nationalist forces he can neither control nor escape. Yet, his existence is also connected to that of a larger human yearning that transcends nation-state boundaries and even time: "Here, in this very darkness, centuries ago, hearts, human as his, had mildewed in despair; limbs, robust as his own, had stiffened in immovable torpor" (505). The superb yet tragic vision of Israel becoming part of a large tormented human crowd of sufferers—"destitute, honest men like himself" (607)—is not very different from that of *Clarel*'s corresponding young protagonist. Like Israel's, Clarel's fate is connected to that of "tormented humanity" (604) as he joins the heterogeneous crowd of "Cross-bearers" in the Via Crucis at the end of the poem (*Clarel* 1991, 4.34.43). Also like Israel's, Clarel's suffering is not exceptional among either fellow humans or even animals: "In varied forms of fate they wend—/ Or man or animal, 'tis one:/Cross-bearers all, alike they tend/And follow, slowly follow on" (4.34.41-44).

By telling the stories of individuals who are victims of the sociopolitical, economic, religious, ethnocentric, and also nationalist apparatuses which both generate and perpetuate human segregation, violence, and injustice, Melville's works enable multiple subjectivities, with all their complexities, to unfold. These literary personalities would otherwise become dead letters to humanity as many of Melville's works indeed were during the author's life. Similar to how Hunilla in "The Chola Widow" (1854) empathizes with others and incorporates others' pain into her own, Melville also turns his works into hospitable spaces to host alterity and humanize otherness through suffering as a common human condition. Such alterity is individualized and, at the same time, connected to a universal continuum in the same way that the enigmatic final exclamation of the 1853 novella "Bartleby, the Scrivener"—"Ah Bartleby! Ah humanity!" (2001b, 98)—also intermingles both. The irony, perhaps, is that the author's understanding of the fallacy to *know* his characters is also humble, as he acknowledges the impossible task of explaining the complexities of the human heart. Instead, Melville enables complexities and enigmas to speak, often leaving unresolved mysteries and contradictions for the reader to consider. Had he silenced the contradictions Melville would not have done justice to the alterities embodied by his characters, since he would have suppressed the otherness they impersonate to create singular narratives, thereby constructing his works as inhospitable spaces.[1]

The concerns in Melville's oeuvre are not outdated in our own century. Melville explored many sociopolitical complexities that his times and society were either unprepared or unwilling to deal with, some of which remain pressing even today. Judging from his literary testimonies, it is difficult to imagine a Melville who would shrug indifferently at the closing of borders to those millions of Others tragically and urgently leaving their homes—the familiar—to reach unfamiliar shores nowadays, for nobody leaves their home if the home can *host* them better. Regarding migrants, Melville's answer seems clear, welcoming, and—to use Derridean terminology—hospitable; as his young character Redburn exclaims in the 1849 eponymous novel: "the whole world is the patrimony of the whole world" (1983, 318). Our era of rising nationalism and patriotic claims, resurrected interhuman rivalries and hatreds that were never lost, legitimation of xenophobia, racism, anti-immigrant policies, and erected borders, not only in the nation but also in the mind, is certainly different but, perhaps, not so different from Melville's.

The concept of 'hospitality' may shed light on such neighboring complexities and rivalries. Insomuch as, according to Derrida, true hospitality requires the unconditional acceptance of the Other, it does not merely consist of a visit or encounter through which both parties remain the same; it is an exchange through which either or both might be transformed. As a consequence, hospitality involves contact, and contact enables a possible transformative potentiality, whether that be positive or negative. However, one may also question the ethics of accepting the risks of taking on another who may not even be

---

1 See J. A. Weinstock's analysis of Bartleby following Derrida's 1992 essay "Force of Law."

hospitable themselves, yet the answer is not closing ourselves to the Other either.

Derrida continues to point out that hospitality does not require reciprocity because it is not a transaction. A well-known Melvillean instance of unconditional hospitality is that experienced by Ishmael in *Moby-Dick* (1851). Ishmael narrates the development of his feelings of togetherness towards the initially scary pagan Polynesian cannibal with yellowish skin and a tattooed body, Queequeg. When he meets Queequeg, the American cannot at first imagine that he will eventually become friends with this embodiment of alterity:

> I began to be sensible of strange feelings. I felt a melting in me. No more my splintered heart and maddened hand were turned against the wolfish world. This soothing savage had redeemed it. There he sat, his very indifference speaking a nature in which there lurked no civilized hypocrisies and bland deceits. Wild he was; a very sight of sights to see; yet I began to feel myself mysteriously drawn towards him. And those same things that would have repelled most others, they were the very magnets that thus drew me. (*Moby-Dick* 2007, 62)

Ishmael's initial fear of the unknown Other is later replaced by fascination and even love. What derives from this Melvillean episode is a connection with the Other that is not based on making the Other less different or less strange to ourselves; it incorporates the Other *as* other, embracing his/her alterity without conditions. Similar to the Derridean notion of hospitality, for philosopher Martin Buber the openness towards the Other is the generator of interpersonal bonding, transcending notions of sameness and respecting difference, because difference is precisely what generates such bonding. In these interpersonal spaces enabled by such communal disposition towards alterity, Buber argues, human beings may be taught that one's own "relation to truth is heightened by the other's different relation to the same truth—different in accordance with his individuation, and destined to take seed and grow differently" (1992, 65). This is an active exercise which requires a willingness to see the Other approach the same *truth* as oneself from their unique perspective. By doing so, the Other is affirmed as another I.

Buber's approach resonates in Hannah Arendt's, who affirms that dialogue is the process through which human beings make sense of the world together: "as soon as it is uttered," truth "is immediately transformed into one opinion among many, [...] contested, reformulated, reduced to one subject of discourse among others" (1968, 27). This exposure to alterity in a dialogic process is the heart of what Arendt names the "critical judgment," stimulating the development of an "enlarged mentality" (1998, 241) which, at the same time, is the basis of political thinking:

> Political thought is representative. I form an opinion by considering a given issue from different viewpoints, by making present to my mind the standpoints of those who are absent; that is, I represent them. This process of representation does not blindly adopt the actual views of those who stand somewhere else, and hence look upon the world from a different perspective; this is a question neither of empathy [...] nor of counting noses and joining a majority, but of being and thinking in my own identity where actually I am not. The more people's standpoints I have present in my mind while I am pondering a given issue, and the better I can imagine how I would feel and think if I were in their place, the stronger will be my capacity for representative thinking and the more valid my final conclusions, my opinion. (1998, 241)

Arendt emphasizes not only the political, but also the ethical implications of the exercise in critical judgment she describes. A similar argument is given by Emmanuel Levinas, for whom there is no question as to why one should be held responsible for others. As a matter of fact, the philosopher considers the inseparability and mutual constituency of self and Other, claiming that moral responsibility, or the ethical demand, is an innate and disinterested obligation imposed upon each individual even before their existence, and that it is in regard to this moral responsibility that individuals develop their own selves (Levinas 2006, 64 and 57). Like Derrida, Levinas's arguments expose the vulnerability of the self when approaching the Other, a vulnerability which, following Levinas, Judith Butler considers expressive of "both the necessity and the difficulty of ethics" (Butler 2011, 14). Yet, it is precisely this vulnerability which may awaken our empathy and make us more hospitable or receptive to the suffering of others.

Nevertheless, if, as Levinas argues, morality is innate to human beings, Melville also explored the "Innate Depravity [...] from whose visitations, in some shape or other, no deeply thinking mind is always and wholly free" ("Hawthorne and His Mosses" 2001a, 51). As a matter of fact, the inescapable intertwinement of good and evil in the human heart is a recurrent motif throughout Melville's entire literary production and one which determines the author's exploration of interhuman (in)hospitable encounters due to the fact that, as Rolfe declares in *Clarel*, "Evil and good they braided play/Into one chord" (4.4.27-28).

1   "Get[ting] Rid of a *Few* Prejudices"

Melville's travel experiences throughout his life, first as a sailor bound for the Pacific, and later as a traveler to Europe, Constantinople, Egypt, and the Holy Land, conditioned his perception of alterity, of both how similar and different the Other really was. They also made the author question and stretch his thinking parameters. As he would claim in his lecture "Traveling: Its Pleasures, Pains, and Profits" (1859), travel creates humble yet independent thinkers aware of the partiality of their own assumptions and capable of unlearning prejudices and stereotypes:

> For the profit of travel: in the first place, you get rid of a *few* prejudices. [...]
> Travel to a large and generous nature is as a new birth. Its legitimate tendency is to teach profound personal humility, while it enlarges the sphere of comprehensive benevolence till it includes the whole human race.
> Among minor benefits is that of seeing for one's self all striking natural or artificial objects, for every individual sees differently according to his idiosyncrasies. [...] It is important to be something of a linguist to travel to advantage; at least to speak French fluently. In the Levant, where all nations congregate, unpretending people speak half a dozen languages, and a person who thought himself well educated at home is often abashed at his ignorance there. (1987, 423, italics and line breaks in the original)

Arriving in Jaffa on January 6, 1857, Melville reached Jerusalem shortly afterward, where he spent eight days before joining a short expedition to the Dead Sea and Mar Saba (Bezanson 1991, 515). In his journal, Melville depicts a Palestine that looks inhospitable and far from the idealized portrayals of the period; Jerusalem inspires images of wrecks, waste, dearth, oppressiveness, lack of ventilation and air, desolation, stones, and greyness: "Judea is one accumulation of stones—Stony mountains & stony plains; stony torrents & stony roads; stony walls & stony feilds [*sic*], stony houses & stony tombs; stony eyes & stony hearts. Before you, & behind you are stones. Stones to right & stones to left" (*Journals* 1989, 90). In a succeeding entry, Melville adds that "[t]he color of the whole city is grey & looks at you like a cold grey eye in a cold old man" (90). Far from an idealized portrayal of the land of the Bible, Melville was rather skeptical that Palestine constituted a *holy* land, as even sacred spaces like the Holy Sepulcher had become places of confrontation and decay—not communion—reflecting spiritual barrenness and devoid of any divinity. Melville spent approximately three weeks in Palestine before returning to the US. As Melville wrote in his journal: "JC should have appeared in Taheiti [sic]!" (*Journals* 1989, 154).

Not long after Melville's voyage to the Holy Land, tensions exploded between millions of Americans in a divided United States. These tensions reached their peak with the Civil War, to which almost every American lost either a family member or close friend (Foote 1994, 272). The postbellum years, which Melville devoted to the writing of *Clarel*, were some of the most unstable and turbulent as, despite the official end of the war, the nation remained violently confronted, racial violence escalated in the south, and new borders were being established by the country's westward expansion and battles against Native American peoples.[2] On the other hand, if, as biographer Laurie Robertson-Lorant has claimed, "for Melville, writing was as natural as breathing" (1996, 327), the material conditions for writing also changed radically over the almost twenty years following December 1866, when he managed to get a job at the New York Customs House; a confinement which must have been hard to bear for someone who had traveled so much and so far away. Despite these conditions, Melville continued to write, but the long narrative poem *Clarel*, written during this period, would not come to public light until 1876. In it, the author creates a polyphonic dialogic poem and a space of unconditional hospitality, continuing the tradition of his texts.

Hilton Obenzinger has argued that Melville's capacity of representing plurality at its most intricate complexities and even contradictions results from the author's extraordinary "elasticity of mind," which he defines as "the ability to cross over and entertain forbidden arguments, identities, and states of being" (2006, 195). Indeed, Melville's texts become microcosms in which to explore alterity and hospitality while portraying contexts of inter-human divisions, (self-)isolation and segregation. However, Melville's hospitality or *accommodation* of the Other does not rely on presumptions neutralizing difference. On the contrary, novels such as *The Confidence Man* (1857) display a critique of Kantianism as a universalist conception of humanity—based on Western impositions—which neutralizes and invalidates all others outside such claims to universality.[3] Rather, as Timothy Marr remarks, "By accentuating the worldly

---

2 For a detailed analysis of Reconstruction and postbellum racial violence see Foner 2002. For further details on postbellum corruption see Trachtenberg 2007.

3 As Judith Butler theorizes in a way similar to Jacques Derrida, presenting Kantian cosmopolitanism as the only possible way to articulate universality is already a cultural imposition which defeats plurality by clinging to a parochial conception of the universal and imposing it to others (1996, 52).

diversity of his crew, Melville 'federated' a broad latitude of literary characters that empowered his challenge to the ethnocentric claims of universality held by the supposedly civilized" (2005, 136). While Marr refers to *Moby-Dick* when illustrating Melville's federation of such a wide range of literary characters, *Clarel* is an even more highly populated microcosm. It constitutes what Stan Goldman describes as a "chorus of voices," both expressive of conversations among characters representative of the diversity of humanity, and of chants, poems, inscriptions, songs, laments and theatrical representations within the text (1993, 97). In Vincent Kenny's words, "Melville allows the characters to speak their own minds" (1973, 120). It is through this dialogic technique that the poem is turned into a text that hosts a plurality of worldviews, deconstructs one-sided narratives and encourages readers to be independent thinkers by considering the different sides of the same argument. Wyn Kelley, for instance, has argued that Melville "understands the relationship between writer and reader as an ongoing dialogue, a collaboration" (2008, 23), while Samuel Otter has analyzed the demands—though also rewards—of this collaboration in the particular case of *Clarel*, which he calls "a work of complex pleasures" (2006, 480). Among these complex pleasures is the readers' understanding of the impossibility of answers, as they are challenged by the poem/pilgrimage to form new questions because "Truth, for Melville, is a question, not an answer" (Seelye 1970, 10). Most importantly, scholars such as Amy Kaplan have valued Melville's works as embracing human collectivities and interpersonal bonds based on dialogism and plurality. (2010, 50). These dialogic texts move away from individual or community-based identities posing interpersonal barriers and monologic thinking and, instead, make those who come together enter a plural encounter where "you" is always an "I." In this process, the potentiality of ethics in a Levinasian or Derridean way emerges, as it is through the awareness that the strangeness of the Other becomes less strange that hospitality may become more authentically unconditional or empathic. Read in a similar way to Hannah Arendt's image of the table both uniting and separating the people sitting around it (1998, 53), *Clarel* can be said to constitute a dialogic meeting ground bringing together a wide range of characters who are strangers to one another. Some have praised this dialogic nature of the poem, its "mercurial narrative [...] that constantly shifts focus and perspective, allowing a rich texture of disparate ideas, voices, and points of view" not offering "a single answer but a combination of answers in dialogical relationship to each other" (Potter 2004, 14–15; Goldman 1993, 17). Thus, *Clarel* is a dialogic poem in Bakhtinian terms: "It is constructed not as the whole of a single consciousness, absorbing other consciousnesses as objects into itself, but as [...] the interaction of several consciousnesses, none of which entirely becomes an object for the other"

(Bakhtin 1984, 18). Throughout this dialogic process based on alterity, difference, and plural thinking, the poem denounces monologic conclusions, forced silences, and one-sided thinking.

2 Inhospitable Holy Land

The setting of the Holy Land and the particular city of Jerusalem represent a potentially dialogic context, but also a scenario of inhospitable encounters. As I have argued elsewhere,[4] the Palestine in the poem contains resonances of postbellum United States, but it is also undeniable that Jerusalem is a global microcosm. In an aerial sight from the top of the city's wall, the young Clarel is amused by the arrival of pilgrims of all kinds, all of them strangers to the young American and to one another:

> Like envoys from all Adam's race,
> Mixed men of various nations pace,
> Such as in crowded steamer come
> And disembark at Jaffa's stair. (*Clarel* 1991, 1.41.48–51)

It is interesting that, instead of conceiving such assorted humanity in a mass, Clarel's eyes make an effort to individualize the newcomers. As Melville had already warned in *Moby Dick*,

> Seat thyself sultanically among the moons of Saturn, and take high abstracted man alone; and he seems a wonder, a grandeur, and a woe. But from the same point, take mankind in mass, and for the most part, they seem a mob of unnecessary duplicates, both contemporary and hereditary. (2007, 408)

When the last pilgrim enters Jerusalem, the gate is locked, leaving the wilderness outside and, with it, neighboring strangers such as Arabs or Bedouins whom Jerusalem's dwellers conceive as threatening. In these global spaces that Palestine and Jerusalem suppose, the young Clarel himself is a stranger roaming amidst humanity and acquiring some wisdom from his encounters with fellow travelers who are also strangers to him. In this context of in/hospitable encounters, learning and unlearning constitute processes that complement

---

4 See López 2015.

rather than exclude one another. The main problem comes when characters themselves become victims of walls, or, victimizers imposing walls on others, a process by which inter-human divisions are enforced by worldviews sustained by inside/outside forms of belonging creating *foreign* and *alien* human elements. This promotes fear of the Other and, therefore, hinders hospitality.

Walls may be considered a central character in the poem. Their artificiality is highlighted due to their creation of two realities—inside-outside, here-there, insider-foreign/stranger—which otherwise would not exist because they would simply be part of the same continuum. Particularly, the gate as a connecting bridge with the potentiality of either remaining open or becoming an impassable wall is highlighted in the poem, as well as its inability to stop the desert from infusing the human soul with a sort of universal wail conveying a suffering that unites "every creature *in human form*" (*Journals* 1989, 83, italics in the original):

> 'The gate', cried Nehemiah, 'the gate
> Of David!' Wending thro' the strait,
> And marking that, in common drought,
> 'Twas yellow waste within as out,
> The student mused: The desert, see,
> It parts not here, but silently,
> Even like a leopard by our side,
> It seems to enter in with us—
> At home amid men's homes would glide.
> But hark! that wail how dolorous:
> So grieve the souls in endless dearth;
> Yet sounds it human—of the earth! (*Clarel* 1991, 1.24.77–88)

The universal wail will be analyzed in connection with *Clarel*'s ending, but it is important to note at this point how Melvillean characters die due to those interpersonal fences they build towards others or because of the walls they encounter in their efforts to generate some bonding. Thus, returning to the instances of walls in *Israel Potter* which opened this chapter, it is also significant that both the enigmatic scrivener in *Bartleby*, and Celio in *Clarel* are made to die—alone and rejected—with their eyes fixed on thick walls. This may be juxtaposed to Ishmael's survival thanks to his friendship with Queequeg: the fact that he is rescued by Queequeg's coffin as if fulfilling the Polynesian's former promise that "he would gladly die for me, if need should be" (*Moby Dick* 2007, 63). By falling in love with the American-born Jewish Ruth, Clarel also experiences the negative consequences of walls. Despite belonging to the same nationality as Clarel, Ruth is part of to a religious community to which Clarel cannot belong. Clarel becomes an outsider and his relationship indeed encounters the hostility of Jerusalem's Jewish community who closely surveils the relationship of the young couple. The highest authority figure in this community, the Rabbi, is far from welcoming Clarel and extending his/the community's hospitality. Even if he is merely alluded to in some passages, this character develops a crucial function making sure that Clarel does not overly influence the two members of the community he must preserve, Ruth and her mother Agar:

> by the sage was Clarel viewed
> With stony and unfriendly look—
> Fixed inquisition, hard to brook.
> And that embarrassment he raised
> The Rabbi marked, and colder gazed. (*Clarel* 1991, 1.23.59–63)

This becomes even more evident the moment Ruth's father, Nathan, dies—killed by the strangers living outside the city, Arabs whom he aims to convert—and Clarel is banned from accompanying Ruth and her mother in their mourning retreat. Not only is Clarel forbidden from joining the Jewish community during Nathan's funeral, he is also prevented from entering the physical space. The Rabbi is the person in charge of protecting the fences against alien elements such as Clarel and, in consequence, he symbolically locks the door connecting the house to the outside world in front of Clarel's face:

> He [Clarel], waiting so,
> Doubtful to knock or call them—lo,
> The rabbi issues, while behind
> The door shuts to. The meeting eyes
> Reciprocate a quick surprise,
> Then alter; and the secret mind
> The rabbi bears to Clarel shows
> In dark superior look he throws:
> Censorious consciousness of power:
> [...]
> No word he speaks, but turns and goes. (1.42.59–69)

It is significant that, had there been any true hospitality, far from bringing any destructive consequences, the Other, in this case represented by Clarel, may have saved Ruth and Agar from dying of grief during their retreat.

Thus, it is not the contact with alterity but precisely the non-contact with it that brings about some of the (self-)destructive consequences some characters suffer in the poem. In Clarel and Ruth's relationship, hospitality is mutual and emancipative because Clarel embodies freedom to two women who feel repressed within the walls of their religious patriarchal community. As their friendship evolves, the outsider grows closer in affection than those inside the community. Here, alterity is the generator of interpersonal togetherness.

Another character which exposes the destructive consequences of lack of hospitality is Celio, a young Catholic Italian whose community can neither understand nor accommodate his doubting nature. Celio is an outsider, and the only solution the Catholics can propose is to assimilate him and neutralize his questioning nature. Celio's outcast status is emphasized when he is locked out by the gates of Jerusalem and spends the night alone in the wilderness outside St. Stephen's Gate, which symbolically connects him to the Christian martyr with a doubting nature like his own. Introduced in the poem as if he was Clarel's alter ego, Clarel and Celio are immediately drawn to one another despite their differences—"The spiritual sympathy/Transcends the social" (1.19.3–4)—but this magnetism or openness to the Other does not bring about any eventual togetherness, as Clarel is unable to respond to Celio's call for "a brother that he well might own/In tie of spirit" (1.11.43–44). Even if their silences—Clarel and Celio probably speak different languages—are powerful, Clarel's paralysis in front of the stranger maintains the interpersonal distance Celio longs to abridge in his desperate need for human connection. Through this example of an interpersonal wall, and contrary to Derrida's affirmation that authentic hospitality be unreciprocated, the poem seems to point out that unreciprocated hospitality leads to disastrous consequences. As Vincent Kenny explains, "Clarel sensed in Celio an alter ego, but his inability to speak prevented the friendship they might have had" (1973, 73):

> Again, as down in Gihon late,
> He [Celio] hovered with his overture—
> An overture that scorned debate.
> But inexperienced, shy, unsure—
> Challenged abrupt, or yea or nay,
> Again did Clarel hesitate;
> When quick the proud one with a look
> Which might recoil of heart betray,
> And which the other scarce might brook
> In recollection, turned away.

> Ah, student, ill thy sort have sped:
> The instant proffer—it is fled! (*Clarel* 1991, 1.15.69–80)

Celio is hurt by Clarel's unresponsiveness. As this encounter, or rather non-encounter, is narrated, the narrator adds a brief interlude describing the muezzin's call for prayer which Jews ignore: "Is Zion deaf?" the narrator muses (1.15.32). This passage pointing out the deafness among neighboring communities mirrors Clarel's blindness to the yearning in Celio's eyes and physical disposition as the Italian rises to greet the American. Clarel's incapacity to answer the call of the Other in Celio's call can be said to reflect a paralyzing fear to open himself to alterity. This failed reciprocity has a violent closure for Celio: consumed by doubt, shunned by his community and seeing his last efforts to create a bond with someone for whom he had felt a special connection fail, Celio dies emblematically facing the wall:

> Yes, some retreat to win
> Even more secluded than the court
> The Terra Santa locks within:
> Celio had found withdrawn resort
> And lodging in the deeper town.
> There, by grasping ill distressed—
> Such as attacks the hump-bowed one—
> After three days the malady pressed:
> He knew it, knew his course was run,
> And turning toward the wall, found rest. (1.19.7–16)

Ironically, only after Celio is dead does Clarel want to approach the stranger by reading his journals. This can be interpreted as an example of conditional hospitality, as it is when the Other cannot pose a threat that Clarel opens himself to him and discovers that Celio was his alter ego. Another example of conditional hospitality is the fact that Celio's body is claimed by the Franciscans who had despised his doubting nature but who now bury him as Catholic. Rolfe notices the irony in Celio's imposed posthumous conversion when, upon reading Job's inscription at Celio's tombstone—"I KNOW THAT MY REDEEMER LIVETH"—he exclaims, "Poor Ethelward! Thou didst but grope;/I knew thee, and thou hadst small hope" (4.40.48; 49–50). The central theme of withdrawing from human society is retaken later in the poem in a play about the wandering Jew Cartaphilus which the pilgrims watch during the celebrations of Saba's festival inside the walled monastery of Mar Saba. This play can be said to evoke the incapacity of reciprocated hospitality, which provokes the deaths of characters like Celio in the general context of the poem—"More lonely than an only god;/For, human still, I yearn, I yearn" (3.19.76–78)—what William Potter has called "the inability to transcend one's own self and experiences, to achieve, as it were, an 'intersympathy' of any kind" (2004, 189).

3 Unconditional Hospitality: Rolfe

Despite these instances of rather inhospitable encounters, or encounters in which hospitality is carried out with conditions to neutralize the difference of the Other, *Clarel* also provides readers with positive models who embody the very dialogical nature of which the poem itself, as so many of Melville's works, is an example. The character Rolfe, also an American like Clarel—frank, kind, social, extroverted, "a messmate of the elements" and "indiscreet in honesty" (*Clarel* 1991, 1.31.21 and 1.31.25)—is a role-model of a plural thinker open to exploring alterity and the different sides of any story. He is also a crucial piece of *Clarel*'s construction of plural dialogue, since the character is always disposed toward Others, making them talk, while at the same time showing a deep respect for silences and human nature. Joseph G. Knapp calls Rolfe an "intellectual pioneer" who "probes the frontiers of the mind to search out those truths which haunt all men" (1971, 85). His main role in the poem is to gather the scattered individualities and corresponding thoughts of different characters embodying different cultures, ethnicities, worldviews (religious, atheist, nihilistic, scientific, etc.), feelings, moods, and life experiences. Rolfe constitutes a Socratic figure in Plato's dialogues who, by questioning and evaluating, establishes connections, exposes contradictions, and analyzes specific notions both transnationally and historically. William Potter has likened this capacity to evaluate different points of view at the same time to that of a whale, which can look in two different directions simultaneously—due to the position of its eyes—and which Ishmael describes in *Moby-Dick* (2004, 15). Rolfe can, therefore, be interpreted as the figure of a host capable of unconditional hospitality; he places opposites together in an effort to understand them, yet without neutralizing differences and, what is more, embracing others and their worldviews as interpretive possibilities with which he infuses his own thinking parameters. Rolfe is not afraid to face the bleakness many of his fellow travelers represent either. The different perspectives he encounters, no matter how desolate, are taken in by a mature mind like Rolfe's, who can still retain his balance and not fall into despair (Miller 1998, 213):

> Rolfe's great virtue lies in his balance. He, too, can doubt, and can ponder long his doubts, but without abandoning himself to despair and death.

> But if he is capable of following, without monomania, the intricate paths of the intellect, he is also capable of making his way, without being duped, through the labyrinths of the heart. His is the ideal maskless nature—'a genial heart, a brain austere'. He is 'frankly kind' [...]. Rolfe can acknowledge the rightness of the dark views of Mortmain and Ungar without assuming their despair. He can understand the value of Vine's solitude without joining him in retreat. And he can comprehend Derwent's commitment to optimism without condoning his hypocrisy. Between a shallow optimism and a deep-plunging pessimism, between foolish hope and dark despair, Rolfe does indeed remain 'poised at self-centre and mature.' (Miller 1998, 213–214)

The character is attributed a special place in the poem, as he is likened to the Hindu God Rama, who lived among humans unaware of his divine nature. As Rama, Rolfe sees deeper than any other character in the poem. Rather than being scared by the darkness other characters represent, or simply dismissing it, Rolfe's "Manysidedness" (*Clarel* 1991, 3.16.263) and capacity for in-betweenness are distinct from Derwent's, the Anglican priest who, with Rolfe, is the other main generator of dialogue in the poem due to his social openness. However, Knapp acknowledges that "Derwent expects a dialectical progression of truth, [whereas] Rolfe does not" (1971, 89). The poem exposes dissimilarities between them: while Rolfe can empathize with Mortmain's heroic but dark nature, understand Ungar's anger, respect Agath's gravity, and even appreciate Nehemiah's simple nature, Derwent predicates mere tolerance and often censors beliefs or doubts that cannot be contemplated within his own cheerful thinking parameters. His hospitality, in consequence, is simply conditional. He dismisses as "queer"—a word he often uses, together with "mad" or "terrifying"—the ideas he cannot grasp or that are too gloomy for his optimistic mindset (Kenny 1973, 130). In his private encounter with Clarel, for example, Derwent censors young Clarel's doubting nature, thus showing he has little patience for doubt—"Alas, too deep you dive" (*Clarel* 1991, 3.21.307), the priest claims. Derwent is unable to develop the deep understanding of human nature of which Rolfe is made an embodiment. As Vincent Kenny notes, Rolfe also differs from Derwent in that the former accepts that evil exists, and even admits its inseparability from goodness (1973, 205) since "Evil and good they braided play/Into one chord" (*Clarel* 1991, 4.4.27-28). If, on the one hand, Rolfe stands for the capacity to examine one idea from diverse points of view, Derwent is limited by his cheery optimism, his inability to comprehend doubt, the fact that he regards his own beliefs as superior to others' and his rejection of darkness: "Derwent will not dive and—in Melville's values—will never arrive at greatness" (Knapp 1971, 52). Rolfe, however, is what Richard Chase named "Melville's ultimate humanist" (1949, 257), perhaps only comparable to the Lebanese Djalea in the poem, another wandering figure suspected to have been a Druze of noble origin and who becomes an example of human dignity while guiding, in Ada Lonni's words, a "caravan of displaced pilgrims" (2011, 47). Djalea can also be taken as a role-model of hospitality, since his job as dragoman and translator places him between languages and cultures, and he has learned to host these languages and cultures within his own personality:

> A dragoman (*Turjuman* in Arabic) interprets, translates, and transposes words and ideas from one language to another, from one culture to another. Translation builds bridges, creates transparencies and reciprocal comprehension between persons and cultures. But to create links between different realities and thought systems, we must enter those other realities and systems: the translator cannot understand and, at the same time, remain extraneous and immune from the culture to be translated; it is not possible, in other words, to avoid one another's influence. (Lonni 2011, 42–43)

Djalea's translating and mediating role unites, moves across, and gives voice to "things all diverse" (*Clarel* 1991, 3.16.173). To him, hospitality is a part of his job and his nature, as he is in the middle and, like Rolfe, connects different cultures and worldviews. However, Rolfe goes even beyond Djalea's mediating/translating role. He feels at home with difference. His openness to others exposes him to the dangers of self-annihilation, of letting himself be carried away by the self-destructive gloomy natures of some of his fellow travelers with whom Rolfe empathizes. Yet it also enables him to learn and be liberated from one-sided worldviews that trap most other characters in the poem. These views make them keep to themselves and develop certain forms of monomania which are, in some cases, self-destructive, and, in other cases, destructive of the potentiality to create bonds with other companions. Rolfe embodies what philosopher Hannah Arendt would describe as *fermenta conditionis*. This way of thinking is "not the search for truth, since every truth that is the result of a thought process necessarily puts an end to the movement of thinking;" its aim is the generation of more thoughts "to stimulate others into independent thought, and this for no other purpose than to bring about a discourse between thinkers" (1968, 10). According to Arendt, such a thinking process is itself a political process that allows its participants to "humanize" the world by speaking of it with others who are different, and, in this very process, "learn to be human" by making sense of the world together (24–25).

Rolfe's manysidedness thus lays bare the (self-)imprisoning interhuman walls posed by the individualist and communitarian mindsets that most of the characters in the poem cannot traverse. As Merlin Bowen acknowledges, Rolfe's resistance and constant questioning of definite beliefs demonstrate an "opposition to all attempts to freeze experience into rigid artificial forms" (1960, 260). His open personality, by which "unlike things must meet and mate" (Melville 2009, 280), transcends Derwent's embrace of mere tolerance combined with censorship of those aspects he considers too difficult to understand or too uncomfortable to sympathize with. This nature has the potentiality of making human thinking more plural, and therefore, less exposed to be polluted by fear of the Other. Rolfe is one of the most respectful, humane, and globally conscious characters in the poem. This relational nature and unconditional hospitable openness to alterity is the one the young Clarel is encouraged to imitate, since, "Clarel's destiny," as Robert Milder affirms— and perhaps also readers'—, "if he [or we] can rise to it, is to mature into Rolfe" (2006, 216).

Thanks to his several travel experiences, Melville widened and enriched his thinking parameters. His own contact with alterity from a young age made the author question the ethnocentrism his culture and education had made him interiorize. In a way similar to the humbling effect Ishmael experiences through his friendship with Queequeg, Melville learned to question monolithic truths and realized the democratizing potentiality of interhuman contact. The author transmitted such wisdom to his oeuvre by creating literary spaces of unconditional hospitality, which give expression to individual experiences of pain—otherwise silenced and invisible—and connect them to a wider human awe that transcends any walls, separation, or difference.

Melville's works portray both hospitable and inhospitable encounters. These interhuman contacts—or, as this chapter has shown, lack of contacts as a consequence of factors such as fear—emphasize the tensions that arise between characters who represent different forms of alterity to one another, at the same time that they also underline the transformative possibilities enabled when the Other is embraced *as other*. Melville creates in *Clarel* characters such as Derwent, only able of conditional hospitality, or the Rabbi, who does not tolerate any opening to another who is external to the community he protects. The young Clarel himself enforces such partial hospitality or complete inhospitality principally with Celio, who begs for Clarel's opening the same way Clarel does to the Jewish community in Jerusalem. However, the poem also portrays in Rolfe a positive role model who is capable of true hospitality while knowing—and exposing himself to—the risk such unconditional hospitality involves. Thus, if Derrida argued that pure hospitality is impossible because some conditions are always necessary to prevent hostility, aggression, and even war, Melville seems to indicate in *Clarel* that it is not hospitality, but the lack of contact with the Other which provokes (self-)destructive consequences in characters who die alone and alienated.

By the end of the poem, Melville incorporates Clarel—grieved by Ruth and her mother's death—to his literary community of sufferers. Turning him into a small part within a universal—human—wail, the poem concludes that each individual is ultimately a solitary loner who cries alone, unable to grasp, or care about, the pain of others. As Ishmael would observe in *Moby-Dick*: "Each silent worshipper seemed purposely sitting apart from the other, as if each silent grief were insular and incommunicable" (2007, 49). Melville's literary production strives to communicate this grief. It shows deep understanding that no human being is foreign or illegal in a world of interconnected strangers exposed to suffering, vulnerability, mortality, and even the opposing forces of good and evil inherent to our very nature. Although characters in the poem are generally unable to move away from their own subjectivities and connect with one another, *Clarel*, following Melville's literary production, performs a dialogic exercise in unconditional hospitality expressive of the varied emotions, questions, preoccupations, worldviews, and internal or external struggles that each character within it represents.

References

Arendt, Hannah. 1968. "On Humanity in Dark Times: Thoughts about Lessing." In *Men in Dark Times*, 3–31. New York: Harcourt, Brace & World.

Arendt, Hannah. 1998. *The Human Condition*. Edited by Margaret Canovan. Chicago and London: U of Chicago P.

Bakhtin, Mikhail. 1984. *Problems of Dostoevsky's Poetics. Theory and History of Literature, Volume 8*. Edited and Translated by Caryl Emerson. Minneapolis: U of Minnesota P.

Bezanson, Walter E. 1991. "Historical and Critical Note." In *Clarel: A Poem and Pilgrimage in the Holy Land. The Writings of Herman Melville, Volume 12*, edited by Harrison Hayford, Alma A. MacDougall, Hershel Parker, and G. Thomas Tanselle, 505–637. Evanson and Chicago: Northwestern UP and The Newberry Library.

Bowen, Merlin. 1960. *The Long Encounter: Self and Experience in the Writings of Herman Melville*. Chicago: U of Chicago P.

Buber, Martin. 1992. *Martin Buber. On Intersubjectivity and Cultural Creativity*. Edited by S. N. Eisenstadt. Chicago and London: U of Chicago P.

Butler, Judith. 1996. "Universality in Culture." In *For Love of Country. Debating the Limits of Patriotism*, edited by Martha C. Nussbaum and Joshua Cohen, 45–52. Boston: Beacon Press.

Butler, Judith. "Precarious Life, Vulnerability, and the Ethics of Cohabitation." Lecture given at the Museu d'Art Contemporani de Barcelona (MACBA), Barcelona, July 2011.

Caputo, John. 1997. *Deconstruction in a Nutshell: A Conversation with Jacques Derrida*. New York: Fordham UP.

Chase, Richard. 1949. *Herman Melville, A Critical Study*. New York: Macmillan Co.

Derrida, Jacques. 1999. "Hospitality, Justice and Responsibility: A Dialogue with Jacques Derrida." In *Questioning Ethics: Contemporary Debates in Philosophy*, edited by R. Kearney and M. Dooley, 65–83. London: Routledge.

Derrida, Jacques. 2001. "On Forgiveness: A Roundtable Discussion with Jacques Derrida." In *Questioning God*, edited by J. Caputo, M. Dooley and M. Scanlon, 65–85. Bloominghton & Indianapolis: Indiana UP.

Foner, Eric. 2002. *Reconstruction: America's Unfinished Revolution, 1863–1877*. New York: Perennial Classics.

Foote, Shelby. 1994. "Men at War. An Interview with Shelby Foote." In *The Civil War*, edited by Geoffrey C. Ward, Ken Burns, and Ric Burns, 264–273. New York: Vintage Books.

Goldman, Stan. 1993. *Melville's Protest Theism: The Hidden and Silent God in* Clarel. DeKalb, Illinois: Northern Illinois UP.

Kaplan, Amy. 2010. "Transnational Melville." *Leviathan. A Journal of Melville Studies* 12 (1): 42–52.

Kelley, Wyn. 2008. *Herman Melville. An Introduction*. Malden, MA: Blackwell.

Kenny, Vincent. 1973. *Herman Melville's* Clarel*: A Spiritual Autobiography*. Hamden, CT: Archon Books.

Knapp, Joseph G. 1971. *Tortured Synthesis: The Meaning of Melville's* Clarel. New York: Philosophical Library.

Levinas, Emmanuel. 2006. *Humanism of the Other*. Introduced by Richard A. Cohen and translated by Nidra Poller. Urbana and Chicago: U of Illinois P.

Lingis, Alphonso. 1994. *The Community of Those Who Have Nothing in Common*. Bloomington: Indiana UP.

Lonni, Ada. 2011. "Translating between Civilizations: The Dragoman in *Clarel*'s Nineteenth-Century Jerusalem." *Leviathan. A Journal of Melville Studies* 13 (3): 41–48.

López Peña, Laura. 2015. *Beyond the Walls. Being With Each Other in Herman Melville's* Clarel. Valencia: Publicacions Universitat de València.

Marr, Timothy. 2005. "Without the Pale. Melville and Ethnic Cosmopolitanism." In *A Historical Guide to Herman Melville*, edited by Giles Gunn, 133–165. New York: Oxford UP.

Melville, Herman. 1983. "Redburn." In *Redburn, White-Jacket, Moby-Dick*, 1–340. New York: Library of America.

Melville, Herman. 1984. "Israel Potter." In *Pierre, Israel Potter, The Piazza Tales, The Confidence-Man, Uncollected Prose, Billy Budd*, 423–615. New York: Library of America.

Melville, Herman. 1987. "Traveling: Its Pleasures, Pains, and Profits." In *The Piazza Tales and Other Prose Pieces 1839–1860. The Writings of Herman Melville, Volume Nine*, edited by Harrison Hayford, Alma A. MacDougall, G. Thomas Tanselle, 421–423. Evanson and Chicago: Northwestern UP and The Newberry Library.

Melville, Herman. 1989. *Journals. The Writings of Herman Melville, Volume 15*. Edited by Howard C. Horsford and Lynn Horth. Evanston and Chicago: Northwestern UP and The Newberry Library.

Melville, Herman. 1991. *Clarel: A Poem and Pilgrimage in the Holy Land. The Writings of Herman Melville, Volume 12*. Edited by Harrison Hayford, Alma A. MacDougall, Hershell Parker and G. Thomas Tanselle. Evanson and Chicago: Northwestern UP and The Newberry Library.

Melville, Herman. 2001a. "Hawthorne and His Mosses. By a Virginian Spending July in Vermont." In *Tales, Poems and Other Writings*, edited by John Bryant, 47–62. New York: The Modern Library.

Melville, Herman. 2001b. "Bartleby, the Scrivener." In *Tales, Poems and Other Writings*, edited by John Bryant, 65–98. New York: The Modern Library.

Melville, Herman. 2001c. "Billy Budd, Sailor: An Inside Narrative." In *Tales, Poems and Other Writings*, edited by John Bryant, 449–525. New York: The Modern Library.

Melville, Herman. 2007. *Moby-Dick. A Longman Critical Edition*. Edited by John Bryant and Haskell Springer. New York: Pearson Longman.

Melville, Herman. 2009. "Art." In *Published Poems. The Writings of Herman Melville, Volume 11*, edited by Robert C. Ryan, Harrison Hayford, Alma MacDougall, and G. Thomas Tanselle, 280. Evanson and Chicago: Northwestern UP and The Newberry Library.

Milder, Robert. 2006. *Exiled Royalties. Melville and the Life We Imagine*. New York: Oxford UP.

Miller, James E. 1998. *A Reader's Guide to Herman Melville*. Syracuse, NY: Syracuse UP.

Obenzinger, Hilton. 2006. "Wicked Books: Melville and Religion." In *A Companion to Herman Melville*, edited by Wyn Kelley, 181–196. Malden, MA: Blackwell.

Otter, Samuel. 2006. "How *Clarel* Works." In *A Companion to Herman Melville*, edited by Wyn Kelley, 467–481. Malden, MA: Blackwell.

Potter, William. 2004. *Melville's* Clarel *and the Intersympathy of Creeds*. Kent, OH: The Kent State UP.

Robertson-Lorant, Laurie. 1996. *Melville: A Biography*. New York: Clarkson Potter.

Seelye, John. 1970. *Melville: The Ironic Diagram*. Evanson, IL: Northwestern UP.

Trachtenberg, Alan. 2007. *The Incorporation of America: Culture and Society in the Gilded Age*. New York: Hill and Wang.
Weinstock, Jeffrey Andrew. 2003. "Doing Justice to Bartleby." *American Transcendental Quarterly* 17 (1): 23–42.
Zerilli, Linda M. G. 1998. "This Universalism Which Is Not One." *Diacritics* 28 (2): 2–20.

CHAPTER 8

Eating, Ethics, and Strangers: Hospitality and Food in Ruth Ozeki's Novels[1]

Cristina Garrigós

Abstract

The following essay discusses the notion of the ethics of hospitality in relation to food and eating in the work of Ruth L. Ozeki. Hospitality is present in the three novels that the Asian American author has published to date: *My Year of Meats* (1998), *All Over Creation* (2003), and *A Tale for the Time Being* (2013). In all these cases, Ozeki points out the difficulties of open and unconditional hospitality, to use Derrida's concept. From her Zen Buddhist perspective, unconditional hospitality is the most perfect state, but it is difficult to attain in our society because it would imply accepting the Other in us. To address this issue in her fiction, the essay analyses the role of food as a tool of communication and communion with the other, and thus as a metaphor for hospitality.

The first novel, *My Year of Meats*, exposes the lies behind the appearance of hospitality both in the TV food programs and in the food processing. The author points to the need to dismantle false myths and go back to the real, which is where radical hospitality is to be found. Ozeki's second work, *All Over Creation*, also has food as the central element of the narrative, and again, eating becomes a metaphor for the relationships between hosts and strangers. The analysis of this novel focuses on the idea of strangers as parasites (Serres), that is, people who arrive unexpectedly and do not offer anything in exchange for the food they eat. However, the narrative proves that, as Levinas said, hospitality is an act of ethics. It implies accepting the Others and understanding that there is a connection between all human beings that goes beyond the notion of place, property, and belonging. Thus, the novel questions the notion of the host, the guest, and the meaning of parasitism. In Ozeki's third novel, *A Tale for the Time Being*, hospitality is conceived as something that includes the spiritual and the

---

[1] The author wishes to acknowledge the financial support of the following research projects: "Historia Crítica de la Literatura Étnica Norteamericana: Una Aproximación Intercultural" (FFI2015-64137-P) directed by Prof. Jesús Benito Sánchez and funded by the Spanish Ministerio de Economía y Competitividad, and "Las Fronteras de la Hospitalidad en los Estudios Culturales de Estados Unidos y Europa" (SA342U1) directed by Prof. Ana Mª Manzanas Calvo and funded by the Junta de Castilla y León.

physical, transcending both. In this work, the author is moving beyond known theories of hospitality to include cyborgs or egoless subjectivities. She opens our understanding of hospitality by going beyond humanistic philosophies and ethics. Moreover, she articulates the idea of hospitality/hostility related to cannibalism. According to Jean Baudrillard, cannibalism is a radical form of hospitality. It rewrites the discourse of hospitality, for it implies the total dissolution of boundaries and reverses the meaning of sharing food as a hospitable act.

Thus, this chapter explores the evolution of the notion of hospitality in Ozeki's fiction through the metaphor of eating. Whereas the first two novels explore hospitality as a Levinasian act of ethics, in the sense of offering and sharing with the Other, and the idea of reciprocity, Ozeki's last novel gives another turn to the concept of hospitality beyond the humanist approaches of Kant, Levinas, or Derrida to rely on Buddhism and radical hospitality and approach hospitality through disembodiment.

Keywords

Ozeki – hospitality – hostility – otherness – Buddhism – eating

Offering and sharing food are signs of hospitality. In its more essential sense, hospitality implies "sharing of space, and sometimes also time, bodies, food and other consumables" (Still 2010, 14). Thus, inviting someone to one's table is important, especially when it involves a stranger who is in a physically or economically vulnerable position, because the act of eating together means that you are sharing an experience and are, therefore, connecting on the same level, although it might only be for a limited span of time. The preparation of food is meant to foster a hospitable environment. It is supposed to comfort both the guest and the host and create a sense of well-being and bonding between those sitting at the table. As Elizabeth Telfer argues, it is through the giving and receiving of food that a bond of trust and interdependence, as well as friendship and generosity, is created between host and guest (1996, 83). As such, food and drink are means of communication and, therefore, serve to promote the human exchange where empathy, friendliness, and courtesy are involved (Douglas 2011, 55). To offer food is to invite the guest to enter the home and become a part of its inhabitants (O'Gorman 2007, 28). Food becomes, in this context, inextricably linked to hospitality, understood not only as something that you provide to others but also that the Others are receiving in an undemanding way, something similar to radical hospitality. This radical hospitality is close to Derrida's unconditional hospitality in which the host gives everything he has to the guest, independent of his ties, past or future, with the stranger ([1997] 2000, 25–27).

Ruth Ozeki is familiar with the concept of radical hospitality.[2] She became a Zen Buddhist priest in 2010,[3] but before she converted to Buddhism, she was concerned with exploring in her writing the connections between the material and the spiritual world and with the relationships between human beings and nature in society. Ozeki has published three novels to date: *My Year of Meats* (1998), *All Over Creation* (2003), and *A Tale for the Time Being* (2013). Even though her Buddhist thoughts were not fully developed until her last novel, the three works have many elements in common, and one of them is the importance that food has in the texts and how it works as a metaphor for hospitality.

1   Eating like Strangers: Beef, Japan, and the US in *My Year of Meats*

In *My Year of Meats*, hospitality is related to food and television. The protagonist, Jane Tagaki-Little, is an Asian American documentary maker who is commissioned to film a series of episodes of a food program—My American Wife!—for Japanese television. This program is sponsored by BEEF-EX, "a national lobby organization that represented American meats of all kinds—beef, pork, lamb, goat, horse—as well as livestock producers, packers, purveyors, exporters, grain promoters, pharmaceutical companies, and agribusiness groups" (Ozeki 1998, 14), with the double purpose of promoting meat-eating in Japan, and to present the US as a role model for Japanese women, "To foster among Japanese housewives a proper understanding of the wholesomeness of U.S. meats" (Ozeki 1998, 14). As Conrad Lashey and Alison J. Morrison point out, television food programs present hospitality by means of symbolic fictions of imaginary communities, "the concept of hospitality represented by the nostalgic quest for an idealized mythical past of community, tradition and belonging produces cultural meanings that clearly resonate in the contemporary world" (2000, 124). Food programs thus reinforce the idea of foreignness (the exotic) and authenticity. Through such television programs, food and

---

2   In 2015, Ozeki attended the Hedgebrook workshop and participated in *The Hedgebrook Cookbook: Celebrating Radical Hospitality*. She led a Vortext workshop on medication and the writing process. This workshop offers women authors time to write and time to share food and centers around the notion of radical hospitality. https://hedgebrook.org/experience-radical-hospitality/.

3   For more information on her Zen practice in relation to writing, see Ozeki's "Confessions of a Zen Novelist." *Lion's Roar: Buddhist Wisdom for Our Time*.

hospitality are aestheticized, so that they become works of art to be consumed as cultural artifacts and practices (Lashey and Morrison 2000, 127). The way the food is presented—the ingredients, the kitchen, everything—is manipulated to present an attractive image to the audience, an image of authenticity. Hence, it follows that television food programs are sites to project a hedonistic and narcissistic pleasure through symbolic uses of food very different from the notion of food as hospitality implying generosity, reciprocity, and trying to please others (Telfler 1996, 85).

In the novel, Ozeki displays the falsity in the manipulation behind the food program, but also, the unethical manipulation of food for commercial purposes.[4] For Kalejahi, "[i]n the narrative logic of the novel, the ecological inauthenticity of meat production in feedlots mirrors the cultural and social inauthenticity of meat representation in reality shows such as My American Wife!" (2012, 88). As Kalejahi points out, "the problem Ozeki addresses in this novel is that of disclosing the invisible reality behind the visible surface of that which poses as the real. In doing so she moves the problem of authenticity beyond the realm of ethnic and culinary culture" and "presents the authentic as an indispensable attribute of an ecologically viable culture and as a marker of representational sincerity in a globalized media economy" (Kalejahi 2012, 82). By pointing out the absence of authenticity in stereotypical images of America, the novel presents hospitality as forced, inauthentic, or fake, a spectacle to be produced, a fiction, like that of TV shows. The value of sharing food as a hospitable act is therefore put into question when it is done as performance. Thus, the idea of hospitality behind the food show and the food industry becomes a *trompe l'oeil*, since it is based on inauthentic parameters pretending to be authentic. In other words, in the novel, Ozeki shows that, instead of real hospitality, behind the food program that Jane is filming lies hostility towards the stranger, that is, Derridean *hostipitality*.

The mission behind the show is to present the United States as a country to be looked up to and imitated, a land of plenty and hospitality, ready to receive strangers "in its house" with open arms. However, the reality of US hospitality as portrayed in the novel is not the unconditional one that Derrida refers to, but rather, a conditional one. This type of hospitality is one whose laws are ingrained in the politics of the country from colonial times as Manzanas and Benito remark in their discussion of Winthrop's defense of the importance to regulate and limit the hospitality offered to the strangers who arrive in the New

---

4 Among the studies that address the environmental issues in the novel are Cheryl J. Fish (2009) Harrison (2017) or Wallis (2013).

World.[5] Hence, there is a tension between the Law of hospitality and the laws of the state: "Whereas the Law of hospitality is premised on blurring the lines between self and Other, the laws serve to mark the limits of how the stranger can be received. Such unresolved conflict, present in America from its colonial origins, permeates the contemporary encounter between the emplaced (national) self and displaced strangers" (2017, 19).

In the novel, Ozeki offers a satiric view of the US as a land of hospitality and demonstrates that the encounter between two different countries through the metaphor of food, instead of "blurring the lines" between the hosts (the US) and the guests (Japan) points to the differences between them. For instance, from the moment they arrive, the Japanese film crew is surprised by the size of things, "the sheer amplitude of America" (Ozeki 1998, 45), which they see in the size of the supermarkets, such as Wal-Marts: "To a Japanese person, Wal-Mart is awesome, the capitalist equivalent of the wide-open spaces and endless horizons of the American geographical frontier. All this for the taking!" (Ozeki 1998, 45). When Jane understands how the supermarkets appear in their eyes, she understands that the mission of My American Wife! is to place this image of the US before the Japanese audience to induce a state of want, "because want is good" (Ozeki 1998, 45). However, when she sees the crew stocking up the cart, she realizes that "profligate abundance automatically evokes its opposite, the unspoken specter of dearth" (Ozeki 1998, 45). The tension between having and not having, between showing a perfect ideal image of the US and the authentic reality behind the show, will be the main objective of Jane's alternative version. Ozeki's novel presents, thus, a satiric view of hospitality in America, emphasizing those aspects that are forced.

Thus, the first "American Wife" is Suzie Flowers, who is to cook a rump roast with Coca-Cola, Campbell's mushroom soup, and Lipton's onion soup, an 'authentic' American dish. However, this episode already evidences that the happy life of the perfect American wife is not real. Just before filming at her house, Suzie (and simultaneously the TV audience) learns that her husband is unfaithful. In spite of this, she tries to present the image of an ideal household to receive her guests, both the film crew and the TV audience. Falsity is present in everything she does: the recipe she prepares, besides being fake (she uses Pepsi instead of Coca-Cola, due to the many different takes and the lack of supplies), points to the unhealthy cooking habits of many US houses fond of ready-made dishes and many artificial and sugary ingredients. Also, Suzie's hospitality towards the Japanese crew and television audience is presented as

---

5 Manzanas and Benito refer to John Winthrop's "A Declaration in Defense of an Order of Court Made in May, 1637."

forced: for instance, she buys new floral bedding because she thinks that her old one is old-fashioned, but Jane wants to show the old handmade quilt which she considers more authentic. In her forced attempt to present a good image, Suzie bought

> new towels for the bathrooms and lots of extra sodas for the Japanese crew. They never wanted any. They were so well prepared, with their own cooler in the van, filled with mineral water from France. They were polite about it, but Suzie figured that the Japanese people just didn't like American pop. (Ozeki 1998, 31)

Suzie's hospitality fails because it is fake. She has no empathy and makes a generalization out of the fact that the crew prefers to drink water rather than sodas: in her mind, it means they prefer classical Europe (France) versus modern America. She takes this as a rejection of her country and as a projection of her husband's affair with another woman, making her feel a failure as a wife and as a host.

The relationship between the Japanese film crew and the families provides numerous examples of Derridean *hostipitality* throughout the novel, as the author offers a wide perspective of multicultural hospitality including episodes with US families from different origins: French, African, Polish, and so on. In most cases where the image of the US conforms to the idea of the 'authentic' US hospitality does not work because it is fake. Instead, real hospitality is to be found in those families that are not traditional, or that do not conform to the image of the perfect country that Ueno wants to project.

For instance, for the Beaudrouxs, who live in a little town in Louisiana, hospitality is both related to food—Vern, the father, runs a restaurant—and to adoption: they have ten children from different ethnicities, apart from two biological children. This family represents the reality of Southern hospitality: "Welcoming strangers into their home was a way of life" (Ozeki 1998, 402). In their case, the relationship with the Japanese crew works reciprocally. The cameraman, Suzuki, teaches Vern that he can use kudzu for culinary purposes: "He showed Vern how to turn them into starch, then to use the starch to thicken sauces and batters. He made a salad with the shoots and the flowers, and even a hangover medicine that resembled milk of magnesia. Vern was astounded. He'd never thought of the plant as anything else than an invasive weed" (Ozeki 1998, 92).[6] In this case, the host receives the new plant in his

---

6 As Ozeki explains in the novel, kudzu was introduced in 1933 as part of the Soil Erosion Service to rehabilitate the land devastated after careless cotton and tobacco farming and the abandonment of the farms. The government paid farmers to plant kudzu but soon it outgrew

kitchen, adopting it for his own culinary purposes and the guest teaches the host how to prepare the food. That is, hospitality is based on sharing knowledge and experiences and dissolving the boundaries between the guest and the host in an act of ethics.

The Japanese film crew is also welcomed with hospitality in Harmony, Mississippi. At first, the black community is reluctant to meet them, but they soon overcome their fears to invite them to take part in the Sunday service. However, the hospitality of the black community is not reciprocated since the Japanese boss, Ueno, decides not to film the chapter there because he believes that the Dawes family are not 'authentic' enough: they are too poor, speak bad English, and eat pork loins instead of beef. In his view, they do not represent America. In this case, the rejection of this family on the grounds of lack of authenticity is a sign of hostility from the representative of the Japanese company who shows his racial prejudices against the African-American community. Instead, he asks Jane to choose a white family that is representative of the country. Jane opts for the Bukowsky family from Indiana, a white family of Polish descent which she selects knowing that Ueno would not approve of them since this episode deals with lamb, a fraught meat in Japan, and not beef.[7]

This case is an example of hospitality in reverse. The community acts as a host offering food, comfort, and solace to the family whose daughter has suffered an accident and is left in a vegetative state. Her parents open the house to visitors who spend time with her and bring her food and share their favorite things with her. After seven months of people coming into the house, she is cured. This episode illustrates a very special case of hospitality, which defies Levinas's ethics. For Levinas, the giver of hospitality does not expect a reward. In this case, by 'using' hospitality to obtain something in exchange, the hosts are reversing the Law of hospitality. For Levinas hospitality takes place when the individual ventures outside and becomes an ethical subject welcoming the Other and experiencing pity, compassion, and proximity, as he said in *Otherwise Than Being* (177). Thus, hospitality for Levinas is based on care since the self is obliged to respond to the Other who needs it. In the case of the Bukowsky family, hospitality is unethical, since they open their home to strangers because they are expecting to receive something in exchange.

---

and engulfed the indigenous vegetation (Ozeki 1998, 92). As we shall see in the next novel, *All Over Creation*, seeds are identified with human beings and become metaphors for transplantation. For more information, see Nancy J. Loewenstein, "The History and Use of Kudzu in the Southeastern United States."

7 Japan buys lamb from Australia. There are references in the novel to Australia as being considered a land of criminals and traitors for the Japanese (Ozeki 1998, 170).

In this way, the idea of hospitality that Ueno had imagined the show would reinforce—an ideal community of submissive and fertile wives cooking meat for their husbands—is subverted by Jane when she shows different types of families, thus dismantling the traditional notions of hospitality as representative of US society. By showing the multiculturality of US society, Ozeki questions the image of the nation as unitary and "perfect" and presents other possibilities for real hospitality. Jane's subversive and radical version of American hospitality presents an alternative view of the US as a hospitable country. Akiko, Ueno's wife, in Japan, receives the message and decides to flee from her oppressive marriage to the US where she expects to be welcome. The turning point for her is the episode of Lara and Dyann, a lesbian, vegetarian, and biracial couple. When Jane tells them about Akiko's letter and how watching the episode was decisive for her, they decide to invite her to stay with them proving that they conform to the Levinasian ethics and they are hospitable because they do not expect anything in return, although they establish some conditions for her to stay:

> 'You guys mean a lot to her. Gave her the courage to leave a really bad situation. She wants to come to Northampton…'
> 'Fine,' said Lara.
> 'Lara!' said Dyann.
> 'What?' said Lara. 'We have a guest room. She can stay with us.'
> 'Oh, all right,' Dyann groaned. 'How long is she coming for?' (Ozeki 1998, 402)

Dyann and Lara help Akiko find an apartment and settle in the US. Jane's TV food programs have thus been a vehicle for hospitality and ethics after all.

Moreover, the program where Jane shows the medical abuses of the animals in Texas also serves to dismantle an image of authenticity based on appearances. By revealing the dark side of the food industry, the bond of trust that is supposed to be created between host and guest (Telfer 1996) is shown to be based on a lie. Food becomes a means of illegal communication and, therefore, does not promote the human exchange where empathy, friendliness, and courtesy are involved (Douglas 2011). By exposing the lies behind the appearance of hospitality both in the TV programs and in the food processing, Ozeki points to the need to dismantle false myths and go back to the real, which is where radical hospitality is to be found.

2   Eating with Strangers: Potatoes and Seeds in *All Over Creation*

Ozeki's second work, *All Over Creation* also has food as the central element of the narrative, and again, eating becomes a metaphor for the relationships between hosts and strangers. As in her previous work, most readings on the novel focus on the environmental critique in the text (Cardozo and Subramaniam 2008; McHugh 2007; Wallace 2011), but no study to this day has focused on the role of hospitality in the novel, even though there are obvious connections between environmentalism and Levinas's ethics. The work articulates the tension between a community of farmers in Liberty Falls, Idaho, and a corporation that aims to grow a genetically engineered potato in their fields. Yumi, the protagonist and narrator, is the estranged daughter of one of the farmers; she acts as the catalyst of the tension between belonging and not belonging, as she describes at the beginning of the text:

> And as for the description 'land belonging,' well, that's a condition measured by human time too. But for one quick blip in the 5 billion years of life on this earth, that three thousand acres of potato-producing topsoil and debatably the slender cone of the planet that burned below, right down to the rigid center of its core, belonged to my father, Lloyd Fuller. (Ozeki 2003, 3)

As the only child of Lloyd Fuller and his Japanese wife, Momoko, Yumi presents herself as a bad seed: "That's what it felt like when I was growing up, like I was a random fruit in a field of genetically identical potatoes. Burbanks—that's what people planted ... Honestly, I never liked potatoes much" (Ozeki 2003, 4). After many years away, Yumi has returned from Hawaii with her children to take care of her sick parents. Once there she is faced with the double role of being both guest and host at her parents' house. She belongs and does not belong there, but she acts as the mistress of the house when she is faced with the arrival of "The Seeds of Resistance," an anti-establishment activist group that comes to Liberty Falls looking for Lloyd. They consider him their guru because he sells exotic seeds—homegrown by Momoko—that are in danger of disappearing. The Seeds dress differently from the rest of the youth in town, they have piercings and tattoos, and seem dangerous to the people they meet on their travels. They arrive in the Spudnik, a biodiesel-fueled Winnebago in which they travel through the United States: "We target a range of food-related issues. Right now, it is genetic engineering. We drive around the country to communities and engage with the people and do actions" (Ozeki 2003, 52–53).[8] In contrast to the mobility of the Seeds of Resistance, the farmers conceive of the land as their property and are hostile to the menace of strangers. Thus, hospitality in

---

8   The name of the Winnebago could also be a reference to the word spud, potato.

the novel is related to the idea of land/country ownership and the rejection of outsiders who are perceived as invaders.

The people of Liberty Falls become hostile towards the nomads who are regarded as parasites and potential threats to the peace of the community. The Seeds are considered uncomfortable and unwelcome strangers who appear unexpectedly seemingly wanting to receive and not give anything in return. Yumi who, as noted above, has adopted the role of the owner of the house, is skeptical from the moment the Seeds enter her parents' home, and wants them to leave:

> I turned to check Cassie's pot roast in the oven. I was looking forward to their flowing right on out of here, but Phoenix's eyes were shining, and Ocean was entranced.
> 'We came here from Hawaii to meet our grandma and grandpa,' Ocean was saying, 'How come you came here?'
> 'Are you gonna stay?' Phoenix asked. 'You can eat dinner with us. We got lots of food, and you can camp out in the yard and—'
> I spun around. 'What the *fuck*, Phoenix!' The words were out of my mouth before I could stop them. Everyone was looking at me now, and in a lash, I saw myself as they were seeing me, wearing Momoko's faded, flowered apron and brandishing a wooden spoon. Two months in this house and I'd turned into what I would have become if I'd stayed—a small-town lunatic housewife.'
> 'That's okay,' Y said. 'We don't eat flesh.'
> 'But,' Geek said smoothly, addressing me, 'now that you mention it, we would like to camp out here for a while. We came here to learn about the seeds.' (Ozeki 2003, 139–140)

Yumi does not want to offer them food because she considers them dangerous. In other words, she is not hospitable.

Yumi's open hostility towards the strangers who have invaded her space is contrasted with the unconditional hospitality of her children who offer them food and a place to stay without asking for anything in return and without setting any limit on their stay. They are, in their innocence, offering radical hospitality. However, Yumi proves to have the same reluctant attitude that other people had towards her in the past due to her mixed ethnicity and unconventional lifestyle. Now, she feels uncomfortable with the Seeds in her house because she is putting herself in the shoes of her parents (and she is literally wearing her mother's apron). She came as a guest to her parent's house, but she has become a host, imposing limits to hospitality. All the limits that, as a racialized guest, were imposed on her in the past are now in her power. That is, she has become traditional, not open to dialogue, and not willing to welcome strangers according to the rules of hospitality.

In this reversal of roles, Lloyd and Momoko have become the guests of Yumi, as she has the power of mastery over them since they are both dependent. They cannot act as hosts in the house and must rely on the hospitality of their daughter and of their neighbor, Cass, who has become the actual owner of their land and provides them with food. Thus, they become strangers in their own house, and as such they side with the newcomers. When Melvin (Y) demonstrates his proficiency by nursing the old man, despite his dreadlocks and 'strange' ideas about society, Lloyd starts to 'like' him: "He grew to tolerate them, Melvin and his friends. He liked the way they gathered in his room, settling around his bed, to listen to him talk about seeds and farming. [...] Momoko liked them, too" (Ozeki 2003, 144). The Seeds are welcome to Lloyd and Momoko, but for Yumi her parents' hospitality is inappropriate:

> 'Don't they drive you nuts?' She asked.
> 'No. I like them. You drive me nuts.'
> She looked hurt. 'Me? Why?'
> 'The way you're standing there. Either come all the way in or get out.'
> [...]
> 'How can you tolerate them?' She asked at last. 'You hate hippies.'
> 'Is that what they are?' (Ozeki 2003, 147)

Now that they have swapped positions, Yumi feels threatened by strangers. She has started to think like the other farmers and to see anything/anybody different, as potentially dangerous, whether they are plants, or an activist group (the Seeds). The Seeds do not belong to the land, they are the Others. Unlike Yumi, her friend and neighbor Cass sides with the strangers and not with the locals: "They seem okay" (Ozeki, 2003,160). Thus, it is the former 'rebel' Yumi who openly opposes the stay of the young activists in the house while her neighbor and best friend, Cass, her children, and even her parents welcome the strangers. They receive them unconditionally because they believe they are peaceful and can contribute their work to help with the care of the elderly, as well as to put the catalog of seeds in order. They are, hence, beneficial for the community. Yumi does not share this idea: "No, they are not, Phoenix," she tells her son, "I know the type. They're parasites and freeloaders" (Ozeki 2003,160).

For Derrida, a guest who does not have the benefit of the right of hospitality is a parasite:

> In principle, the difference is straightforward, but for that, you need a law; hospitality, reception, the welcome offered had to be submitted to a basic and limiting jurisdiction. Not all new arrivals are received as guests if they don't have the benefit of the right to hospitality or the right of asylum, etc. Without this right, a new arrival can only be introduced 'in my home,' in the host's 'at home,' as a parasite, a guest who is wrong, illegitimate, clandestine, liable to expulsion or arrest. (Derrida [1997] 2000, 59–61)

According to this definition, the Seeds are wrong because they seem to be interested in taking and not giving anything in exchange. They are parasites who arrive in the house to eat from the owner's table, as Serres said: "*Parasiter veut dire: manger à coté de*" (2014, 22).[9] Thus, they are illegitimate and liable to expulsion or arrest by the police.

Of course, unlike Yumi, Cass does not see them as parasites at all. She opposes her husband, Will, when he presses charges against them for trespassing on their property and damaging the new genetically modified potatoes that he had planted. She takes Charmey, a member of the Seeds, with her to her house when the rest are taken to jail. Cass proves to be hospitable, providing the care and attention that the pregnant Charmey needs without asking for anything in exchange, in opposition to the wishes of other people, including her husband. However, she receives a reward for her hospitality when Frankie decides to leave their newborn daughter, Tibet, with Cass and Will to raise her, after Charmey's death in the explosion of the Spudnik.

For Yumi and the rest of the farmers in the community, the strangers are not welcome in 'her' house until they propose a deal which consists of taking care of her parents through a growing season so that they can learn from the seeds that Momoko planted. Only then, considering the possible benefits of the deal, does Yumi, sitting on her father's old checkered recliner and taking the position of the master of the house, decide to accept their offer:

> So, I capitulated, with the provision that the Seeds divest themselves of illegal substances while on the property and refrain from political agitation within the country line. The children were happy, and, watching them, I started to feel an overwhelming sense of relief as well. Charmey said she would help with the cooking. Y and Lilith would see to Lloyd's needs, Geek and Frankie would work with Momoko in the garden, first cataloging, then planting, and finally with the harvest: It seemed too good

---

9 To parasite means: eating alongside of.

to be true. My mind slid over the inevitable, and I focused on short term possibilities. If this worked out, maybe I could leave, take the kids back to Hawaii, as long as I came back at the end, to wrap things up. (Ozeki 2003, 167)

Yumi's decision to accept the deal comes from her selfish interest to have some help in the house so that she can delegate to them and go back to Hawaii. The hospitality that Yumi can offer is conditional, because there is a time limit for their stay, and certain conditions, but it is more than she was willing to offer at the beginning. Thus, the Seeds become guests in 'her home' and not parasites. However, she is reluctant to consider them as full guests with the rights of hospitality, and when she asks Geek if she can trust them, he answers: "Listen, I'll make a deal with you. We'll stick around as long as you do" (Ozeki 2003, 168). Thus, she becomes the one who must prove that she can be trusted and that she is not a parasite taking advantage of their free labor. She has become a guest to her guests in another inversion of roles. Thus, the 'deal' implies a commitment on both parts and a dissolution of the boundaries between host and guest.

Before they leave, Yumi accuses Geek of using the Fullers for their interest: "I don't go around exploiting people and using them to further my political agendas" (Ozeki 2003, 409). To which he replies, "I didn't use you! I *loved* you! All of you!" (Ozeki 2003, 410). Then, finally, she understands:

> Somehow, though, I got it. The bigger picture.
> Standing in my mother's greenhouse that night, surrounded by mounds of wormy seeds and chaff, I felt the brittle coat around my heart crack open at the hopeless beauty and fragility and loss of all that is precious on earth. He was right, we are responsible. Intimately connected, we're liable for it all. I had to take responsibility for myself and my kids, but also for Geek and Elliot, and for Charmey and Lloyd, too, and yet at the same time, I realized I was powerless to forecast or control any of our outcomes.
> But maybe that was the trick—to accept the responsibility and forgo the control? To love without expectations?
> A paradox for sure, but such a relief. (Ozeki 2003, 410)

Yumi's understanding of what it means "to love without expectations" is close to Derrida's idea of unconditional hospitality. For her, the relationship with the unexpected guests is key to her personal growth. It enables her to come to terms with her past and connect with her family and her native land. As

Levinas said, hospitality is an act of ethics. It implies accepting the Others and understanding that there is a connection between all human beings that goes beyond the notion of place, property, and belonging. Thus, the novel questions the notion of the host, the guest, and the meaning of parasitism, as well as suggesting the possibility of radical hospitality as a reality.

3   Eating the Strangers: Cannibalistic Hospitality in *A Tale for the Time Being*

In Ozeki's last novel, *A Tale for the Time Being*, Ruth, a writer who lives in British Columbia, finds a Hello Kitty lunchbox on the beach containing the diary of a sixteen-year-old Japanese girl, Naoko Yasutani (Nao). Ruth becomes intrigued by the narrative of the girl and eventually loses herself to her story, although her first impulse is to throw the plastic bag into the garbage. Indeed, when her husband places it on the kitchen table to inspect it, she sees it as an invader:

> She winced, anticipating the stench of someone's rotting picnic, or worse, that would ruin the fragrance of their meal. Lentil soup. They were just having lentil soup and salad for dinner, and she had just put in the rosemary. 'Do you think you could dissect your garbage out on the porch?' (Ozeki 2013a, 9)

The work alternates excerpts from Nao's diary and other texts found in the lunchbox with Ruth's reflections on what she is reading and the narrative about her present life in Canada. The autobiographical references abound in the novel and have been the subject of critical attention (Davis 2015; Lowell 2018). Rocío G. Davis considers the novel "a scavenger hunt" where the fictive and the real are interlocked (Davis 88). However, again, the topic of hospitality in the novel has not received critical attention.

In an interview with Eleanore Ty on the novel, Ozeki declared: "So much of what I am writing about in this book is informed by basic Buddhist principles—of interdependence, impermanence, interconnectedness—these kinds of things" (2013, 161). These principles, which she takes from her Buddhist beliefs, are articulated through the metaphor of food and literature. She said: "I wanted to play with that in an overt kind of way but also look at the way this relates to the Buddhist understanding of self and no-self: the idea that we are all only the stories that we tell ourselves… I think that is very much what the book is doing: it is playing with the idea of how you hold the story of yourself" (2013, 162–163). According to Buddhism, hospitality implies doing something good for other people. The Sanskrit word *atithisatkara*, which translates as "hospitality," combines *atskara*, "doing something virtuous," with *atithi* "guest," a person who wanders, a traveler, somebody who may show up unexpectedly, maybe even at an inappropriate time (Rotman 2011, 115). As shown in the stories of the Buddha, the host should spare no effort, whether it is putting his/her heart into cooking or making sure the guest is at home. In other words, according to Zen, hospitality is something that you do actively, that requires putting your mind and heart into it. The host must work on it, and the guest, in turn, is expected to reciprocate. This bears resemblance to Kant's idea of hospitality based on reciprocity, that is, the "right of a stranger not to be treated with hostility when he arrives on someone else's territory" (105) provided that he "behaves in a peaceable manner in the place he happens to be in" (106).

Besides being a meditation on memory and time, and on the interaction between reality and fiction, as well as the role of the author and the reader, the novel, according to Marlo Starr, "introduces a model of feminism that balances material and bodily experiences with ideas of equality that emerge from cyber-, Buddhist, and transnational feminist projects" (2016, 99). As such, although some readings of the novel have focused on the Buddhist philosophy that pervades the novel, for Mojca Krevel, the ethical and philosophical implications of Ozeki's Zen Buddhism have not been sufficiently explored (2019, 91). Krevel interprets Zen Buddhism in the novel in connection with the postmodernist ethos, which could lead to the "dissolution of the notion of Otherness on all levels, as well as to the comprehension of the critical importance of connectivity and connectedness and the resulting awareness of the fundamental agency of being" (2019, 105). Buddhism seeks to eliminate difference by dissolving the individual ego. The idea that the self is unitary and separate from the others is illusory in Buddhist thought (Starr 2016, 101). Where cyber technologies supposedly create equality by eliminating conceptions of 'Other,' Buddhism is thought to create equality by denying conceptions of 'self.' It is in this light that we can address the concept of hospitality in the novel. Hence, hospitality is conceived as something that includes the spiritual and the physical, transcending both. In the novel, Ozeki is moving beyond known theories of hospitality to include cyborgs or egoless subjectivities. She is opening our understanding of hospitality by going beyond humanistic philosophies and ethics.

The first reference to hospitality in relation to food that we find in the novel is the fact that Nao, a teenage girl who had recently moved back to Japan after some years abroad, writes her diary in a French cafeteria in Akiba, a commercial area in Tokyo, where she can write while drinking black coffee surrounded by the French music of Edith "Pilaf" (sic. Ozeki 2013a, 4) and by a maid called Babette. In this international atmosphere, Nao feels safe enough to express

EATING, ETHICS, AND STRANGERS 149

herself, away from her school, where she is rejected for being a *kikokushijo* (repatriated child) (Ozeki 2013a, 43), and becomes the object of *ijime* (bullying) by teachers and classmates:

> The minute he turned his back, they would start to move in. Have you ever seen those nature documentaries where they show a pack of wild hyenas moving in to kill a wildebeest or a baby gazelle? They come in from all sides and cut the most pathetic animal off from the herd and surround it, getting closer and closer and staying real tight, and if Dad had happened to turn around to wave to me, it would have looked like good-natured fun, like I had lots of fun friends, gathering around me, singing out greetings in terrible English—Guddo monigu, dear Transfer Student Yasutani! Hello! Hello!—and Dad would have been reassured to see me so popular and everyone making an effort to be nice to me. And it's usually one hyena, not always the biggest one, but one that's small and quick and mean, who lunges first, breaking flesh and drawing blood, which is the signal for the rest of the pack to attack, so that by the time we got through the doors of the school, I was usually covered with fresh cuts and pinching bruises, and my uniform was all tucked with new little tears in it made by the sharp points of nail scissors that the girls kept in their pencil cases to trim their split ends. Hyenas don't kill their prey. They cripple them and eat them alive. (Ozeki 2013a, 48)

In this passage, Nao is the prey eaten by predators. This cannibalistic act reverses the meaning of sharing food as a hospitable act and becomes the opposite. Manzanas and Benito discuss Jean Baudrillard's equation of cannibalism with a radical form of hospitality. According to this notion, hospitality and cannibalism navigate similar cultural demarcations. Cannibalism rewrites the discourse of hospitality, for it implies the total dissolution of boundaries (2017, 11). In Ozeki's novel, Nao is eaten by the predators. References to her as smelling bad also reinforce the idea that she is rotten or dead flesh:

> Basically, it went on like that all day. They would walk by my desk and pretend to gag or sniff the air and say Iyada! Gaijin kusai![10] or Bimbo kusai![11] Sometimes they practiced their idiomatic English on me, repeating stuff they learned from American rap lyrics: Yo, big fat-ass ho, puleezu show me some juicy coochie, ain't you a slutto, you even take it in the

---

10   Gross! She stinks like a foreigner!
11   She stinks like a poor person!

butto, come lick on my nutto, oh hell yeah. Etc. You get the idea. My strategy was basically just to ignore them or play dead or pretend I didn't exist. (Ozeki 2013a, 48–49)

Nao is attacked because she is different; she spent some years away from Japan in the US. In a country renowned for its politeness, where *omotenashi*, or selfless hospitality—the idea of helping others without expecting a reward—is a cornerstone of Japanese culture, the high rate of suicide and bullying at school is a paradox. In Nao's story, her school is a place of open hostility towards the different. This lack of empathy, as well as the loneliness pervasive in Japanese society, is the subject of Ozeki's critique in this novel, as it was in *My Year of Meats*. Nao suffers different insults from her teachers and schoolmates, including name-calling, teasing, ostracism, physical abuse, and extortion. They even stage her funeral, as if she had died, by placing her photograph on a desk with candles and posting a video on the Internet titled "The Tragic and Untimely Death of Transfer Student Nao Yasutani" (Ozeki 2013a, 107). Nao thus becomes a dead body whose remains are 'eaten' by the scavengers.

Accordingly, the Internet becomes a heterotopia, a conflicted space in terms of hospitality. Whereas Nao looks to cyberspace as a place to transcend her material and hostile reality and tries to find a community there, the web is also a place where Nao is exposed and humiliated. It is the symbol of *hostipitality*. The Internet becomes a place that creates an illusion of connection, that acts as a poor surrogate for intimate relationships (Starr 2016, 104). As a result, Nao sees her physicality connected to her virtual self and becomes aware of how her body has become repulsive:

> I swear, even on the Internet people can give off a virtual smell that other people pick up, although I don't see how that's possible. It's not like a real smell, with molecules and pheromone receptors and so on, but it's just as obvious as the stink in your armpits or the vibe you give off when you're poor and don't have any confidence or nice stuff. Maybe it's something in the way your pixels start behaving, but I was definitely starting to have it. (Ozeki 2013a, 125–26)

Nao's stay in the convent with her great-grandmother, Jiko, a 104-year-old Buddhist nun, helps her to transcend her body through meditation. She becomes one with the mosquitos that bite her: "There was no difference between me and the mosquitoes. My skin was no longer a wall that separated us, and my blood was their blood" (Ozeki 2013a, 204). Thus, from being the 'food' eaten by the hyenas and the rotten flesh on internet, she comes to see the act of being eaten by the mosquitoes as an act of communion: she becomes one and the same with the mosquitos. Every being is connected.

The difficulties that Nao finds in not belonging to a community—both a 'real' one and a virtual community on the Internet—are only overcome when she leaves the country. The educational system in Japan proves to be openly hostile to a student like her who is not like the rest. Hospitality is nowhere to be found among her classmates and teachers in Japan, or among her old friends in the United States. Hence the importance of her father's work designing a program for cleaning and erasing all trace of shameful evidence on the web, "Mu-Mu the Obliterator" (Ozeki 2013a, 382). Nao's failure to be received with hospitality in a community, either in the real world or in the virtual one, makes her transcend her physical self to become a story. This is the superpower that her Buddhist great-grandmother, Jiko, teaches her. Like her, Nao becomes a time being. Thus, she lives in the texts in the lunchbox which are received and hosted by Ruth. She becomes the writing in the diary to be consumed (eaten) by the reader, as we are the hosts of the stories written by Ozeki. The novel is thus a defense of literature as communion and communication in the era of social networks and media. Literature is a space where we can find hospitality by having access to a community of time beings.

4   Conclusion

This chapter has explored the connections between food and hospitality in the three novels published by Ozeki to date. Whereas the first two novels explore hospitality as a Levinasian act of ethics, in the sense of offering and sharing with the Other, and the idea of reciprocity, Ozeki's last novel gives another turn to the concept of hospitality beyond the humanist approaches of Kant, Levinas, or Derrida. As Ozeki has acknowledged, her Zen practice transformed her understanding of the world (Ozeki 2003b, 38–39). Thus, Buddhism taught her to see the Others and the self as interconnected. There are no Others but in one-self which is dissolved in many. This radical form of hospitality suggests we consider hospitality through disembodiment. While in her first two novels Ozeki considers our relationships with the Others and with the ownership of the land through the metaphor of food, in her last novel to date, she moves beyond the material aspects of food, to explore the spiritual aspects of eating as hospitality, considering acts of cannibalism and communion with the Others. In this sense, for Ozeki, all the beings that share this universe are united by a bond of interdependence that includes what we eat and who we are. In other words, we are both hosts and guests at the same time, dissolving the boundaries between the different selves and becoming all part of the same connected world.

References

Cardozo, Karen and Banu Subramaniam. 2008. "Genes, Genera, Genres: The Nature-Culture of BioFiction in Ruth Ozeki's *All Over Creation.*" In *Tactical Biopolitics: Art, Activism and Technoscience,* edited by Beatriz da Costa and Kavita Philips, 269–298. Cambridge, MA and London: MIT P.

Davis, Rocío. 2015. "Fictional Transits and Ruth Ozeki's *A Tale for the Time Being.*" *Biography* 38 (1): 87–103.

Derrida, Jaques. (1997) 2000. *Of Hospitality: Anne Duformantelle Invites Jaques Derrida to Respond.* Translated by Rachel Bowlby. Stanford: Stanford UP.

Douglas, Mary. 2011. "Food studied as a System of Communication." In *The Active Voice,* edited by Mary Douglas, 82–104. New York: Routledge.

Fish, Cheryl J. 2009. "The Toxic Body Politic: Ethnicity, Gender and Corrective Eco-Justice in Ruth Ozeki *My Year of Meats* and Judith Helfand and Daniel Gold's *Blue Vinyl.*" *MELUS* 34 (2): 43–62.

Harrison, Summer. 2017. "Environmental Justice Storytelling: Sentiment, Knowledge, and the Body in Ruth Ozeki's *My Year of Meats.*" *ISLE* 24 (3): 457–76.

Kalejahi, Saeed. 2012. "Politics of Food, the Culinary and Ethnicity in Ruth Ozeki's *My Year of Meat*: An Ecocritical Reading." *International Journal of Applied Linguistics & English Literature* 1 (1): 82–89.

Kant, Immanuel. 1970. "Perpetual Peace: A Philosophical Sketch." In *Kant's Political Writings.* 2nd ed., edited by Hans Reiss, 93–130. Cambridge: Cambridge UP.

Krevel, Mojca. 2019. "Taking the I out of Being: Zen Buddhism and Postmodern (Dis)contents in Ruth Ozeki's *A Tale for the Time Being.*" *Atlantis* 41 (1): 89–107.

Lashley, Conrad and Alison J. Morrison, eds. 2000. *In Search of Hospitality: Theoretical Perspectives and Debates.* Oxford: Butterworth Heinemann.

Levinas, Emmanuel. 1969. *Totality and Infinity: An Essay on Exteriority.* Translated by Alphonso Lingis. Pittsburgh: Duquesne UP.

Levinas, Emmanuel. 1984. "Ethics of the Infinite." In *Dialogues with Contemporary Continental Thinkers: The Phenomenological Tradition,* edited by R. Kearney. 47–70. Manchester: Manchester UP.

Levinas, Emmanuel. 1987. *Time and the Other and Additional Essays.* Translated by Richard A. Cohen. Pittsburg: Duquesne UP.

Levinas, Emmanuel. 1998. *Otherwise Than Being or Beyond Essence,* translated by Alphonso Lingis. Pittsburgh: Duquesne UP.

Loewenstein, Nancy J. 2014. "The History and Use of Kudzu in the Southeastern United States." *Extension*. [Accessed online on June 19, 2019].

Lovell, Sue. 2018. "Towards a Poetics of Posthumanist Narrative Using Ruth Ozeki's *A Tale for the Time Being*." *Critique: Studies in Contemporary Fiction* 59 (1): 57–74.

Manzanas, Ana María and Jesús Benito 2017. *Hospitality in American Literature and Culture: Spaces, Bodies, Borders*. New York: Routledge.

McHugh, Susan. 2007. "Flora, Not Fauna: GM Culture and Agriculture." *Literature and Medicine* 26 (1): 25–54.

O'Gorman, Kevin. 2007. "Dimensions of Hospitality: Exploring Ancient and Classical Origins." In *Hospitality: A Social Lens*, edited by Lashley, Lynch, and Morrison, 17–32. Amsterdam: Elsevier.

Ozeki, Ruth L. 1998. *My Year of Meats*. London: Picador.

Ozeki, Ruth L. 2003. *All Over Creation*. London: Penguin.

Ozeki, Ruth L. 2013a. *A Tale for the Time Being*. Edinburgh: Cannongate.

Ozeki, Ruth L. 2013b. "Confessions of a Zen Novelist." *Lion's Roar: Buddhist Wisdom for Our Time*. [Accessed online on June 19, 2019].

Rotman, Andy 2011. "Buddhism and Hospitality: Expecting the Unexpected and Acting Virtuously." In *Hosting the Stranger Between Religions*, edited by Richard Kearney and James Taylor, 115–122. London: Continuum.

Serres, Michel. 2014. *Le Parasite*. Paris: Pluriel.

Still, Judith. 2010. *Derrida and Hospitality. Theory and Practice*. Edinburgh: Edinburgh UP.

Starr, Marlo. 2016. "Beyond Machine Dreams: Zen, Cyber—and Transnational Feminisms in Ruth Ozeki's *A Tale for the Time Being*." *Meridians: Feminism, Race, Transnationalism*. 13 (2): 99–122.

Telfer, Elizabeth. 1996. *Food for Thought: Philosophy and Food*. London: Routledge.

Telfer, Elizabeth. 2000. "The Philosophy of Hospitableness." In *In Search of Hospitality: Theoretical Perspectives and Debates*, edited by Lashley, Conrad and Alison J. Morrison, 38–56. Oxford: Butterworth Heinemann.

Ty, Eleanore. 2013 "'A Universe of Many Worlds': An Interview with Ruth Ozeki." *Melus* 38 (3): 160–171.

Wallace, Molly. 2011. "Discomfort Food: Analogy, Biotechnology, and Risk in Ruth Ozeki's *All Over Creation*." *Arizona Quarterly* 67 (4): 155–181.

Wallis, Andrew H. 2013. "Towards a Global Eco-Consciousness in Ruth Ozeki's *My Year of Meats*." *Interdisciplinary Studies in Literature and Environment* 20 (4): 837–854.

CHAPTER 9

"It's a Long Way to Tipperary": the Relation between Race and Hospitality in the Irish-American Experience and its Literary Representation[1]

Patricia San José Rico

Abstract

When dealing with notions of immigration and hospitality, there is a third concept that often unavoidably follows suit: that of the Other. Usually identified with what is different, what is not understood as equal to the self and/or its inherent cultural, linguistic, or racial identity, the Other is perceived as an outsider, someone—or something—that, due to its difference, is often feared and most of the times not welcome into the domain/territory of the self. Likewise, the concept of race is also unmistakably linked to that of the Other, as the former embodies what can perhaps be conceived as the most obvious and identifiable of differences: a visible mark of otherness that is, by definition, inextricably engrained within the alien individual.

Certain past—and present—discourses on migration have capitalized on the relation between notions of otherness, race, and the migrant as an intruder and a perceived need of self-preservation in order to reinforce and implement several anti-immigration policies, which are, in turn, often paralleled in the society's rejecting attitude towards those immigrants. In the case of the US, instances of such practices against the racialized immigrant have been evident in the Asian Immigration Ban implemented during a good part of the twentieth century, or the Anti-immigration rants that President Trump frequently directs towards Mexicans, among other examples.

---

[1] This article has been elaborated thanks to the financial support of the Spanish Ministerio de Economía y Competitividad (Research Project: "Historia Crítica de la Literatura Étnica Norteamericana: Una Aproximación Intercultural" (FFI2015-64137-P) directed by Prof. Jesús Benito Sánchez), the Junta de Castilla y León (Research Project: "Las Fronteras de la Hospitalidad en los Estudios Culturales de Estados Unidos y Europa" (SA342U1) directed by Prof. Ana Mª Manzanas Calvo), and the European Union through its Erasmus + KA2: Strategic Partnership program (research project: "Hostfilm: Hospitality in European Film" (2017-1-ES01-KA203-038181) directed by Prof. Ana Mª Manzanas Calvo).

One of those other examples is the attitude towards the Irish immigrants that arrived in the US during the nineteenth and early twentieth centuries. Even though there are apparently little linguistic and racial differences between the Irish and the white population of the US, the Irish's whiteness was by no means taken for granted during the better part of that period. And yet, unlike other racialized groups of immigrants—as well as other 'resident' collectives like the African Americans or the Native Americans—the Irish were able to achieve the recognition of whiteness that they had been previously denied.

Based on the works of previous scholars like Noel Ignatiev's *How the Irish Became White* (1996), this chapter will trace the Irish trip towards whiteness in the US and the efforts of its individuals across generations to achieve it. To illustrate this process, examples of its representation in novels depicting the Irish-American experience such as Frank McCourt's *'Tis* (1999), Mary Gordon's *The Other Side* (1989), and Taylor Caldwell's *Captains and the Kings* (1972) will be employed.

Keywords

Irish-Americans – hospitality – race – whiteness – the other

•••

It's not enough to be American. You always have to be something else, Irish-American, German-American, and you'd wonder how you'd get along if someone hadn't invented the hyphen.
FRANK MCCOURT
'Tis

∴

1 **Introduction**

The cover of the 2009 edition of Noel Ignatiev's (1940–) *How the Irish Became White* consists solely of an image of a pint of the internationally famous Irish black beer over which appears the title and author's name in big, white lettering. In the picture, the beer is perfectly set, displaying a fully formed, distinct layer of its trademark white froth sitting comfortably on top of the black liquid. Yet what makes the image a perfect choice for this volume's cover is that, as many avid drinkers of this famous beer may well know, the froth does not by any means start off as white. In fact, if the pint is correctly poured, it emanates from the, at that point, uniformly brownish liquid and ascends slowly as the beer decants itself separating the two substances, liquid and froth, into two distinct and opposite colors: black and white. The whole process takes a couple of minutes and, as any Irish would tell you, if the thirsty drinker wants to enjoy a proper pint, s/he must be patient and wait until it has finished and the froth looks completely white and sits atop the contrasting black liquid before delving into the brew.

Similarly, Ignatiev argues throughout his volume, the Irish in America needed some time to 'rise' from the racial classification they received upon arrival in the US and locate themselves socially above non-white ethnic groups. This process required a series of political alliances, heritage renunciations and even instances of open racial antagonism and violence towards other ethnic minorities that eventually granted the Irish-Americans the right to claim white privilege in their host country. Through instances of what could be termed whitewashing, the Irish migrants in the US utilized the hostile hospitality discourse with which they were received and turned it against other marginalized groups to position themselves against them and achieve their current status as inside-members of the American society.

As part of the numerous past and present American discourses on migration that have capitalized on the relation between notions of otherness, race, and the migrant as an intruder as well as a perceived need for self-preservation—what Derrida called the laws of hospitality—in order to reinforce and implement several anti-immigration policies, the attitude towards the Irish immigrants that arrived in the US from the seventeenth century onwards can be likened to other anti-migration acts in America, such as the Asian Immigration Ban implemented during a significant part of the twentieth century, or the promises to build a wall along the US-Mexican border we were sadly used to hear during the last (2018) presidential campaign, among other examples. All those instances of an open rejection of the migrant Other tend to identify race and physical difference as the most obvious marker of that defining and often fear-inspiring otherness which is, in turn, often paralleled in the society's rejecting attitude towards those immigrants. However, even though there are apparently few linguistic and racial differences between the Irish and the white population of the US, their whiteness was by no means taken for granted during the better part of their migration period. And yet, unlike other racialized groups of immigrants—as well as other 'resident' collectives like African Americans or Native Americans—the Irish were eventually able to achieve the recognition of whiteness that they had been previously denied.

In what follows, Derridean concepts such as the clash between his notion of the Law of (unconditional) hospitality and the laws of (preservative) hospitality, together with the Levinasian interpretation of the Other, will be read against the perspective of racial theorist Noel Ignatiev in his work *How the Irish Became White* in order to trace the Irish journey towards whiteness in the US and the efforts of individuals across generations to achieve it and revert the inhospitable discourse and attitude that 'welcomed' them to their host country. To illustrate this process, this chapter employs examples of its representation in novels depicting the Irish-American experience such as Frank McCourt's (1930–2009) autobiographical novel *'Tis* (1999), Irish-descended American novelist Mary Gordon's (1949–) *The Other Side* (1989), and best-seller author and immigrant herself Taylor Caldwell's (1900–1985) *Captains and the Kings* (1972).

2   Social Difference as a Marker of Racial Otherness

It has previously been established in this same volume that race and physical difference is ineffably linked to notions of otherness and the subsequent rejection of the racialized migrant. And yet, when talking about race one must immediately question the concept itself. In the words of Howard Winant,

> [r]ace is not only real, but also illusory. Not only is it common sense; it is also common nonsense. Not only does it establish our identity; it also denies us our identity. Not only does it allocate resources, power, and privilege; it also provides means for challenging that allocation. Race not only naturalizes, but also socializes. (1998, 90)

This "ineluctably contradictory character of race" (Winant 1998, 90) makes it susceptible to different understandings and interpretations; from a merely genetic marker to a purely social construct. The former, however, is probably the most problematic, as hybridity makes it difficult to "present a convincing rationale for distinguishing among human groups by physical characteristics" (Winant 1998, 89). To illustrate this we can offer a couple of examples: According to Richard Dyer, there are "gradations of whiteness," under which "Latins, the Irish and Jews, for instance, are rather less securely white than Anglos, Teutons and Nordics" (2003, 27). Similarly, in the words of Dalton Conley, "Japan has a minority group, called the Burakamin, that is physically indistinguishable from the rest of the population, yet they constitute a separate race" (2003, 212).

Surely, if physical difference is non-existent or minimal, and yet a racial differentiation is nonetheless established, race cannot be purely constructed in terms of genetic markers, there must be something else that defines it. According to Coates et al., "[i]f race were indeed a fact of nature, it would be simple to identify who falls into which racial category, and we would expect racial categories to remain static across history and societies. [...] Race must derive from human interventions. These interventions reflect the social construction of race" (2018, 33). Those "social interventions" have lately been envisioned by several scholars (Case 2013; Ferber, Jiménez, Herrera, and Samuels 2009; Collins 1990) in terms of a matrix. Understood as "the surrounding environment in which something (e.g., values, cells, humans) originates, develops, and grows," the idea behind the social matrix of race "captures the basic sociological understanding that contexts—social, cultural, economic, historical, and otherwise—matter" (Coates et al. 2018, 50). It follows, therefore, that "people are members of different races because they have been assigned to them" (Ignatiev 2009, 1) and that "the white race consists of those who partake of the privileges of the white skin in this society" (Ignatiev 2009, 2). Consequently, white privilege, as Winant puts it, has for centuries "denied the existence of commonalities among whites and non-whites—such as shared economic activities and statuses, shared rights as citizens, even on occasion shared humanity—thus constructing race, at least in principle, in terms of all-embracing social difference" (1998, 90–91).

It could be argued, therefore, that race can be interpreted not only in terms of physical difference, but of status. Even if the former nearly always entailed a lower social status in the US, the latter could also mean being blocked out of the white paradigm, which spells out how the Irish physical whiteness was not enough for them to acquire white status upon arrival in America. Race and class go hand in hand, suffering from mutual feedback for, "as race is often encoded into class, so class difference can be decoded as racial" (Williams 1998, 261). This was precisely the case with the Irish in America, who, despite their apparent physical whiteness, were initially excluded from the white paradigm on account of their being identified as socially inferior to the normative WASP society in the US.

And yet, their poverty, rural extraction, and hunger were not the only elements responsible for the racial marking of the Irish; the fact that they were mostly Catholics, not Protestants, also played a major role. As opposed to other—Protestant—migrant groups coming from northern and western Europe who were "generally embraced as the racial and ideological kin of Anglo Americans [...] celebrated for a lineage that stretched back to the ancient tribes who sowed the seeds of American democracy under the trees of the Black Forest" (Adams 2003, 398), Irish immigrants in the US needed to acquire their status as 'white' by progressively turning from "Irish Americans" to "European Americans" and finally to simply "Americans" (Durso 2002, 97).

Such a differentiation in religion and class leading to racial labeling was not new to the Irish though; a similar process had already taken place for some in their native country. Eighteenth-century Ireland was governed by the Penal Laws; a series of regulations that limited the liberties of Irish Catholics and effectively turned them into an oppressed race or, in the words of Ignatiev, "imposed upon them a caste status out of which no Catholic, no matter how wealthy, could escape" (2009, 42). Prior to the massive migratory movement towards North America during the Great Famine (1845–1855), most of the Irish immigrants in the US had been Ulster Presbyterians, but most importantly, they had been noticeably wealthier. Once the poorer, mostly Catholic Irish of the Famine started to arrive, the formerly established Irish descendants chose to differentiate themselves from the more socially contemptible new arrivals by reenacting the racialized class difference they had witnessed at home, thus helping to perpetuate the Catholic-racially inferior model that had previously been enacted there (Ignatiev 2009, 46–47).

This differentiation between Protestant (white) and Catholic (racially marked) Irish can be explained by introducing the concept of 'ethnicity' as opposed—or better yet, complimentary—to that of 'race.' In the words of Chandler and Watkins, ethnicity "is usually defined in terms of cultural criteria—common language, social customs, national and political identification, religion, group processes" (2006, 51). However, physical characteristics "are not usually tied to definitions of ethnicity" (Coates et al. 2018, 42). It could be argued, therefore, that what marked the Irish as inferior upon arrival to the US was not their race—understood in terms of physical difference to the dominating society—but their 'ethnicity' as poor, rural, and Catholic Irish-borns. Poor Catholic Irish migrants (but not their wealthier, Protestant kinsmen), thus, were labeled as racialized Others and therefore cast out as aliens, as potentially dangerous parasites unworthy of unconditional hospitality.

3   The US as the Land of Hope

While the Irish migration to the US during the Great Famine is the most readily remembered Irish migratory movement due to its traumatic connotations and great numbers, the Irish had been migrating to North America since the 1600s. A sum of all the estimated figures of Irish emigrants across the centuries amounts to approximately ten million people having left the Irish shores since 1607 (Fitzgerald and Lambkin 2017, 2), out of which a vast majority chose North America, particularly the United States, as their preferred destination. According to Mike Cronin, by 1900 around two million Irish had settled in the

United States, which allowed for thirty-three million people (ten percent of the total US population) to identify themselves as Irish in their 2013 census (2017, 2–3).

Irish migrants have traditionally chosen the US as a host country primarily for economic, religious, linguistic, and family reasons. The perceived image of the US as a land of religious freedom, great farming expanses, and opportunities for upward mobility led many oppressed and impoverished Irish to create and perpetuate the myth of the US as the 'land of hope,' which accounts for their extensive migration there. This mythical image of the US as "the mother of exiles extending an expansive welcome" (Damai 2012, 3) is reinforced by the US itself as expressed by the inscription at the base of the Statue of Liberty, which marked the entrance to the country for many of those same immigrants arriving by boat to New York Bay. This inscription is taken from the last verses of Emma Lazarus's poem "The New Colossus" which read:

> Give me your tired, your poor,
> Your huddled masses, yearning to breathe free,
> The wretched refuse of your teeming shore,
> Send these, the homeless, tempest-tost to me,
> I lift my lamp beside the golden door! (Lazarus 2002, 20)

This message became a beacon for many Irish migrants who, especially during the mid-nineteenth century and the 1950s, were fleeing famine, poverty, or exclusion and "viewed emigration as a voyage of survival" (Kinealy 2017, 4). This was encouraged and magnified by those who had made the trip before them and is amply represented in the Irish-American literature of migration. In Mary Gordon's *The Other Side*, for example, we can find Vincent, one of the protagonists, reminiscing about his decision to move to the US in the early nineteen hundreds:

> Of course boys like him and Martin would come to America: they'd been brought up on the dream of it. Chicago, Butte, Philadelphia were more real to them than the Wicklow Mountains or the Giant's Causeway or the Galway Bay. America was an invented country and yet one where people they had known had gone and prospered, not returning, sending money home. And exhortations: Pack up, come with us. Their voices rang across the ocean like the voices of the damned crying for clemency, or like the siren crying: Follow; like the Angel with the flaming sword or like the angel breaking, with a touch, the prisoner's chains. Of course he and Martin would come to America. (1990, 245–246)

Something similar is portrayed in Taylor Caldwell's *Captains and the Kings*, only this time the period is that of the Great Famine:

> It was real for him, for he had dreamt that scene a thousand times on this sorrowful voyage. His father would meet his family on the dock and enfold them all, and then he would take them to the 'flat' in the Bowery where he lived with his brother, Jack, and it would be warm and there would be soft beds and a hot stove and joy and the fragrance of boiling potatoes and turnips and beef or lamb and safety and comfort and peace and hope. Had they not received letters from him, and money, and had he not told them of this? He had a good job as a janitor in a small hotel. He ate to repletion for the first time in years. He worked hard, and he received money for his labour. He would provide for his family, and no more would they be hunted like vermin and despised and execrated for their Faith, and thrown from their land to die on the highways of exposure and hunger. 'Ah, and it is a land for free men,' Daniel had written in his careful hand. 'The lads will go to school, and the little one will be born in America, and we will be Americans together, and never part again.' (1973, 11–12)

What these two fragments have in common is the description of the US as the land of plenty. In both cases, the soon to be emigrants have heard tales of the warm welcome and hospitality they would receive in their host country; the reality, in most cases, turned out to be a far cry from what was advertised. Taking into account the fact that inhuman working and housing conditions meant that life expectancy for Famine Irish migrants after arrival in the US—if, that is, they had not perished on the voyage there, as so many did—amounted to an average of six years (Kinealy 2017, 4), plus the prejudice and signs saying "no Irish need apply," we can easily conclude that, at least at that time and although "the United States [...] proclaimed itself as the ultimate hospitable space for all citizens, it nonetheless maintained a certain Land of Nod where all those who did not belong were cast out" (Manzanas and Benito 2017, 55). In this case, what made the Irish 'not belong' was their racialized social, economic, and religious difference; a distinction that was maintained throughout the following century. Even in the twentieth century, Frank McCourt experienced a similar reality check, as expressed in his memoirs:

> New York was the city of my dreams but now I'm here the dreams are gone and it's not what I expected at all. I never thought I'd be going around a hotel lobby cleaning up after people and scouring toilet bowls

in the lavatories. How could I ever write my mother or anyone in Limerick and tell them the way I'm living in this rich land with two dollars to last me for a week, a bald head and sore eyes, and a landlady who won't let me turn on the light? [...] They'd never believe me. They'd say, Go away ower that, and they'd laugh because all you have to do is look at the films to see how well off Americans are, the way they fiddle with their food and leave something on their plate and then push the plate away. (2000, 54)

What McCourt expresses here is the realization of the discrepancy between the perceived image of the US as the paradigm of hospitality and the actual acts of hospitality towards Irish and other immigrants. Whereas the former would comprise the Derridean concept of the Law of (unconditional) hospitality, the latter would make reference to the application of the laws of (conditional) hospitality, that take into account the preservation of the self against the stranger, the different Other. Insomuch as the Irish were perceived as racialized Others on account not of their physical appearance, but of their culture, social status, and religion, they were often met with prejudice and even denied entrance.

This represents a contradiction between America's perceived and (self-)publicized image as the land of perpetual hospitality and the conditions—or plain refusal—met by many immigrants upon arrival there. When legislating hospitality, this contradiction between the Law and the laws of hospitality must be met and recognized, trying to find a balance between good—as in generous, charitable—hospitality practices and what is safe for the host community. Was it charitable to deny entrance to hundreds of sick Irish arriving on boats to the different American ports and later to Ellis Island? Clearly not, but was it in accordance with the laws of conditional hospitality? If those sicknesses were considered a threat to the well-being of the American community, then the answer is yes according to Derrida. There is, in sum, a "non-dialectizable antimony" (Derrida [1997] 2000, 77) between the Law and the laws of hospitality, or rather between the ideal of hospitality and the actual practice of it, as the Irish came to know very well upon their arrival to the US.

4 Social Prejudice and Nativism as a Catalyst for Failed Hospitality

When accounting for hospitality—or lack thereof—towards immigrants, one must not fail to acknowledge the role of political and historical events in the host country. We are not unaccustomed to seeing how nationalistic political movements are often accompanied by an inhospitable discourse towards the migrant, especially when that migrant is, by class, race, or both, considered a hostile invader. A self-imposed need for preservation of the racial and national identities' purity is then called forth against a perceived threat from the outside, and that is where the laws of conditional hospitality come into place. More often than not, the migrant Other might be deemed acceptable under the Law of hospitality, even needed, but social practice and thought under the influence of intense nationalistic movements might declare him/her unwanted. Prejudice then comes into play, which is the reason why we can conclude, as Manzanas and Benito do, that "American history and culture [...] is traversed by hospitality and its own parasitic double, hostility" (2017, 7).

This was precisely the case in mid-nineteenth-century America and the reason behind part of the nation's attitude towards the Irish migrants. Arriving in a highly nationalistic society, the mostly Catholic Irish Famine migrants to the US found themselves amidst a climate of marked nativism. Even though Catholicism was a presence—albeit minor—in the US before the arrival of the Famine migrants, the sudden increase in Catholic population that this migratory peak caused during the mid-century years was used by nativists to reinforce already-existing anti-papist discourses and direct them against the new arrivals. The Irish migrant was therefore immediately identified with Catholicism, which in turn entailed racial labeling. According to McCaffrey,

> [i]n the United States [...] Anglo-Protestant and Scots-Irish Presbyterian prejudices against Irish Catholics had racial dimensions. They insisted that indigence and disorderly conduct were inherent in the Irish Catholic personality, and that their religious choice of Rome indicated an inferior intellect. They said that Catholicism locked the Irish into ignorance, shiftlessness, superstition and disloyalty to the American nation" ([1976; 1984] 1997, 93–94).

In this way, the nationalistic anxieties of mid-nineteenth-century America targeted the Irish migrant as a threat on the grounds of their cultural, religious and—fabricated—racial difference and therefore barred them from receiving true, unconditional hospitality. Sometimes, as aforementioned, these nationalistic anxieties barred them from receiving any hospitality at all.

In her novel *Captains and the Kings*, Taylor Caldwell provides an account that, although fictional, illustrates the effort of many Irish to rise above this initial rejection and achieve a place among the elite of white privileged people. The novel opens with the protagonist's arrival in the States after escaping the Famine in Ireland and reflects precisely on the aforementioned discrepancy between America's reputation as the perfect hospitable country and its actual implementation of conditional hospitality upon the arrival of the feared

Other: "Joseph knew of the many little ships that had been turned back at various ports in America: they were not wanted. They were the destitute and the starveling, and they were 'Romans' and Irish and trouble-makers and strange. The Religious were especially despised and secretly feared" (Caldwell 1973, 13).

This distinction between Catholic Irish and non-Catholic (or Scotch-Irish) was, as previously mentioned, one not established by the Americans themselves, but one that was readily accepted by the white American society and used by nativists to spread a fear of the outsider among the population and diferenciate between acceptable guests and unacceptable—poorer—guests in relation to the Irish. And yet, as many of those learned Irish must have realized, persecution and prejudice on the grounds of religion should not be a new idea to the descendants of the early American settlers—let alone a condoned one. When confronted with a man who refuses to allow his daughter to marry an Irish-Catholic descendant, Joseph, the boy's father and Caldwell's protagonist reflects on the following:

> But, sir, we were destroyed as ruthlessly as Russian serfs are destroyed by their masters. We were hunted down like animals, like vermin, for no reason at all but that we wanted to be free, as a nation, and to practice our religion. That was quite a heinous crime, wasn't it? [...] Your own ancestors left England for just the same thing. But you have forgotten. Your ancestors were poor driven English yeomen, who wanted nothing but peace and to serve their religion. This they were denied, as my people were denied. So they emigrated—here. (Caldwell 1973, 342–343)

Frank McCourt comes to a similar conclusion in his autobiographical novel *'Tis*, and also hints at the apparent irony behind the American's disdain of the Irish on account of their religion:

> The professor is saying the Pilgrims left England to escape religious persecution and that puzzles me because the Pilgrims were English themselves and the English were always the ones who persecuted everyone else, especially the Irish. I'd like to raise my hand and tell the professor how the Irish suffered for centuries under English rule but I'm sure everyone in this class has a high school diploma and if I open my mouth they'll know I'm not one of them. (Mccourt 2000, 194)

The lack of a clear referent for the pronoun 'them' in the last sentence in the previous quote leaves it open for interpretation as to which group Frank does not feel a part of: high school graduates or white Anglo-Saxon Protestants.

Perhaps both. In any case, what these two passages illustrate is that, in the words of Puspa Damai,

> America, which has always sought to distinguish itself from the cursed nations without hospitality, forgets its natural and constitutive part [*sic*?], and needs to be reminded of its forgetfulness. America forgets hospitality because it periodically lapses into amnesia with regard to hospitality [...] and therefore needs to be reminded of its repression; it needs a project of memory [...] which reminds the 'just maturing youth' of America to be hospitable. (2012, 50)

America, as the narrators in these two novels suggest, needs indeed to be reminded that it was prejudice that drove the Pilgrims away from England, and that it is prejudice of a very similar kind that kept—keeps still—hundreds of those tired, poor, and homeless Others in search of shelter from benefiting from the hospitality their host country professes but does not practice. This prejudice is, more often than not, based on stereotypes, and the case of the Irish was not an exception. According to Coates et al., "[p]eople often associate an elaborate array of behaviors, attitudes, and values with particular racial groups, presuming that these reflect innate or culturally specific traits" (2018, 40), which accounts for the Irish's typical stereotyping. Even if "not all were poor, not all were Catholic, and not all even spoke English" (Ignatiev 2009, 45), especially after the mass migration during the Famine years there grew in the American society—aided by the nativists' anti-Irish and anti-Catholic discourse—the preconceived image of all Irish as, indeed, poor, illiterate Papists. To this were added charges of violent temperament and a tendency towards excessive drinking. Most of these stereotypes are maintained today and shape the picture of the 'typical' Irish from which the Scotch-Irish tried to distance themselves.

The three novels analyzed here are full of instances in which the Irish or Irish-descended protagonists encounter examples of such stereotyping, like when the Jewish lover of one of Mary Gordon's protagonists openly tells his Irish-descended girlfriend they all thought "the Irish were a bunch of crazy drunks" (1990, 327), or when a powerful businessman, reluctant to let his daughter marry the daughter of Taylor Caldwell's protagonist, encounters the man himself and is shocked to see a well-groomed gentleman instead of the dirty rogue he was clearly expecting, explaining his disappointment to himself by assuming he was "Scots-Irish, perhaps, with a background of Covenanters" (1973, 339). This question of religion, as has already been explained, is perhaps the strongest and most perpetuated stereotype of all. Surely not all the Irish who migrated into America were Catholics, but most of the poorest and therefore most contemptible of those Irish emigrants were, which served to catalog all of the unwanted Irish under the same label. Frank McCourt reflects on this in the following passage:

> At the next meeting of the psychology class the professor asks me a question about Jung and the collective unconscious and the moment I open my mouth I know everyone is staring at me as if to say, Who's the one with the Irish brogue? The professor himself says, Oh, do I detect an Irish accent? and I have to admit he does. He tells the class that, of course, the Catholic Church has been traditionally hostile to psychoanalysis. Isn't that right, Mr Mc Court? and I feel he's accusing me. Why is he talking about the Catholic Church just because I tried to answer his question on the collective unconscious and am I supposed to defend the Church? (2000, 223)

The fact that Catholicism was immediately brought to the professor's mind as soon as he identified McCourt as Irish illustrates the fact that the connection of Irish-Catholic has been deeply ingrained in the collective unconscious the class was discussing. This classifies the identification as a stereotype, and the fact that it was traditionally used to degrade and reject the Irish in America makes it a prejudice.

Of course, the exposure to these stereotypes and prejudices permeates the Irish themselves, which might result in a feeling of inferiority in comparison to the more privileged members of their host society. If the rejected Other is not made to feel welcome among his/her unwilling hosts, this might result in a tendency to hide one's otherness; whatever it is that makes one different and, therefore, makes one rejected. This is illustrated when, in *Captains and the Kings*, the protagonist Joseph Armagh passes as Scottish in order to get a job (Caldwell 1973, 22), or when Dan, one of the protagonist's descendants in *The Other Side* feels as an imposter for hiding his family's roots while at the same time knowing that "if they did know him and the history of his family, they'd be appalled" (Gordon 1990, 24). His cousin, Cam, knows of this concealment and is conscious of its source: "He knew that she knew his double shame; he was ashamed of how his grandmother stood out in the world, that she was not like others, but he loved her and was shamed by his own shame" (Gordon 1990, 81). Dan is aware of his Irish grandmother's otherness, and is shamed by it as well as by his efforts to hide it in himself. Cam, for her part, does not show such ambivalent feelings towards their grandmother, but does not partake of a very positive image of the Irish either: "It's no accident the Irish built the subways.

And then stayed there. It was the perfect place for them, dark, underground, dangerous, hidden" (Gordon 1990, 60).

5 Climbing the Social Ladder: the Irish's Process of Becoming 'White'

In order to get out of the subways, in order to get over their self-shame and revert the lack of hospitality they faced in their new country, the Irish needed to acquire 'white' status, positioning themselves over other non-white groups. This, of course, marked the relations of the Irish to other races in America. Cast out as socially contemptible, the Irish were thrown together with other non-privileged groups upon arrival and treated with similar contempt. According to Ignatiev, "[i]n the early years Irish were frequently referred to as 'niggers turned inside out'; the Negroes, for their part, were sometimes called 'smoked Irish'" (2009, 49). The Irish were among the first non-whites to be enslaved in New England in the early 1600s (Coates et al. 2018, 112), and in the late 1890s it was common to believe that the Irish were in fact descended from Africa, acceding to the "Iberian hypothesis" (Coates et al. 2018, 39). This racialization of their social, cultural, and religious differences with the dominant white society allowed nativist groups to perpetuate a stereotype of the Irish migrant as a dangerous—racial—Other that would threaten their racial purity, their cultural specificity, and their religious independence from Rome. A group, in sum, subject to being denied access under the laws of conditional and preservative hospitality.

In order to revert this racial labeling, in order to shed their otherness and become admissible guests under the laws of hospitality, the Irish migrants needed to turn the spotlight on other racialized groups, making use of their physical if not social difference. In other words, even though "Irish immigrants experienced a tremendous amount of prejudice in the United States and were not considered to be among the country's elite White ethnics" (Coates et al. 2018, 39), they learned to utilize the privilege of their skin color in order to become part of the US's "matrix of oppression and privilege" (Ferber, Herrera, and Samuels 2007; Ferber, Jiménez, Herrera, and Samuels 2009). As Ignatiev puts it, "[t]he Irish who emigrated to America in the eighteenth and nineteenth centuries [...] came to a society in which color was important in determining social position. It was not a pattern they were familiar with and they bore no responsibility for it; nevertheless, they adapted to it in short order" (2009, 2). Consequently, even though at the beginning there was a fair share of intermingling between Irish and African Americans, as soon as the African Americans became competition in the job market, the

Irish stood against them and made use of the most apparent difference between the two groups to prevail. As David Roediger puts it, "white workers [...] created racialized class identities by reflecting not only on their roles as the producers and the exploited, but also in reference to their positions as non-slaves, and as refusers of 'nigger work'" (1998, 57). Once the poor and desperate Irish workers replaced African Americans in the marketplace by accepting lower wages in menial jobs, they endeavored to make use of the color line by barring blacks from ever returning to those jobs. "As members of the privileged group," Ignatiev points out, "white workers organized to defend their caste status [...] [by prohibiting] free Afro-Americans from competing with them for jobs" (2009, 115). Of course, since physical appearance was not for the Irish a guarantee of white status, if they wanted to be recognized as whites they needed to do so by establishing a contrast between themselves and other groups, most noticeably, their direct opposition: African Americans. White man's work, Ignatiev argues, "was, simply, work from which Afro-Americans were excluded" (2009, 130). Consequently, "[t]o be acknowledged as white, it was not enough for the Irish to have a competitive advantage over Afro-Americans in the labor market; in order for them to avoid the taint of blackness it was necessary that no Negro be allowed to work in occupations where Irish were to be found" (2009, 130).

Frank McCourt illustrates this process in his autobiography *'Tis*, although, in his experience, the differentiation in the workplace was made with reference to Puerto Ricans, not African Americans. In one of his first jobs as a young boy in America, Frank encounters this particular—Irish—union shop steward who greets him by saying that "it's a good thing [Frank is] Irish or it's down in the kitchen [he'd] be with the spics" (2000, 37). And he continues by saying that Frank is

> paid two dollars and fifty cents a week more than the dishwashers and [he has] opportunities for advancement they'll never have because all they want to do is not learn English and make enough money to go back to Puerto Rico and sit under trees drinking beer and having big families because that's all they're good for, drinking and screwing till their wives are worn out and die before their time and their kids run the streets ready to come to New York and wash dishes and start the whole goddam thing over again and if they can't get jobs we have to support them, you an' me, so they can sit on their stoops up in East Harlem playing their goddam guitars and drinking beer outa paper bags. That's the spics, kid, and don't you forget it. [...] They are like the Negroes, they don't take nothin' serious. (38–39)

If the irony that the Irish are usually accused of exactly the same things—not working, drinking in excess, and having excessively big families of more, poor, Catholic children—by the dominant society is lost on Eddie (the union shop steward), it is by no means lost on Frank, who fills his novel with several instances of the same such stereotyping directed at him as Irish.

If we take hospitality to mean the process by which a stranger is allowed to feel at home in someone else's territory, then we could argue that, being able to work in America—and therefore provide for themselves and their families in order to thrive there—was the first step that this community had to take in order to be finally welcomed there. That they needed to achieve this by reverting the racial labeling they were initially given and making use of a similar pre-existing racial labeling for other minorities shows how their initial rejection was linked to their racial—through social and religious differences—othering and therefore their falling into the category of the unacceptable parasitic guest.

And yet, racial relations were not the only means by which the Irish achieved inclusion in the hegemonic social group; politics also had a great deal to do with the process. Many Irish immigrants chose politics as a way to fulfill the American Dream, and many are the names of Irish or Irish-descended who made their way in the political sphere. The most famous one would be, of course, John Fitzgerald Kennedy, whose election notably helped the Irish cause in America since his "whiteness was ratified by popular vote" (Jacobson qtd. in Durso 2002, 99). However, he was not the only US president with Irish ties. According to Nathan Mannion, twenty-two of the forty-five US presidents to date can claim Irish ancestry, including Barack Obama (2017, 8). This process is clearly depicted in Taylor Caldwell's *Captains and the Kings* when, from early on in the novel, Joseph Armagh realizes that the only way to achieve respect and equality in his new host country is to acquire power and wealth:

> He needed more money. Money was the answer to all things. [...] He thought of his mother, given to the sea after the ship had left New York, and his father in a pauper's grave, without stone or remembrance, and Joseph's mouth became a slit of pain in his stark face. He must have money. He no longer cared how he would obtain, not a comfortable wage, but money in profusion. [...]
>
> He thought of Mr Tom Hennessey, the Irishman who had made his fortune, it was said with truth, in blackbirding, and he had many interests in the great Commonwealth of Pennsylvania, and all of them, it was hinted, equally nefarious. It was his money which had made him mayor

of this town, and which had given him a luxurious home in Green Hills, he the son of an Irish immigrant like Joseph Armagh himself. [...] Even an Irishman with money was to be respected and honoured, and caps lifted at his passing. (1973, 36–37)

According to Puspa Damai, "[h]ospitality as furnishing [...] depicts America as the land of plenty and promises of prosperity, which are actualized and achieved by treating the land as a means to acquire or amass property" (2012, 197). This is precisely what Joseph has in mind when he conceives of his plan to make money whatever the cost. It is his vision of the American Dream, the only way he finds for an Irishman to be, if not fully respected, at least tolerated. He, in fact, makes it his life's mission, which reaches its peak when he sets his mind to making his son president. All these schemes do not, of course, fail to have some part of vengeful sentiment in them, as is made evident towards the end of the narrative:

> 'Pa,' he said, 'why do you want me to be a Congressman, then a Senator, perhaps a Governor, or, as you used to say, President of the United States of America?' He smiled as at some happy jest, but his father gave him one of his fierce glances and Rory no longer smiled.
> 'I thought I told you,' said Joseph, in slow but emphatic words. 'The country that would not accept me and my family, the country which rejected me, the country which despised me—it will accept my sons as Representatives, Senators, or whatever. That will be my ...' He stopped, snipped a little wine. (1973, 307)

What Joseph's words evidence is a desire to turn the lack of hospitality he encountered in his host country back on itself, and force his unwilling hosts to be ruled by his descendants, the class of people they formerly despised, now whitewashed through money and power.

6   The Assimilation of Irish-Americans

According to Manzanas and Benito, "the melting pot, as a metaphor for American identity, participates in [a] cannibalistic trope because it reduces immigrants to a common denominator of Americanness" (2017, 11). This is achieved through a process of assimilation, or incorporation, which "implies a blurring of boundaries between two entities that can be tantamount to consumption, for one element is dissolved into the other, and the foreign is assimilated within the familiar" (Manzanas and Benito 2017, 83). Of course this process comes at the cost of the assimilated group's losing what makes it different, its uniqueness. This de-othering goes against the Law of unconditional hospitality, under which the guest is to be accepted despite its "inescapable differences" (Manzanas and Benito 2017, 20), yet it repeatedly takes place within the United States. As Patricia Williams reminds us, "one loses sight of the fact that some 'successfully assimilated' ethnicities in the United States have become so only by paying the high cost of burying forever languages, customs, and cultures" (1998, 253).

Is this what happened to the Irish in America? Is the fact that St. Patrick's Day is celebrated throughout the US enough proof that the Irish retained their cultural identity or is it rather indicative of an appropriation of certain 'acceptable' Irish traits on the part of American society? If we agree that what constituted the Irish non-white status was their poverty, rusticity, and Catholicism, we can surmise that, insomuch as their journey into whiteness entailed an improvement in living conditions through the acquisition of increasingly better jobs at the cost of other races as well as an acclimatization to urban life through participation in politics and law enforcement, at least some of their identifying traits were lost in the process. Religious identification has also shifted since, according to Shaun O'Connell, "[b]y the end of the 20th century some 44 million Americans claimed some Irish identity, divided loosely into 24 million of Protestant descent and 20 million of Catholic lineage" (2003, 254). Patricia Williams describes this process—as witnessed in a Russian neighbor of hers—as

> compulsive because so tied to fear of being bounded, so linked to fear of being made fun of for becoming 'too ethnic,' too closed, too ignorant of 'the larger society.' While this should be in no way taken as a necessarily bad thing, it can also signal a lost balance, a sacrifice of appreciation for the bonds, the links, the ties that bind, that make family, connection, identity. (1998, 254)

All this can only result in an ambivalent relationship between the wish or even the need to fit into the host community and a feeling of melancholy and shame for the lost ties to the motherland. Such a situation is very well portrayed in Mary Gordon's *The Other Side*, especially in the MacNamara original couple: Vincent and Ellen. She, having fled Ireland after a troubled childhood, does not wish to retain any of what links her to her original country. Her husband, for his part, having been kept from his wife's past, fails to understand her rejection of the homeland and, although he recognizes his life is much better in the US, cannot help but feel an attachment to Ireland to which he gives way in the form of songs. This became a common source of contention for them, as one of their grandsons remembers:

> Oh, this beautiful thing, Ellen would say, through furious cruel teeth, we loved it so, that's why we couldn't wait to leave. And when his grandfather would send unto the air a nice memory, rising like a balloon to give them pleasure, when he would say: The greenness of the grass, the goodness of the milk, the lovely bread, the songs, the smell of the peat fire, she would raise the hammer of her scorn. She would begin to talk in a false brogue. 'Yes, dad,' she'd say, ''tis little enough ye knew of it. You left at fifteen and lucky for you. 'Twas a lovely life you had. Breaking your back on the farm that went all to your brother, then apprenticed out at twelve, 'Twas what ye wanted for yer children, wasn't it. Everybody slaving till they died or wore out. 'Twas wonderful. If only I could have it back, my carefree youth.' And she would flap and dance and invent a song. 'My carefree youth/The cowshit and the toothless mother/And the starving tinkers out to steal me blind/Back, back to the auld sod of my dreams.' (Gordon 1990, 159–160)

This juxtaposition of attitudes is transferred onto their descendants, who, as has already been mentioned, have a tendency to feel ashamed both of their roots and of their shame of that shame. Except for Sheilah, another of their grandchildren: A former nun who left her order to marry a priest, she is determined to recover the cultural heritage that was denied to her—a common process in third-generation immigrants—which is not understood nor shared by the rest of her family:

> She is working on her master's degree in family history (for which she has tried to interview her grandfather, with results that frustrate and anger her), she travels regularly to Manhattan for meetings of a society dedicated to the preservation of Irish culture; with her son, Diarmid, and her husband she takes weekly classes in the Irish language and in Irish dance. In these circles of earnestness, she is respected and looked up to. But in her family she is seen by the kindly as pathetic, by the less kind as a joke. She is never seen as a success. [...] None of them cares about these things. [...] We are at the center of a movement which allows the Irish to reclaim our heritage. *We* study the language, *our* child learns the traditional dances. Not theirs. He competes each year in the city-wide Feis. One day he will win ribbons for me, medals. I know a history they never knew

they lost. How dare they make me a failure. They are the failures. (Gordon 1990, 34–35. Emphasis in the original)

When faced with hostile hospitality, processes like that described above are common enough. Especially if returning is not possible or desirable, the migrant wishes to achieve acceptance in the new host land. Sometimes, in order to do that, it is necessary to eliminate all differentiating markers that would make one appear as an alien Other, not worthy of unconditional hospitality. In some instances, this process must be achieved at the cost of losing the home heritage or by forcibly displacing other marginalized groups. In any case, individuals may develop some sort of Du Boisian Double Consciousness as Frank McCourt realizes: "I'd like to be Irish when it's time for a song or a poem. I'd like to be American when I teach. I'd like to be Irish-American or American-Irish though I know I can't be two things even if Scott Fitzgerald said the sign of intelligence is the ability to carry opposed thoughts at the same time" (2000, 360).

In succeeding to shed off their initially given label of otherness, the Irish in America may have indeed managed to become Irish-American, but one could argue that the scales tip more towards the American than to the Irish side and that, in the process, Ireland remains "a long way to go," as the popular WWI song that gives title to this chapter claims. Be that as it may, what remains is a relatively quick assimilation process by which, through political alliances, some whitewashing and a good deal of racial antagonism, the Irish managed to cease being considered threatening racial Others and therefore unwanted guests in order to become an intrinsic part of their host community.

References

Adams, Bluford. 2003. "Reading the Re-Revival: Competing Approaches in US Ethnic Studies." *American History* 15 (2): 395–408.

Caldwell, Taylor. 1973. *Captains and the Kings*. London: Fontana.

Case, Kim, ed. 2013. *Deconstructing Privilege: Teaching and Learning as Allies in the Classroom*. New York: Routledge.

Chancer, Lynn S. and Beverly Xaviera Watkins. 2006. *Gender, Race, and Class: An Overview*. Malden, Oxford, and Carlton: Blackwell.

Coates, Rodney D., Abby L. Ferber, and David L. Brunsma. 2018. *The Matrix or Race: Social Construction, Intersectionality, and Inequality*. Thousand Oaks: Sage.

Collins, Patricia Hill. (1990). *Black Feminist Thought: Knowledge, Consciousness, and the Politics of Empowerment*. New York: Routledge.

Conley, Dalton. 2003. "Universal Freckle, or How I Learned to be White." In *Privilege: A Reader*, edited by Michael S. Kimmel and Abby L. Ferber, 195–212. Boulder and Oxford: Westview.

Cronin, Mike. 2017. "The Irish Made Lives in all Parts." *EPIC. The Irish Emigration Museum*, February 24, 2–3. [Special Magazine published by the *Irish Independent*].

Damai, Puspa L. 2012. "Welcoming Strangers: Hospitality in American Literature and Culture." PhD diss., University of Michigan, Ann Arbor.

Derrida, Jaques. (1997) 2000. *Of Hospitality: Anne Duformantelle Invites Jaques Derrida to Respond*. Translated by Rachel Bowlby. Stanford: Stanford UP.

Durso, Patricia Keefe. 2002. "Bringing Whiteness 'Home': Exploring the Social Geography of Race in Mary Gordon's *The Other Side*." *Modern Language Studies* 32 (1): 85–102.

Dyer, Richard. 2003. "The Matter of Whiteness." In *Privilege: A Reader*, edited by Michael S. Kimmel and Abby L. Ferber, 21–32. Boulder and Oxford: Westview.

Ferber, Abby L., Andrea O'Reilly Herrera, and Dena R. Samuels. 2007. "The Matrix of Oppression and Privilege: Theory and Practice for the New Millennium." *American Behavioral Scientist* 51 (4): 516–531.

Ferber, Abby L., Christina M. Jiménez, Andrea O'Reilly Herrera, and Dena R. Samuels, eds. 2009. *The Matrix Reader: Examining the Dynamics of Oppression and Privilege*. Boston: McGraw Hill.

Fitzgerald, Patrick and Brian Lambkin. 2017. "One Nation, Millions of Stories…" *EPIC. The Irish Emigration Museum*, February 17, 2–3. [Special Magazine published by the *Irish Independent*].

Gordon, Mary. 1990. *The Other Side*. New York: Penguin.

Ignatiev, Noel. 2009. *How the Irish Became White*. New York: Routledge.

Izarra, Laura P. Z. 2004. "Locations and Identities in Irish Diasporic Narratives." *Hungarian Journal of English and American Studies (HJEAS)* 10 (1/2): 341–352.

Kant, Immanuel. (1970) 1991. *Kant: Political Writings*. 2nd ed. Translated by H. B. Nisbet and edited by Hans Reiss. New York: Cambridge UP.

Kinealy, Christine. 2017. "A Deadly Blight that Changed Everything." *EPIC. The Irish Emigration Museum*, February 17, 4. [Special Magazine published by the *Irish Independent*].

Kirwan, Padraig. 2011. "Transatlantic Irishness: Irish and American Frontiers in Patrick McCabe's *The Butcher Boy*." *Comparative Literature* 63 (1): 3–24.

Lazarus, Emma. 2002. *Emma Lazarus: Selected Poems and Other Writings*. Edited by Gregory Eiselein. Peterborough, Ont. and Orchard Park, NY: Broadview.

Levinas, Emmanuel. 1987. *Time and the Other and Additional Essays*. Translated by Richard A. Cohen. Pittsburg: Duquesne UP.

McCaffrey, Lawrence John. (1976; 1984) 1997. *The Irish Catholic Diaspora in America*. Washington: The Catholic U of America P.

Mannion, Nathan. 2017. "Four-day Visit in '63 Confirmed Kennedy Was one of our Own." *EPIC. The Irish Emigration Museum*, February 24, 8. [Special Magazine published by the *Irish Independent*].

Manzanas Calvo, Ana María and Jesús Benito Sánchez. 2017. *Hospitality in American Literature and Culture. Spaces, Bodies, Borders*. New York and London: Routledge.

McCourt, Frank. 2000. *'Tis*. London: Flamingo.

O'Connell, Shaun. 2003. "That Much Credit: Irish-American Identity and Writing." *The Massachusetts Review* 44 (1/2): 251–268.

Roediger, David. 1998. "White Workers, New Democrats, and Affirmative Action." In *The House that Race Built*, edited by Wahneema Lubiano, 48–65. New York: Vintage.

Williams, Patricia J. 1998. "The Ethnic Scarring of American Whiteness." In *The House that Race Built*, edited by Wahneema Lubiano, 253–263. New York: Vintage.

Winant, Howard. 1998. "Racial Dualism at Century's End." In *The House that Race Built*, edited by Wahneema Lubiano, 87–115. New York: Vintage.

CHAPTER 10

Hospitality Rituals and Caribbean Migrants: Tom Wolfe's *Back to Blood*, Ana Lydia Vega's "Encancaranublado," and Francisco Goldman's *The Ordinary Seaman*[1]

Ana María Manzanas Calvo

Abstract

In "The Caribean Imaginary in 'Encancaranublado' by Ana Lydia Vega," Diana Vélez argues that the Caribbean "is a space that can be theorized productively within both paradigms: both diaspora and borderland" (828). This chapter proposes that hospitality can also offer an apt theoretical frame to analyze the interactions between and among migrants on one hand, and between migrants and Americans on the other. The chapter examines Ana Lydia Vega's story as part of a series of literary works that gravitate around acts of hospitality. Vega's "Encancaranublado" and Edwidge Dunticat's "Children of the Sea" and "Caroline's Wedding" establish a direct connection between contemporary migrants and the slave trade. Tom Wolfe's *Back to Blood* and Francisco Goldman's *The Ordinary Seaman* tackle the stasis and the hostility of the arrival. If Wolf's character is literally suspended between land and sea, between being a 'dry' or a 'wet' foot, between standing a chance of being welcome to America or being sent to Guantánamo, Goldman's characters undergo a process of depersonalization that transforms them into slaves and zombies. The four examples show that the arrival to an American harbor never translates as hospitality, and that mobility for Caribbean migrants often translates as another variation of mobility 'in chains.'

---

1 Research funds for this article were provided by the Spanish Ministry of Science and Technology through the research project "Critical History of Ethnic American Literature: An Intercultural Approach" (ref. FFI2015-64137-P), directed by Prof. Jesús Benito Sánchez, by the Regional Government of Castilla y León through the research Project "The Frontiers of Hospitality in Spanish and American Cultural Studies" (ref. SA342U14), and by the European Project "Hospitality and European Film" 2017-1-ES01-KA203-038181.

Keywords

hospitality – borders – Caribbean – mobility – slavery

In "The Caribbean Imaginary in 'Encancaranublado,'" Diana Vélez argues that the Caribbean is a space that can be theorized productively within the diaspora and borderland paradigms (1994, 828). This chapter proposes that hospitality can also offer an apt theoretical framework to analyze the interactions between and among Caribbean migrants on the one hand and, on the other hand, between those same migrants and the United States. Especially significant at a time of multiple crossings and migrations, hospitality as a critical framework examines the instability of the host/guest dynamics, as well as the term hospitality itself, unable to extricate itself from its parasitic other, hostility (Derrida 2000, 3). The chapter examines works by Francisco Goldman (1954–), Ana Lydia Vega (1946–) and Tom Wolfe (1930–2018). Significantly, these three writers offer examples of changing acts of hospitality at sea, as guests become hosts and hosts become unwanted guests. The sea becomes the connective medium that provides vistas into different manifestations of changing borders, as crossers are routinely separated and selected according to different protocols and immigration policies. All of these crossers/guests are finally unwelcomed by the ultimate host, the United States. The opening of Tom Wolfe's *Back to Blood* starts the discussion with the predicament of Cuban migrants in the United States, literally suspended between land and sea, between a "dry" or a "wet" foot.[2] Vega's "Encancaranublado" and Francisco Goldman's *The Ordinary Seaman* offer further examples of arrival at a sanctuary or American harbor. The welcoming of the Other, the three writers show, is undercut by ambivalence or open hostility. Vega and Goldman, however, offer far more nuanced characterizations of migrants as they show how the characters are reconceptualized and envisioned according to previous modes of dealing with contingents deemed inferior or uncivilized. Migrants are incorporated into the host country but, the chapter shows, this incorporation is undercut by calculations and limitations, that is, by the hostility inherent to hospitality.

---

[2] The policy that allowed any Cuban who made it to US soil to stay and become a legal resident was repealed by President Obama in January 2017.

1   Stasis in Tom Wolfe's *Back to Blood*

> We must be reminded of this implacable law of hospitality: the *hôte* who receives (host), the welcoming *hôte* who considers himself the owner of the place, is in truth a *hôte* received in his own home; he receives it from his own home—which, in the end, does not belong to him. The *hôte* as host is guest.
>
> JACQUES DERRIDA
> *Adieu to Emmanuel Levinas*

Wolfe's *Back to Blood* opens with a scene that visually shows the acrobatics of immigration laws. Nestor Camacho, a Cuban-American cop, is ordered to bring down a Cuban refugee from the top of a schooner's 75-foot foremast. Suspended in midair, the man desperately tries to step on American land and become a "dry foot," which would expedite his welcome into the United States. "That," the narrative voice claims, "is all a Cuban has to do: set foot on American soil or any structure extending from American soil, such as the bridge, and he will be granted asylum ... Any *Cuban* ... No other refugees were granted such a privilege" (2012, 42). The issue is crucial, for Cubans stopped before stepping on shore or apprehended on or in the water almost always get returned to Cuba. The man, dangling from the mast, is in sight of a nearby bridge, where Cuban-Americans have gathered to demand the refugee be allowed on land and granted political asylum as a dry foot. It is a moment of suspension in the novel that dramatizes the lot shared by all Cubans seeking asylum. The Cuban Adjustment Act of 1966 initially allowed political refugees from Cuba to pursue legal residency in the US. According to the 1966 Act, Cubans were considered "self-imposed political exiles" and "consumer refugees," and were granted "special privileges" in comparison to other migrants such as Haitians (Arteaga 2008, 510).[3] President Clinton and the Cuban government revised the application of the Cuban Adjustment Act of 1966 and proposed what can be considered an immigration legislation anomaly: those Cuban immigrants who were captured at sea were returned to Cuba, but those who reached American soil were able to invoke their rights under the CAA. This anomaly has come to be known as

---

3   Arteaga 2008 (510–511) provides a poignant anecdote to illustrate the different treatment that awaits each nationality: "Five miles off the coast of Miami, Florida, a vessel carrying 131 Haitian nationals who had fled Haiti stopped and picked up two Cubans at sea. They were near death because their boat had capsized. When the vessel arrived in Miami, the Haitians were all sent back to Haiti. The two Cubans were granted access to the US and after one year were eligible to receive green cards solely based on their nationality."

the Wet Foot, Dry Foot Policy (Arteaga 2008, 529). Such is the piece of legislation behind the literal dangling of the Cuban migrant at the opening of Wolfe's novel. The man is on the mast and, as the narrative voice clarifies, "has made it out of the water—but onto a boat. Technically he is 'still "in the water" and is classified as a 'wet foot'" (Wolfe 2012, 43). Policing the liquid line that separates the migrant from land would be business as usual for a Miami cop, but it takes on a special meaning for Camacho as a son of immigrants. Although most of Wolfe's description centers on the Cop's bravado and over-trained biceps, one of the key aspects of the novel is this encounter with this dangling man while a chorus of Cuban dissidents call him *"Gusano"* and "Dirty traitor" (2012, 47). Although the two men are in different positions, it seems possible to claim that the migrant's feeling of stasis and suspension is contagious, and that Camacho himself is suspended in the midst of the climb: he is damned if he brings down the migrant because he will be snubbed by the Cuban American community in Miami, damned if he does not for he will be held accountable to his boss.

When the cop reaches the migrant, the latter tries to entreat the former to let him go. The text code-switches between Spanish and English to convey how Camacho interprets the migrant's words:

> '*¡Te lo suplico! ¡Te lo suplico!* I'm begging you! Begging you! You can't send me back! They will torture me until I reveal everybody! They'll destroy my family. Have mercy! There are Cubans on that bridge! I'm begging you! Is one more such an intolerable burden? I'm begging you, begging you! You don't know what it's like! You won't be destroying just me, you'll be destroying a whole movement! I beg you! I beg you for asylum! I beg you for a chance!' (2012, 49)

Camacho tries to explain to the man that he can claim a "credible threat" so that he could get a Coast hearing and maybe get asylum. His Spanish, however, fails him, and he is unable to comfort the migrant, who feels cornered and terrified, and is described by the narrative voice as a "poor drowned rat" (2012, 49). Finally, Camacho manages to haul down the man. As he does so, both men fall into the water, thus visually confirming the migrant's fate as a wet foot, which implies being sent back to Cuba. Water, however, becomes the medium that both separates and connects the two men. As the son of Cuban immigrants, Camacho can be considered a guest in a foreign land. In fact, his father and grandfather built a small boat and stole two big café umbrellas to use as sails and finally set out for Florida. As Derrida would put it, Camacho as *hôte* is both guest and host. These memories of migration, as refreshed by Camacho's father, are of no avail when confronted with the policing of the very same line his family crossed. His hauling down the migrant marks his definite and unequivocal belonging to America and his self-fashioning as host. As chronicled by the narrative voice, "Nestor Camacho is now ... *a cop* ... a *real* cop ... as real as they make'em ... Nestor Camacho enters Heaven" (2012, 55). This entering allegedly rolls out the red carpet of hospitality and confirms his belonging to white America. Camacho is no longer a guest but a host, and can extend (or not) his own acts of hospitality.

Although his acceptance into the white world initially contrasts with the migrant's lot, who is turned over to the Coast Guard, the shared baptism in the water approximates the two men's perspectives and positions. Camacho, torn between his duty as a cop and as a member of the Cuban-American community, between his double identity as host and guest, seems to assume the position of the migrant, for just as the man finds the public hostility of the target country, Camacho finds the private hostility of the Cuban-American community, which considers him a traitor. He becomes a "latingo," a "Latino who had turned *gringo*" (2012, 57). In the eyes of the Cuban-American community, he is only a traitor with no sense of honor.

2 Hospitality in Three Acts: "Encancaranublado"

> [T]he boat is a floating piece of space, a place without a place, that exists by itself, that is self-enclosed and at the same time is given over to the infinity of the sea and that, from port to port, from bank to bank, from brothel to brothel, it goes as far as the colonies in search of the most precious treasures they conceal in their gardens [...] The ship is the heterotopia par excellence.
>
> MICHEL FOUCAULT
> *Of Other Spaces*

> The image of the ship—a living, micro-cultural, micro-political system in motion—is especially important for historical and theoretical reasons [...] Ships immediately focus attention on the middle passage, on the various projects for redemptive return to an African homeland, on the circulation of ideas and activists as well as the movement of key cultural and political artifacts.
>
> GILROY, PAUL
> *The Black Atlantic: Modernity and Double Consciousness*

The image of the sea as an intersection of different trajectories and crossings returns in Vega's short story. Two centuries after slave ships crossed the

Atlantic Ocean and distributed slaves in the Caribbean and the southern United States, Ana Lydia Vega introduces a small boat carrying disposable crossers like the Cuban migrant in Wolfe's *Back*. As a "floating piece of space, a place without a place," the boat turns into "the heterotopia par excellence," as Foucault explains. As a location that is a "counter-emplacement" (2008, 17) and that is located outside all places (2008, 17), the boat has the ability to juxtapose in a single real place several spaces, several emplacements—and several roles, we may add—that are in themselves incompatible (2008, 19). The roles of host and guest, the story demonstrates, come to the fore on the heterotopic boat, as the three protagonists of the story find themselves in an absolute break from traditional time. The boat brings echoes of former pilgrims—also illegal—that arrived on the American continent to pursue their religious freedom and of the human cargo taken to the Caribbean to be distributed in North America

Just as Gilroy proposed in *The Back Atlantic*, the boat may start the circulation of peoples and ideas, but may also contribute to the reinforcing of historical, racial, and cultural barriers. Such potential for transcultural communication initially sets the tone for the crossing, which can be seen as an opportunity for the creation of a nascent Caribbean Confederacy, as the epigraph to the story reads ("A la confederación caribeña del futuro/Para que llueva pronto y escampe"[4]). The difficulties of establishing such a transnational confederation, however, become clear in the story. Three representational logics collide as the initial passenger of the boat, a Haitian called Antenor, welcomes two other castaways, a Dominican man called Diógenes, and a Cuban man named Carmelo. They happen to be on the same heterotopic boat on their way to Miami.

Vega uses the comic mode to chronicle the voyage, and structures the story along the well-known lines of the formula "three men on a boat." The omniscient narrator is a privileged speaker "from a social class considerably higher than that of the narrative subjects, a position explicitly shared with the reader" (Castillo 2005, 64). The writer deploys a constant balancing act, "jostling high culture and popular culture language registers" (Castillo 2005, 64) French, Spanish, and English phrases. This instability at the linguistic level mirrors the literal instability of the boat and the changing relations and alliances the passengers create among themselves, as hosts become guests and guests become hosts. The different languages and linguistic registers, the different interpretations of the journey, the rapid succession of actors and their different forms of mastery over space contribute to the instability of the text-boat and the increasingly difficult balancing acts on board. As in Wolfe's *Back*, only a liquid

---

[4] "To the Caribbean confederacy of the future, may it rain soon and clear up" (My translation).

line, referred to in the story as "ese morelludo brazo de mar" separates the three men from the ironic "pursuit of happiness" (Vega 1992, 13). The English phrase, inscribed in the Declaration of Independence, sets the distance between English and Spanish, but also between individual dreams, aspirations and reality.

The Haitian man, Antenor, starts the journey alone. His reasons for leaving Haiti are well known: "Atrás quedan los mangos podridos de la diarrea y el hambre, la gritería de los macoutes, el miedo y la sequía"[5] (1992, 14). Against this backdrop of terror and famine, his diminishing water reserves and his adventure at sea feel more like a pleasure cruise. He is about to fall asleep when he hears the cries of a drowning man, whom he manages to help onto the boat. As a gracious host, Antenor welcomes a Dominican man, Diógenes, and shares the water jug with him, only to take it away when the latter holds on to it for too long. Thus the threat of the abusive guest starts to loom in the horizon. There is no need for a common language between the two men, for, according to the narrator, both share the internationalism of hunger and the solidarity of dreaming. This initially smooth interaction between Haitian host and Dominican guest shifts when the men hear new cries from another man at sea, a Cuban. The Dominican as guest expresses his exasperation at welcoming yet another passenger, as his comment, "Como si fuéramos pocos parió la abuela"[6] (1992, 15), conveys. The Haitian, on his part, also translates the appearance of the new guest as a burden, for another passenger means another mouth to feed. Not withstanding their reservations, the two men haul the Cuban onto the boat once he makes sure they are also en route to Miami. The third man rearranges the power dynamics on board. The Dominican and the Cuban establish what Antenor terms a "Cervantine monopoly" (1992, 15) and he can only interject timidly. Significantly, initially the host language, the language of mastery on board, French becomes a guest language in the face of the power of Spanish. Still there is some ground to share between the host and the new guest, and both men can relate to working in sugar cane fields. The exchange of experiences triggers the first point of friction within this bourgeoning camaraderie, for the Dominican voices the popular claim or representational logic that immigrant *madamos* are brought in, thus taking away Dominican jobs. This word strikes a cord for Antenor, for he knows it is a pejorative term for Haitians. The Haitian senses further upheaval when the Cuban, calling him *prieto*,[7] endorses

---

5 "He left behind the rotten mangos of diarrhea and hunger, the uproar of the Macoutes, the fear and the drought" (My translation).
6 "As if there weren't enough of us, now grandmother's gone and popped a baby" (Velez's translation 1994, 829).
7 In the Caribbean, *prieto* refers to a dark-skinned person.

such representation of Haitians, and demands that Antenor hand over the shoe box where he kept food, rum, and tobacco for the journey: "Levanta el corcho, prieto"[8] (1992, 16). When Antenor pretends not to understand, the Dominican, siding with the new guest and forgetting everything about the Haitian's hospitality, rephrases the Cuban's words: "Alza el cagadero, madamo, que te jiede a ron y a tabaco"[9] (1992, 16). The demand marks a shift in the power relations on the boat, for it is now the guests who gang up and displace the host. Dispossessed and disempowered, Antenor is almost kicked off "his" boat. But nothing is stable at sea, and dissent soon breaks out between the new competing hosts. After increasingly aggressive statements between the guests-turned-hosts, the water jug ends up at Antenor's feet. In his resentment towards his former guests, the Haitian throws the water jug into the sea and a fight breaks out. Unable to balance the power relations on board, the boat capsizes and the three men end up in the sea. When they are about to succumb to the dangers of the Bermuda Triangle they hear a whistle and are finally rescued by an American ship. Since the migrants cannot make it to America, America comes to them in anticipation of the Promised Land.

The first intimations of the "pursuit of happiness" and the encounter with America are not encouraging, however. The narrator describes the captain at length, and focuses on his Aryan and Apollonian features, blond hair and blue eyes. The emphasis on the captain's whiteness is crucial to assess his vision of the rescue and the specificity of his instructions to accommodate the three men:

> Get those niggers down there and let the spiks take care of 'em. Palabras que los incultos héroes no entendieron tan bien como nuestros bilingües lectores. Y tras de las cuales, los antillanos fueron cargados sin ternura hasta la cala del barco donde, entre cajas de madera y baúles mohosos, compartieron su primera mirada post naufragio: mixta de alivio y de susto sofrita en esperanzas ligeramente sancochadas.[10] (1992, 20)

The three men, who fought so hard on the boat to reaffirm their national differences and their linguistic monopoly over each other, are finally united under

---

8 "Move your ass" (My translation).
9 "Move your ass, madamo. It stinks of rum and tobacco" (My translation).
10 "Words that the uncultivated heroes did not understand as well as our bilingual readers. After being pronounced, the Caribbeans were unceremoniously taken to the hold of the ship, where among wood crates and moldy trunks they cast their first post-wreck, gaze: a mixture of relief and fear stir-fried with slightly poached hope" (My translation).

the American captain's gaze as "niggers." It is another re-enactment of the color line that disrupted alliances on the boat. Migrants and readers alike are reminded that English is the dominant language, the host language that establishes and administers categories and an overwhelming representational logic. The three men are finally in the same boat, both figuratively and literally (Vélez 1994, 832), on the same level of otherness. Thus the Captain denies the men the cultural specificity for which they viciously fought, a denial that "operates as the confirmation of an assigned space and order (if only down there with the spiks), erasing national identities in favor of a single racialized otherness relegated to the fringes of U.S. subjectivity" (Castillo 2005, 66). The confederacy that failed to be established on the original boat is ironically achieved from without, as the United States discards national differences and relegates the migrants to a pervasive marginality, a confederacy of blackness. Hospitality becomes indistinguishable from hostility towards these undifferentiated and unwanted Others. Their total lack of agency is emphasized in the use of the passive voice in "fueron cargados," just like cargo or merchandise. Even if different migration policies await each migrant, as noted in the previous section, what is clear from the captain's instructions is that the three men occupy the same space in the American imaginary, the hold of the boat, the space traditionally reserved for African slaves. The journey to freedom turns into its very opposite, and the future and the past collapse in the hold of the ship. Étienne Balibar (2005, 39) has argued that the colonial heritage has structured the way immigrants are being introduced into contemporary metropolises. Managing immigrants has become a form of "imported colonialism" (Hoffman 2009, 248) that reproduces previous encounters and modes of dealing with contingents that are deemed deficient and in need of development and civilization.

Unlike Camacho's role as the United States' gatekeeper in Wolfe's *Back,* Vega introduces a "spik" who is in charge of administering the hospitality rituals on board. The Puerto Rican grumbles in the dark: "Aquí si quieren comer tienen que meter mano y duro. Estos gringos no le dan na gratis ni a su mai"[11] (1992, 20), and in saying so, "a black arm" hands them dry clothes. Survival, the Puerto Rican implies, can only rely on brotherhood, on that sense of confederacy that failed on the boat. The Puerto Rican also lays out the kind of hospitality the migrants will encounter in the Promised Land. They will not find the unconditional hospitality they dream of, only a limited hospitality that is based on "limits and borders: calculations and the management of finite resources,

---

11   "Here if you want to eat you have to work hard at it. These Gringos won't give anything away for free" (My translation).

finite numbers of people, national borders and state sovereignty" (Rosello 2001, 11). There is nothing free in the land of the free, and immigrants are nobody's guests. Their place in American society will always resemble the space reserved for the dark Other.

3   Stasis: Francisco Goldman's *The Ordinary Seaman*[12]

A similar moment of anagnorisis on an American ship awaits Francisco Goldman's characters in *The Ordinary Seaman*. The allocation of migrants to the hold of the American ship in Vega's short story recalls previous colonial practices and ways of dealing with alien Others. Goldman goes a step further and explicitly compares the journey towards America with that of the African slaves that arrived in New York in the nineteenth century. From this perspective, Goldman's characters impersonate the image of the neo-slave: disposable, dispossessed, and trapped in mysterious capitalist practices. They embody the figure that Nancy calls "abandoned being" (1993, 36) and that Butler and Spivak call "spectral humans," beings deprived of "ontological weight," and who, failing the tests of social intelligibility required for minimal recognition, not only are disqualified for citizenship but also actively qualified for statelessness (2007, 15). The crew also becomes the embodiment of Bauman's concept of "wasted humans" as elaborated in *Wasted Lives*. Bauman has argued that the global spread of the modern form of life has set loose and put in motion enormous and constantly rising quantities of human beings. They are what he terms "the collateral casualties of progress" that are regularly disposed of because they are disposable (2004, 7, 15, 12).

Set in the 1980s, the story opens with the beginning of a journey that takes two Nicaraguans, the young Esteban and an old man, Bernardo Puyano, to a dream job in New York. Together with the rest of the Central American crew they are taken to a "deserted and apparently defunct end of the port" (Goldman 1997, 19) where the ship, the Urus, which was to leave New York in four days, was docked. Because of technical difficulties, however, the ship never leaves port, and the men are abandoned. The dilapidated buildings of the port reveal the decline of industrial port jobs and the rise of neoliberal capitalism and its attending practices, such as the trans-localized division of labor, national policies and economies increasingly porous and less sovereign, and the

---

12   A different and longer version of this section is forthcoming in *A Critical Gaze from the Old World: Transatlantic Perspectives on American Studies*. Isabel Durán *et alia*, eds. (Peter Lang).

setting of many people in motion (Comaroff and Comaroff 1999, 25). The Urus, newly named for this new economic venture, refers to the "urus," an extinct large, long-horned wild ox of Europe that is the ancestor of domestic cattle, according to Merriam Webster's Dictionary (1971, 1573). As the novel unfolds, the crew will reveal itself as the cattle, the Third-World labor that has historically sustained commercial ventures from colonial times to the present. Significantly, the word Urus refers to a particular ox, but is also the "you are us" and the "UR-US," the UR-text (Silva Gruesz 2003, 67) that creates a repeated sense of history from slavery to the present.

On board the men are welcomed to a broken ship by the captain and his "primero oficial," Mark (Goldman 1997, 23). Captain Elias explains that they would be delayed in port until some spare parts arrived from Japan. Bernardo is aghast at the explanation, and the image of the ship as a disastrous carcass gradually and painfully reveals itself. Unsurprisingly, when the crew looked south over the waterfront warehouse and terminal roofs and trees, they did not see the majestic and welcoming image of the Statue of Liberty. They just see its upper portion, a green, oxidized arm in the air. The statue did not salute the newcomers with the promise of a new life. Rather, its static and threatening quality becomes a symbol of the crew's immobility, as Bernardo will remind them throughout the novel: "When that statue walks, *chavalos*, this ship will sail" (Goldman 1997, 45). The men's liminal position as seamen that will never be at sea is reinforced when the captain lays out their legal status. While on board, the crew is in Panama and protected by Panama sovereign laws since the Urus has a Panamanian registry. Onshore, the Captain clarifies, they are in the United States and they are perfectly legal until their transit visas expire. But the protection of the sovereign laws of Panama is limited, for the country operates what is known as open registries or "flags of convenience" that allow a series of advantages to shipowners: They have neither the will nor capability to impose domestic or international regulations on registered ships (Naimou 2015, 71). To make matters worse, the boat is not even Panama's responsibility since the sailors, as Bernardo keeps repeating throughout the novel, are unlicensed seafarers. The captain, however, projects this lawless space onto the shore, and cautions the crew not to leave the ship. Port cities, he clarifies, are dangerous, especially if the crew left the port yard and entered the streets around *los proyectos*, government housing for the very poorest people, controlled by gangs who did not like strangers wandering through. The men do leave the ship and cut through the *proyectos* on their way to Brooklyn and are attacked and mugged by men who look like them. The transgression reinforces the captain's authority and his admonition to stay in what he calls "Panama." Unsafe on American ground, unprotected by Panama sovereign laws, immobilized and gradually abandoned by the captain and his first mate Mark as the economic venture flounders, the sailors become hostages and refugees.

4 Ship, Anti-Ship, and the Welcome to the Past

> A specter is always a *revenant*. One cannot control its comings and goings because it begins by coming back.
> JACQUES DERRIDA
> *Specters of Marx*

Unable to leave the ship, the men turn into what Bauman calls "the outsiders incarnate." They are outsiders everywhere "except in places that are themselves out of place—the 'nowhere places' that appear on no maps used by ordinary humans on their travels" (Bauman 2004, 80). As a place of containment, the ship becomes a "nowhere place" that folds the sailors within and perpetuates their externality. There is no need for barbed wire or watchtowers around the stranded boat, for its separation from the land secures its out-of-placeness. Discipline, Foucault argues, "sometimes requires enclosure," as it organizes an "analytical space" (1977, 141, 143). The ship stands as the enclosed and disciplined space that harbors the "docile bodies" (1977, 152–156) of the sailors. For the crew the ship becomes another example of heterotopic space, a rerouted home and place of exile, a refuge, a disciplined space, a place of exception, a prison and also a hospital, as the novel unfolds. The image of the static ship and the stranded crew converses with Paul Gilroy's vision of the boat as a mobile signifier in *The Black Atlantic*. The liminal position of the Urus, situated in a middle passage of sorts, emphasizes not the circulation of ideas but rather the persistence of different forms of subservience and colonization, a conceptual continuity with the past that, according to Étienne Balibar (2005, 39), articulates contemporary contacts between immigrants and citizens. Just as there is no need for barbed wire around the ship, those contained within do not need to be shackled either. As Ana Lydia Vega's "Encancaranublado" illustrates, there is a persistent dynamic that assimilates migrants to previous experiences of bondage. A new version of slavery thus returns as a revenant to structure contemporary interactions between immigrants and host countries. The Urus, once again, appears as the UR text that speaks back to a hemispheric racial history, but also as the "you are us," as Silva Gruesz (2003, 67) argues, a cautionary voice against a repeated history of exploitation.

The stasis in time and space is confirmed when, on the third Friday on board, the captain lets the crew quit work early and announces a meeting and a barbecue. After assuring the men that he and the ghost owner are satisfied with their work, he adds that due to the delay in port the owner is unable to pay them. The bright side to the situation, Captain Elias assures the men, is that they really do not need the cash since they are illegal off the ship. Bernardo speaks first to state that the situation is not a blessing. The ship is a swamp of safety and maritime violations and not getting paid was just a great insult. In Bernardo's assessment, the captain is asking them to be slaves. The captain corrects Bernardo claiming that slaves do not get paid, whereas they were going to be paid or the ship was never going to move. Moreover, he argues, the laws protected them, Panamanian law, international laws, United States law. In fact, as stated before, there is only one law on board, the law of the master/captain/owner. As if to placate the possibility of a mutiny, the captain announces promotions for the whole crew. The old man is promoted to *Segundo oficial*. Significantly, the charade creates a zone of indistinction where opposite concepts mean the same. Promotions are the same as demotions; discipline is equal to non-discipline; hospitality is the same as hostility, and lack of violence is a form of coercion. As a hostile abode and as a disciplined space, the ship appears as an open space the migrants are free to leave, for the Immigration Service, the captain reminds them, has nothing against "illegal aliens" leaving. Captain Elias's word, as the embodiment of the law, "affirms itself with the greatest force precisely at the point in which it no longer prescribes anything" (Agamben [1995] 1998, 49). For the crew, the "law demands nothing ... and commands nothing other than its own openness." Paradoxically the "law applies ... in no longer applying, and holds [them] in its ban in abandoning [them] outside itself" (Agamben [1995] 1998, 50). The open possibility that the crew can leave includes them through exclusion and excludes it through inclusion (Cf. Agamben [1995] 1998, 50). Elias's words do not prescribe anything because the men are already ontologically contained and immobilized as "illegals," as already outside the law before they cross any threshold. This reconceptualization allows the Captain to prescribe without prescribing, to command through the very openness of his words. The men are excluded and outlawed, yet they are defined by the law and in a precarious relationship to the law itself (Cf. Downey 2009, 109).

The crew's containment and abandonment are obvious by the end of the summer. The Urus, becomes what Bernardo anticipated, a "dead ship" (Goldman 1997, 106) impossible to resuscitate. Dressed in rags and "increasingly sad eyed, shaggy, and dirty," the crew are described as "young corpses risen from graves" (Goldman 1997, 46). This is the situation the Ship Visitor encounters when he inspects the Urus. Significantly, the section that introduces the Ship Visitor's perspective, entitled "As IS, Where Is," is written in the simple future and the future anterior, with sentences such as "[The Ship Visitor will] board a ship whose name and port of registration will have recently been painted off ... He'll have seen abandoned crews and ships before" (Goldman 1997, 129). The choice of tense is significant, for it inscribes the future within the past, within the journeys of exploitation that have converged on New York Harbor for centuries (Naimou 2015, 51). There is, as Derrida remarks in *Specters of Marx*, the doubtful contemporaneity of the present to itself. The present of the Urus is contemporaneous to a recurrent past and a possible future that folds the boat within a similar pattern of exploitation. Thus the future anterior turns into a boomerang tense that breaks down the boundaries between the past, the present, and the future. Thus time on the boat becomes heterotopic, and opens itself to a variety of heterochronies, in Foucault terms.

This coupling of past and present can be traced in Mark's musings about the crew, a human cargo of what he calls "useless nitwits" (Goldman 1997, 278), of "idiots" codified as inferior, redundant, and disposable. Interestingly, Mark seems to forget that it is through his and Elias's agency that the men are put in such a position. Once transformed into the unprotected and the disposable, the men can be treated as slaves. As Mark thinks to himself, the two men own a "secret slave ship in New York Harbor" (Goldman 1997, 304) whose crew is made up of their "little brown guys, property of Captain Elias Cortés and First Mate Mark Pizarro" (Goldman 1997, 305). The intercalation of the owners' names and Spanish conquistadors illustrates the troubling juxtaposition of times and personas and the recurrence of the colonial heritage in the present. The made-up names speak to a time that is totally out of joint, that is disadjusted, discorded, and anachronistic (cf. Derrida 1994, 25), a time that cancels progress and boomerangs back to the past. At this point of their joint undertaking, however, their "little brown guys" are no longer valuable because their labor is irrelevant and futile. The novel registers the mutation from worthy and exploitable slaves, at least worth feeding, to worthless possessions the owners can forget about and abandon. The process is never decoupled from racism or the heritage of colonialism and slavery. The men are lumped together in a faceless mass that Mark seems to see everywhere: "[E]verywhere he goes he sees them: busboys, McDonald's, even working in pizza parlors now instead of Italians and Greeks" (Goldman 1997, 305). Mark only individualizes Bernardo, whose stories he shares with his girlfriend. The rest of them, he claims, literally fall into the category of zombies (Goldman 1997, 308). Paradoxically, Bernardo, the dissonant voice in the crew, will epitomize the condition of abandoned being, for he can be left to die with no consequences. Mark leaves him at a hospital in the hopes that the hospital staff will cure him and deport him. After all, Bernardo represents the infection that comes from the south and threatens the well-being of the target country. As if to emphasize the contrast between the crew's stagnation and the owner's free movement, Mark takes a plane to Yucatán so he can chill out. His mobility, Like Elias's, is predicated on the immobilization of others.

5   The Outside of the Inside

> One can be inside without being inside, there is an inside in the inside, an outside in the inside and this goes on infinitely
> JAQUES DERRIDA AND HÉLÈNE CIXOUS
> From the Word to Life: A Dialogue between Jacques Derrida and Hélène Cixous

There are no boat mutinies in *The Ordinary Seaman*. There is, however, a carefully staged farce similar to Melville's *Benito Cereno*. In Melville's masterpiece the charade consists in pretending that slavery articulates every minute gesture or social interaction on the San Dominick. In *The Ordinary Seaman* the charade works in the opposite direction. Elias, Mark, and the crew pretend there is no slavery. Elias stages a farce that promises salaries, a proper job, and a protective flag. There are a couple of moments when the tension on the Urus could have led to a mutiny, but the revolt never unfolds and the men return to their subordinate position. What brings the men back to subservience is the fear and the uncertainty as to when they will be definitely abandoned. For six months this not knowing diverts the crew from staging a mutiny against an absent captain. During that time the men navigate different subject/object positions: they have been slaves without literally being enslaved; they are seamen without ever setting sail or being legally so; they are stateless persons without formally losing their citizenship (Naimou 2015, 54). When they find out that Bernardo never went back to Nicaragua, as they were assured by the captain, however, the men take over the ship. The Urus sails even if the statue never walks, thus honoring Bernardo by proving him wrong. Like Babo in Melville's *Benito Cereno*, the men get out of their scripted roles as inferior and as neo-slaves. They concede they did not get very far, but they didn't do too badly (Goldman 1997, 380). As to the rest of the crew, they decided to take a chance and went with Esteban into town.

Like the Puerto Rican that instructs the three castaways in Vega's "Encancaranublado," Esteban acts as the mediator between a community of Spanish speakers and the crew. The young man manages to step off the boat and start a life as an "illegal" refugee on the streets of Brooklyn. Soon enough, he finds a night-shift job in a small chair factory, and is able to extend his own acts of hospitality towards the crew at a time when the captain seemed to have abandoned the ship altogether. He experiences firsthand the kind of limited and conditional hospitality that awaits migrants. He is no longer confined to the ship, yet he will always occupy a variety of spaces that oscillate between inclusion and exclusion, a liminal space that is not sufficiently explained by the dyad in/out (Cf. Mezzadra and Neilson 2012, 62). Esteban's inclusion is also an exclusion that is associated with "varying degrees of subordination, rule, discrimination, and segmentation" (Mezzadra and Neilson 2012, 67). This topography of subjection confirms, as Derrida and Cixous argue, that even if the men are inside the country, they will encounter an infinite number of outsides within the inside. Esteban, like the rest of the crew, is the recipient of what Derrida calls *hostipitality*, the crossing of hospitality and hostility. The realm of *hostipitality* opens a grey area within the nation-state that converses with Mezzadra and Neilson's notion of the in-between. *Hostipitality* occupies the space between the traditional binary of internality *vs* externality, and, consequently, blurs "the clear-cut distinction between inside and outside" (Mezzadra and Neilson 2012, 68). There are, as *Back to Blood*, "Encancaranublado," and *The Ordinary Seaman* show, multiple ways of hostipitalizing the immigrant Other. This hostipitalization is intricately related to the erasure of specificity (of language, of culture, of nationality) in favor of a single racialized otherness, as the Captain in Vega's "Encancaranublado" and as the captain and Mark demonstrate in *The Ordinary Seaman*. The only possible antidote to this master representational logic, as Vega and Goldman suggest, is the nascent Caribbean-Latino Confederacy that Vega places as the epigraph to the story. The survival of the Urus crew and the three castaways is contingent upon a sense of community and brotherhood, on an act of private hospitality that compensates, at least partially, for the lack of public hospitality. Survival, as Esteban and the unnamed Puerto Rican illustrate, is also contingent upon a rereading of the meaning of the Urus as the UR text that encodes a repeated history of exploitation and carries another message, U R Us.

References

Agamben, Giorgio. (1995) 1998. *Homo Sacer: Sovereign Power and Bare Life*. Translated by Daniel Heller-Roazen. Stanford, CA: Stanford UP.

Arteaga, Javier. 2008. "The Cuban Adjustment Act of 1966: More than Forty Years Later a Proposal for the Future." *FIU Law Review* 3 (2): 509–53.

Balibar, Étienne. 2005. *We, the People of Europe? Reflections on Transnational Citizenship*. Translated by James Swenson. Princeton and Oxford: Princeton UP.

Bauman, Zygmunt. 2004. *Wasted Lives: Modernity and Its Outcasts*. Cambridge: Polity.
Butler, Judith and Gayatri C. Spivak. 2007. *Who Sings the Nation-State*. London: Seagull.
Castillo, Debra. 2005. *Redreaming America: Toward a Bilingual American Culture*. Albany: State U of New York P.
Comaroff, Jean and John Comaroff. 1999. "Alien-Nation: Zombies, Immigrants, and Millennial Capitalism." *CODFESRIA* 3–4: 17–26.
Derrida, Jaques. 1994. *Specters of Marx*. Translated by Peggy Kamuf. London and New York: Routledge.
Derrida, Jaques. (1997) 1999. *Adieu to Emmanuel Levinas*. Translated by Pascale-Anne Brault and Michael Naas. Stanford: Stanford UP.
Derrida, Jaques. 2000 "Hostipitality." Translated by Barry Stocker with Forbes Morlock. *Angelaki: Journal of the Theoretical Humanities* 5 (3): 3–18.
Derrida, Jacques and Hélène Cixous. 2006. "From the Word to Life: A Dialogue between Jacques Derrida and Hélène Cixous." *New Literary History* 37 (1): 1–13.
Downey, A. 2009. "Zones of Indistinction: Giorgio Agamben's Bare Life and the Politics of Aesthetics." *Third Text* 23 (1): 109–125.
Foucault, Michel. 1977. *Discipline and Punish: The Birth of the Prison*. Translated by Alan Sheridan. New York: Pantheon.
Foucault, Michel. 2003. *Society Must Be Defended: Lectures at the Collège de France, 1975–1976*. Translated by David Macey. London: Penguin.
Foucault, Michel. 2008. "Of Other Spaces." Translated by Lieven De Cauter and Michiel Dehaene. In *Heterotopia and the City: Public Space in a Post—civil Society*, edited by Michiel Dehaene and Lieven De Cauter, 13–29. London: Routledge.
Gilroy, Paul. 1994. *The Black Atlantic: Modernity and Double Consciousness*. London: Verso.
Goldman, Francisco. 1997. *The Ordinary Seaman*. London: Faber.
Kristeva, Julia. 1982. *Powers of Horror: An Essay on Abjection*. Translated by Leon S. Roudiez. New York: Columbia UP.
Hoffman, Mark. 2009. "Securing the Absent Nation: Colonial Governance in the New World Order." In *Europe and its Boundaries*, edited by Andrew Davison and Himadeep Muppidi, 243–270. Lanham, Maryland, and Boulder, Colorado: Lexington.
Melville, Herman. 1961. *Billy Budd and The Piazza Tales*. New York: Dolphin.
Mezzadra, Sandro and Brett Neilson. 2012. "Between Inclusion and Exclusion: On the Topology of Global Space and Borders." *Theory, Culture & Society* 29 (4/5): 58–75.
Naimou, Angela. 2015. *Salvage Work: U.S. and Caribbean Literatures amid the Debris of Legal Personhood*. New York: Fordham UP.
Nancy, Jean Luc. 1993. *The Birth to Presence*. Translated by Brian Holmes *et al*. Stanford: Stanford UP.
Rosello, Mireille. 2001. *Postcolonial Hospitality: The Immigrant as Guest*. Stanford, Ca.: Stanford UP.

Silva Gruesz, Kirsten. 2003. "Utopia Latina: *The Ordinary Seaman* in Extraordinary Times." *Modern Fiction Studies*. 49 (1): 54–83.

Vélez, Diana L. 1994. "We are (Not) in This Together: The Caribbean Imaginary in 'Encancaranublado' by Ana Lydia Vega." *Callaloo* 17 (3): 826–833.

Vega, Ana Lidia. 1992. "Encancaranublado." In *Cuentos Calientes*, 13–20. México: Universidad Nacional Autónoma, Coordinación de Difusión Cultural.

Webster's Encyclopedic Unabridged Dictionary of the English Language. 1971. Chicago: Encyclopaedia Britannica.

Wolfe, Tom. 2012. *Back to Blood*. London: Jonathan Cape.

CHAPTER 11

Tim Z. Hernandez's *Mañana Means Heaven*: Love on the Road and the Challenge of Multicultural Hospitality[1]

Maria Antònia Oliver-Rotger

Abstract

Tim Z. Hernandez's *Mañana Means Heaven* is a critical rewriting of a biographical episode in Jack Kerouac's *On the Road* featuring the relationship between Sal Paradise and a Mexican girl, Terry. Based on documentary research and on his interviews with Bea Franco after Hernandez tracked her down alive in Fresno in 2010, the novel appeals to truth by referring to real people, places, and facts occurring during the two weeks that Bea Franco spent with Kerouac "on the road" in Los Angeles, and in the agricultural towns of Bakersfield and Selma in the San Joaquín Valley. The story also deals with Franco's trip to Denver in which she tried to locate Jack some months after his departure. Both as a counternarrative of Kerouac's version of the story, as a road narrative (Brigham), and as a counter romance narrative (Illouz 1997, 1998, 2012), *Mañana Means Heaven* focuses on the difficulties of incorporating and relating to difference and contrasts with the ideal of an inclusive, heterogeneous America embodied by the experience of Sal Paradise in Kerouac's novel. The novel is built on both the silence of the literary character of Terry and on the historical silence of Bea Franco who, as Hernandez reveals in a closing narrative frame, denied ever having met or ever welcomed or hosted Kerouac in her hometown. Led by the imperative to respect Franco's memory and that "memory belongs to the rememberer," Hernandez negotiates extensive research, documentary evidence, and the writers' interpretation to construct Franco's hypothetical memory of that episode and reveal the ensuing emotional dilemmas and development of a young migrant woman of Mexican origin. Told from the perspective

---

[1] This article is part of research project "Critical History of Ethnic American Literature: An Intercultural Approach" (ref. FFI2015-64137-P), directed by Prof. Jesús Benito Sánchez and funded by the Spanish Ministry of Science and Technology. Moreover, the author also wishes to thank the COFRE program for international research stays; the Departament d'Humanitats at Universitat Pompeu Fabra for its partial financial support; and the Department of Ethnic Studies at UC Berkeley as well as Prof. Laura E. Perez for making possible the two-month research stay during which it was produced.

of Bea Franco, the story reveals the gender, class, and cultural conditions that restrict the protagonist's access to the masculine realm of relative freedom and privilege of Sal Paradise/Jack Kerouac, as well as the gender norms and social prejudices that make it difficult for Jack to be hosted as a migrant worker. Drawing on Ann Brigham's considerations on the road narrative as a genre where the self seeks to reinvent himself through mobility by engaging with other places, regions, and identity, I will approach the road as a "contact zone" (Pratt) where one's status of guest, host, or stranger is related to one's position or one's understanding of self in relation to place, identity, and culture. The understanding of the road and mobility itself also play a role in the understanding of hospitality, as they may be associated to the transgression and overcoming of boundaries, or to the presence of boundaries and the difficulty of incorporation. In the corresponding episode in Kerouac's work, hospitality is at the expense of the misrepresentation of the other and serves the reinvention of the male character (Brigham, 61). Contrarily, in Hernandez's work, class, racial, and gender boundaries challenge narratives of love, geographical imaginaries, and myths of social mobility, and draw attention to the difficulties of hosting and welcoming the Other. Given the social and gender rift between Jack and Bea that *Mañana Means Heaven* illustrates, Franco's silence may be read as the "emotional residue" of the crude, painful fact that theirs is a story of failed hospitality.

Keywords

Tim Z. Hernandez – Jack Kerouac – Bea Franco – memory – testimony – hospitality – mobility – misrepresentation

1   Introduction

In *Mañana Means Heaven* (2013) Tim Z. Hernandez (1964–) explores the brief relationship the Beat writer Jack Kerouac had with Bea Franco in the late 1940s. Kerouac fictionalized Bea Franco as Terry in the short story "The Mexican Girl," published by *The Paris Review* in 1955, and included in an episode of the second chapter of his now classic novel *On the Road* (1957). A metafictional rendition of this episode, and a fictionalization of historical, documented facts, Hernandez's novel is mostly told from the point of view of the so-called real 'Mexican girl,' Bea Franco. In the preface to the novel, titled "The Last Interview," the Chicano writer muses on the notion of literary lineage after one of his classes on the Beats at Naropa University. As he searches for "something of [himself]" within the pages of *On the Road* (1–2), Kerouac's depiction of Terry, 'the Mexican girl,' conjures up the experience of the writer's mother and grandmother, both strong women who worked in the labor camps of the San Joaquín Valley mentioned in Kerouac's novel. This connection was the beginning of Hernandez's inquiries into the life and whereabouts of Bea Franco. The author's documentary research, including the Kerouac Archive in the New York Public Library, came to a head in 2010, when he found Bea Kozera—Bea Franco when Kerouac met her—alive in Fresno, California, Hernandez's own hometown.[2] The interviews with her inspired the author to write a metafictional revision of the story.

Hernandez's work, as he has said in several unpublished conversations, stems from a literary lineage concerned with the 'margins of humanity.' The fictionalization of the fifteen-day period Bea spent with Kerouac seeks to redress, to rephrase the female character's words in the novel, "all sorts of stuff" people could think about her "going by what [Kerouac had said]" (95). The author's dated foreword and afterword, and the similarly dated episodes in the novel—which correspond to verified historical evidence—establish a chronological connection between the reader's historical time, the author's life and research, and Bea Franco's real life. Bea is thus meant to be a partially historical character whose documented difference and particularity are brought to the foreground to redress the concealment of social relationships behind Kerouac's portrayal of 'the Mexican girl' as a fetishized American Other.

When read against the grain of Jack Kerouac's celebration of racial diversity and his ideal of an inclusive, heterogeneous America, Hernandez's *Mañana Means Heaven* comes forth as a critical re-examination of multicultural hospitality by a twenty first century Chicano "mestiz@ consciousness"[3] sensitive to the fact that "some others are designated *as stranger than other others*" [*sic*] (Ahmed 2000, 6) through fantasies that cut them off from their material history. In the light of Sarah Ahmed's "stranger fetishism" (2000), Jacques Derrida's (1993) definition of the *arrivant*, Anne Bingham's view of the road as a liminal

---

2 According to author Tim Z. Hernandez, neither Bea nor her family were aware that Kerouac based his female character on Bea Franco and that Franco is mentioned in more than twenty studies and biographies on Kerouac. Beatriz Kozera died in 2013 at the age of 92. Throughout 2017 Hernandez shared with me his impressions on the writing and research process prior to the publication of the novel. In July 2017 we met in Fresno, where we visited Bea Kozera's grave in Belmont Memorial Cemetery. I am grateful to Tim for his time and generosity.
3 This is a rewriting of Gloria Anzaldúa's term *"la consciencia de la mestiza,"* which the author introduced in *Borderlands/La Frontera* (1987). The term refers to a contested, shifting Mexican-American or Chican@ subjectivity and to complex self-other dynamics at the rhetorical, imaginative, and historical level. These dynamics stage deep epistemological and ethical tensions in a globalized, transnational American society.

space of transgression or replacement of boundaries (2015), and Eva Illouz's social analysis of the romantic love ideal (1997, 1998, 2012), this discussion will contrast Hernandez's fictionalization of the encounter between Bea and Jack to Kerouac's portrayal of the relationship between Sal and Terry to reveal the ways in which both authors approach the ideal of multicultural hospitality and their related forms of social exclusion and inclusion.[4] In both works this encounter happens on the road, a non-place away from the characters' respective homes. Following the prominence of spatial theory in literary criticism such as Anne Brigham's (2015) and Manzanas and Benito's (2016), the road will be approached as a threshold, a neutral, liminal territory favoring hospitality and the blurring of boundaries between self and other, inside and outside (Manzanas and Benito 2016, 9). In Ann Brigham's spatial approach to road narratives, the 'personal' spaces of the home and the body are considered in relation to the economic and political structures that shape and organize our social and cultural world, and where factors such as race, gender, sexuality, disability, and disease define the boundaries of the identities that are regulated and that may also be transgressed (Brigham 2015, 12). In this analysis of Hernandez's rendition of Kerouac's Mexican-girl episode, hospitality, understood as the potential transgression of boundaries, will be addressed by looking at the ways in which different forms of mobility on the road are related to the subjects' relationship to their places of origin, and consequently, to the ways these places determine their construction of identity and their way of relating to others. *Mañana Means Heaven* is discussed here as a critical rewriting of the romantic episode between Sal and Terry in *On the Road* and as a historical novel about the limits of hospitality. In my reading of Hernandez's and Kerouac's novels the characters' relationship to the road and to space plays an important role in the dynamics of inclusion and exclusion during the first encounter of the protagonists as *arrivants* and their later roles as guests and hosts towards each other. While in Hernandez's work, meeting Jack on the road generates in Bea the hope of physical mobility, the dissolution of social and gender barriers, and the possibility of affective fulfillment and economic opportunity, in Kerouac's work, Sal's engagement with Terry is one out of many chances of temporarily merging with exoticized difference along a free-floating, wandering journey. *Mañana Means Heaven* highlights Jack's role of host/guest as securely located within the nation, and Bea's role as host/"temporary" guest as excluded from

---

4 Kerouac's French-Canadian background, the difficult migration of his family from Québec to the United States, together with the fact that French was his first language, are paramount to his "poetics of exile" and his concern with wandering, travel, and cultural mixing. Such is the argument of Hassan Melehy in *Kerouac: Language, Poetics, Territory* (2016).

the ideal of a hospitable America through three complementary counternarratives:[5] A counternarrative to the ideal of multicultural love; a response to Kerouac's fetishization of the Mexican-American immigrant; and a recasting of Bea's road narrative as an immigration narrative and as a narrative of return. These counternarratives highlight the cultural and racial boundaries that mark "some bodies as stranger than other bodies" (Ahmed 2000, 24) within the nation-state.

2   Hospitality on the Road

American national mottos and metaphors ('E Pluribus Unum,' 'The blood of all nations,' 'A melting pot,' 'A nation of immigrants') underscore the relevance of hospitality in the making of a country whose identity and exceptionality has long been understood in terms of the coming together of individuals of multiple origins who, following the biblical precept of being hospitable to all, should be received and be taken care of (Manzanas and Benito 2017, 20). In *The American Kaleidoscope* Laurence E. Fuchs cites spokesmen for the American nation, George Washington and Lyndon B. Johnson, in his description of the founding myth of American civic culture: The "U.S. was created by God as an *asylum* in which *liberty*, *opportunity* and *reward* for achievement would prosper" [*sic*] (1990, 2). The national imaginary, articulated in terms of the openness and welcoming to many foreign others, has contributed to the dissemination of the ideal of American society as essentially hospitable.

Indebted also to critical approaches to American foundational narratives and myths, Ann Brigham's (2015) spatial approach to mobility in road narratives proposes to read the reinvention of the self through mobility as an engagement with other places, regions, and individuals that reveals gender, racial and class power imbalances. The road becomes, for Brigham, a liminal space or "contact zone" (Pratt 1991, 33) where the assumptions about one's identity and the identity of others come to play, and where one's status of guest, host, or stranger is related to one's position or one's understanding of self in relation to place, identity, and culture. Viewed as a 'contact zone,' the road

---

5   I am using the term *counternarrative* in a double sense: That of questioning dominant, hegemonic narratives about culture through myths and ideologies, and that of re-writing history and proposing an alternative local or marginal history, which implies, as well, the notion of counter-memory and alternative literary practice (Lankshear and Peters 1996, 2). As will be inferred from my reading of Hernandez's work, rewriting a story and prying into the "margins of humanity" necessarily leads to a critique of hegemonic meta-narratives.

enables us to approach hospitality as a set of social and cultural relationships linked to multiple meanings of mobility and ways of interacting with places, individuals, and cultures, and therefore, to focus on hospitality as a successful or unsuccessful incorporation/understanding of the Other and his/her needs beyond the 'guest/host' binary. As a threshold, a liminal space, or a utopian non-place, the road allows travelers, wanderers, migrants, and run-aways to be, simultaneously, strangers, hosts, and guests. On the road, both hosts and guests are *arrivants* who may surprise and interrogate each other "enough to call into question, to the point of annihilating or rendering indeterminate, all the distinctive signs of a prior identity, beginning with the very border that delineated a legitimate home and assured lineage, names and language, nations, families and genealogies" (Derrida 1993, 34). In opening to the Other and his needs, *arrivants* may potentially abandon their previous notions of belonging and community, as well as the safe boundaries of the space where their identities are established. Mobility along the road involves the absence of a safe, controlled space in which one receives or is received. As a liminal space, the road calls attention to the status of both guests and hosts of those who meet, and reminds us of how both *guest* and *host* have the same origin in the Latin word *hospes*. Brigham's spatial approach to mobility as an engagement and incorporation of the Other in road narratives, offers a pertinent corrective to the notion of the road as "outside the social order" or as "undifferentiated openness" (Bingham 2015, 10) and frames the meetings between strangers within the power relations individuals establish at different scales in their encounters. This approach is in step with Sarah Ahmed's argument that an ethics of hospitality that "responds to each other *as if they were other in the same* way" [sic] eludes "the finite and particular circumstance in which I face up to others" (2000, 16). The ways one relates to the home, the local and regional environment, national and global territories determine the ways one associates with all those others encountered along the road. Mobility functions differently for certain individuals in specific historical moments, being an indicator of distinct forms of engagement with the Other, and of the multiple social and cultural factors impinging upon this engagement.

3 Love on the Road and the Transgression of Boundaries

Both Kerouac's and Hernandez's novels express the romantic coming together of self and other—Terry and Sal; Bea and Jack—in such a way that the transgression of social boundaries through love is associated with spiritual transcendence or, as Eva Illouz terms it, with "a secular access to the experience of the sacred" (Illouz 1997, 285). In *On the Road,* after Sal and Terry have overcome their mutual anxieties about a sexually degraded relationship—they suspect each other of being, respectively, a pimp and a whore—Sal describes their exhilaration after love-making as feeling like "two tired angels of some kind, hung-up forlornly in an LA shelf, having found the closest and most delicious thing in life together" (85). In *Mañana Means Heaven,* Hernandez describes the lovers' encounter as "a melding of separate worlds, universes in heated collision [...] their lives with all the certainty of a kite broken free of its strings" (72). In both novels, love on the road heightens the feeling of escape and liberation from all social, temporal barriers, a feeling which we may associate with mutual hospitality and with the western mythology of love as described by Illouz: A social alchemy blind to status and wealth, "the hope that lowly conditions can be transmuted into noble ones and that love can unite people otherwise separated by barriers of class, nationality and birth" (1997, 247).

In *Mañana,* Bea's encounter with Jack leads to her empowerment and self-affirmation, while also raising the possibility of an egalitarian understanding of gender relations and sexuality. If, as Adrienne Rich has said, "the body is the geography closest in" (1986, 212), Bea's sexual pleasure is the first step towards healing the scars of bodily control and abuse by her father and husband, a liberated desire representing the female version of independence and free choice. The sexual encounters with Jack will acquire the stature of political acts of freedom and autonomy, which reveals Hernandez's generational legacy to second-wave feminist thought and Chicana and women of color feminism.[6] The charming, well-intended, adventurous Jack of Hernandez's novel is in tune with the feelings and emotions Bea Franco expresses in the letters addressed to Jack Kerouac that the Chicano author reproduces with minor corrections as part of the narrative.[7] His portrayal of Kerouac is, as Hernandez stated in unpublished interviews, to Bea's credit, as the letters Bea sent after their separation clearly show a woman in love hoping to join her beloved soon. The love story spells out the romantic charm that a sweet, good-looking, educated college boy like Kerouac must have had for the daughter of Mexican field workers. Hernandez builds upon Kerouac's curiosity and openness to difference, his literacy, his alluring stories, and his admiration for American transcendentalist

---

[6] I am referring to the contributions of well-known writers and academics such as Cherríe Moraga (1981, 1983), Gloria Anzaldúa (1981, 1987), and Norma Alarcón (1981, 1988) among many others.

[7] Unless the reader looks at the copyright statement of the novel, these letters are not identified as "real" until the end of the novel. Hernandez is not as explicit about his blurring of history and fiction as he is in his later book *All They Will Call You* (2017).

Henry David Thoreau. Jack's mystical approach to life as all-encompassing recalls Thoreau's welcoming of railroad workers, Native Americans, and simple villagers into his notion of American hospitality: Anyone's little chores, Jack says, invoking Thoreau in *Mañana*, "play some role in the giant picture" (60). Jack is thus characterized as a welcoming figure, not only because of his views, but also because he listens, a quality also in keeping with Thoreau's relishing in speech, listening, and soft, thoughtful conversation in his memoir of simple life in nature, *Walden* ([1854] 1882). This, in turn, endows the character of Jack with what Eva Illouz calls "romantic competence," a competence "marked by access to linguistic, cultural, economic and time resources" that strengthens the intimacy and emotional bonds between partners (1997, 248). The "timidities" that Sal Paradise sees in the eyes of Terry in Kerouac's work (1957, 81) are now, in Hernandez's rendition of the story through Bea's voice, a characteristic of Jack (31). His quietness and reserve and his interest in her personal story contrast with the brutality of Bea's husband and the sexual advances of "the men at the campo or in the fields, who, upon hearing of Bea's troubled marriage, often tried luring her with sweet talk of money and sexual escapades" (31). Bea's fears that "maybe she'd said too much" (60) about herself to Jack are as much an expression of the need to communicate as of the "gender gap in romantic competence" in Bea's working-class environment (Illouz 1997, 279). Hernandez characterizes Kerouac as a man to whom Bea can confide her feelings, which suggests the "freedom and equality within the romantic bond" (Illouz 2012, 9), a "modern intimacy" that "includes the verbal disclosure of emotions but also and maybe even more crucially the act of sharing such emotions with a partner, with an expectation that the emotional self be revealed and laid bare to get 'support' and recognition" (Illouz 2012, 38).

Hernandez's novel pries into the dilemmas and contradictions arising from Bea's social transgression in her illicit extra-marital affair with a white, educated man like Jack, which sets her against the roles of dutiful mother, wife, and daughter she is expected to perform. Attached to her relationship with Jack is the possibility of migration, social mobility, and affective stability, all of which are embodied by the "geographical imaginary" of New York (Gregory 1994) and the related ideas that "there's a heap of money waiting to be made in a city like [it]" (18), and that "in the end it would be better for the kids" (72). Bea has opened her mind to the free spirit her host/guest Jack proclaims, but her need for reassurance that Jack's invitation "is for real" (131), and that, in her brother's words, Jack will not "shortchange" her (131), suggests the social gap between the characters. Indeed, Sal Paradise's idea of love as expressed in *On the Road* blends together what, Illouz, drawing on Anthony Giddens, calls "confluent love"—a relationship of mutual consent and fulfillment in which durability is not a major concern (Illouz 2012, 13)—and "the affair"—which she considers to be the paradigm of the postmodern condition where novelty is the major source of satisfaction (Illouz 1998, 176). Tim Creswell tells us that "[o]ne theme connected to the mobility of Sal and Dean is a lack of commitment to traditional forms of sexual relationship" (1993, 257). The following exchange between Jack and Bea in *Mañana* may be read ambivalently in the light of what Cresswell describes as "the jazzman's search for IT—something momentary rather than permanent" (1993, 255), the postmodern view of love as a series of temporary encounters (Illouz 1998, 170), and Kerouac's emphasis on living in the moment. Bea is certainly referring to her temporary separation from her children, whereas Jack might well be thinking about her 'temporary' stay in New York: "You know, Jackie, as long as I tell myself this is just temporary, I feel okay about going, you know, about leaving the kids./Yep, temporary is right" (83).

4   Confronted Fantasies and Mobilities

Jack Kerouac's *On the Road* builds on the myth of the open road, which, like the American frontier, connects physical mobility to adventure, material improvement, knowledge, and new experiences.[8] Kerouac's novel stands as "an example of a rebellious 'popular culture'" (Cresswell 1993, 251) where physical mobility, wandering around, and taking unanticipated routes goes hand in hand with a spiritual journey into the heart of a waning American essence, away from a corrupted bourgeois, capitalist America. The road favors the encounter with alternative ways of life which are envisioned as more hospitable and genuine because they are without the hypocrisy, moral constraints, and material aspirations of middle-class America. However, as Robert Holton has said, there is a paradox in searching for freedom in the lives of the people affected by marginalization and social injustice (1995, 265). Despite his nonconformity to middle-class conventional culture, Kerouac was oblivious to the real conditions of the social and racial minorities whose difference he valued as more authentic. Hernandez's novel is indebted to Jack Kerouac's (Sal Paradise's) openness to others in that it highlights the American subjects of physical mobility, the transgression of boundaries, and the opening of new frontiers of

---

8 The symbolic perception of the road as an extension of the American frontier myth first outlined by Fredric Jackson Turner ([1893] 2008), results in the perception of the road as an unrestricted space of freedom and escape outside the constraints of society and history. Like the frontier, the road symbolizes openness and constant change.

experience and relationship. Unlike Kerouac's novel, however, *Mañana Means Heaven* draws attention to the irreconcilability of Jack's and Bea's respective fantasies of hosting and being received by the other, and it depicts the cultural conditionings warding off the incorporation of the real 'Mexican girl' as a guest in Jack's individualistic road. On the one hand, Hernandez's novel undermines Kerouac's/Sal Paradise's fantasies of the 'Mexican girl' by highlighting the gender and sociocultural differences between the characters. On the other, it shows Bea Franco's difficulties in being Jack's host and Jack's possible guest to be inseparable from her status as a female field-worker of Mexican origin: the general suspicions aroused by the white college boy in the community of Mexican workers, the conflict between traditional womanly duties and her wish to break away from them, the loyalty to her children, and her fears that Jack may ultimately not want to receive her in New York.

The spectral, fantastic view of the Other is to be found in the word *ghost*, meaning *stranger, guest, host*, and reminds us once again of the etymological origins of all those words. This meaning encompasses the outcome of the encounter of strangers as it is affected by the spectral, fantastic view of the Other that Sarah Ahmed describes in *Strange Encounters* (2000) as "stranger fetishism," which ontologizes strangers and cuts them off from their embodied difference (9). In *On the Road* Sal Paradise engages with 'the Mexican girl,' Terry, as an ontology through fetishization (7), for she is a "native" whose difference is dissolved into the familiar and "claimed as that which makes the nation be itself" (Ahmed 2000, 16). Sal approaches 'the Mexican girl' following his fantasy of the hospitable Other that is part of his imaginary national ethos. He "goes strange" (Ahmed 2000, 16) through a fantasy of incorporation into his identity of the "negro cotton picker" and the "Mexican" (Kerouac 1957, 97–98). The title of Kerouac's episode when it was published as short story, "The Mexican Girl" (1955), highlights the ethnic origin and infantilization of his lover, a "stranger fetish," a reminder of the differences we must celebrate in our postmodern times (Ahmed 2000, 4) and that Kerouac's masculine character nostalgically pines for. Hernandez clearly undermines this fetish through the cover of *Mañana Means Heaven*, which features a photograph of the real 'Mexican girl,' Bea Franco, who is visibly a 'white' woman. In Hernandez's work Bea identifies herself as "American," which takes to task her 'Mexican' ethnic difference as portrayed by Kerouac: She is a native from LA, speaks to Jack in English, knows little Spanish, and her cultural referents are those of American popular culture. Bea is said to be *"tan blanquita, que parece hija de la Joan Crawford"*[9] (22).

---

[9] "So white that she could be Joan Crawford's daughter" (My translation).

In her mother and aunt's eyes, she is not as '*jodida*' (fucked up) as Mexicans or *pochos* because she can pass as white. She is not the object of suspicion in places where "No Mexicans, Japs, or Okies" are allowed (98). Since her face is "the pale color of nectarine meat and big green lettuce-leaf eyes" (8), Mexicans riding the same train as Bea's family as they are all being deported to Mexico within the 'Great Repatriation' campaigns of the 1930s, wonder why a girl with her complexion should be in the boxcar at all. The chance that Bea's beauty and skin may be a passport to social mobility has its limits, for, as her female relatives skeptically say, "as long as your last name is Mexican, sounds Mexican, or even looks Mexican, you get tossed in with the rest" (8).

The title of Hernandez's novel contains a clear allusion and reply to the Mexican ethnic fetish of 'the Mexican girl' in Kerouac's novel and short story. In *On the Road,* Sal Paradise builds on the stereotype of the relaxed Mexican and says: "It was always *mañana*. For the next week that was all I heard—*mañana*, a lovely word and one that probably means heaven" (84). 'Mañana means heaven' is a metafictional statement about limits, a literal reference to the barriers erected by linguistic ignorance or stereotyped cultural fantasies of the Other, and to Sal Paradise's distance from the culture and language of the Mexican Spanish-speaking community that so fascinates him. In Hernandez's novel, Jack and Bea have an apparently blithe argument about jazz singer Peggy Lee in which Bea says she is made "sick" by her pseudo-Hispanic accent, "all that *Mañana, mañana* junk [...] and all that *caramba* and *ehs* and *ahs*" (122). Bea is here a mouthpiece of the critique implicit in Hernandez's title, which alludes to Sal Paradise's spurious translation of the Spanish word *mañana*. This use of the foreign language corresponds to what anthropologist Jane Hill has called "mock Spanish," an invented Spanish with total disregard for grammatical coherence, which shows both a fascination with and a complete ignorance of the those who speak it. 'Mock Spanish' goes hand in hand with the racialized stereotypes of the Spanish-speaking Other and serves to construct the white, English-speaking public space as normative (Hill 1998, 680–689). Sal Paradise's fascination with the language, way of life, and customs of the Other is an echo of what scholars have seen as Kerouac's celebration of diversity and difference without any "real cultural understanding" of those he encounters (Holton 1995, 266), what Sarah Ahmed views as a construction of strangers as having "a life of their own (being strange)" that can be assumed and taken on by the subject "going strange" (Ahmed 2000, 16).

If *mañana* possibly meant *heaven* in Kerouac's fiction of multicultural hospitality, in Hernandez's work *mañana* does mean *heaven* for Bea figuratively, as she anticipates emotional happiness and upward social mobility in her hopes of being hosted by Jack. In this second metaphorical sense, then, the title contains an answer to Sal's/Jack's cultural and social misrecognition and failure of hospitality, as it is the expression of Bea Franco's desire for a better future for her and her children in New York with Jack, a desire clearly present in the real letters to Jack Kerouac transcribed literally in the novel. The fact that Bea's ambitions are not West but East, that her being on the road is mostly to escape the constraints of gender, class and environment, and that her journeys' main motivations are escaping her husband, rejoining her children, and finding a better life, point to a confrontation between her idea of mobility as relocation or immigration and the notion of mobility as travel, wandering, exposure to multiple experiences and spiritual growth featured in Kerouac's *On the Road*. This confrontation highlights the gendered conditioning of Bea and Sal's/Jack's respective subject positions within mobility. In her resolution to flee a stifling home environment and open herself boldly to the possibility of change, the character of Bea Franco in *Mañana Means Heaven* has the adventurous, free, unrestrained spirit of Kerouac's masculine character. Unlike Kerouac's novel, however, Hernandez's focuses on the racial, class, and gender differences between his protagonists and on Bea's unwillingness to admit this difference in her unsuccessful pursuit of Jack. Hernandez's brief incursion into Jack's point of view suggests that he thinks of Bea's stay in New York as a temporary visit: Seeing and moving "in the middle of it all," "where the action is," "Empire State Building, Central Park," and showing off Bea to his friends "as a rare specimen" (148). In contrast, Bea associates New York with a harmonious domestic environment. As suggested by her vision of a "yellow light spilling from a single window" that she imagines to be "their home, their little warm glow in the big cold city" (124), and the references to Jack's mother in her letters, the journey to New York stands for a permanent relocation, a chance for her to reinvent herself, through an affective relationship with Jack based on trust and stability. The final episode in *Mañana*, featuring Bea's despairing search for Jack in Denver, highlights Jack's abandonment of his guest, and his failure, as host, to respond to Bea's needs.

On the Road features Terry's son briefly as part of Sal's domestic fantasy as head of a Mexican family. In Hernandez's work, however, Bea's life and identity revolve around her two children, little Albert and Patsy. Her escape from a violent husband to LA, her time with Jack in the city, her subsequent plans to travel with him to New York, and her later trip to Denver hoping to find him, all involve leaving Albert and Patsy behind temporarily. Being away from her husband and children breeds increasing anxiety and distress. Bea is initially resolved to "split," "kids and all" (73), but fear of her husband's reprisal, memories of their first years of marriage and of his change of character after his time at the war front, an inkling of compassion for him, and her sense of responsibility and love for her children elicit doubts and remorse. Bea Franco's real letters to Kerouac reproduced as part of the novel convey a desire to move away from her environment, and a simultaneous awareness of all the impediments that stand in her way. In a letter sent after her husband has forsaken her and the children, she says: "I love to travel and if I had the chances you have, I would do the same (If only I had been born a man.) Or at least if I didn't have my children to tie me down. I really wouldn't mind the children so much if I had a husband to go with them" (191). The attachment of identity to place is present in Hernandez's approach to LA and the San Joaquín Valley as 'lived' realities embedded in real historical conditions. Hernandez describes the environment from the viewpoint of those who work it, depend on it for subsistence, and are seasonally threatened with deportation. Bea sees "the miserable campo" as a "sad den of discarded prayers" (72), "a small city of gray tents strewn sloppily in mud, separated by heaps of trash and discarded mattresses" (107). In *On the Road,* Sal Paradise finds field labor exhausting and is struck that families cram together in small tents, but his idealization of field workers keeps him at an emotional distance from their social conditions. Despite acknowledging hardship, he idealizes the domestic setting at the tent with Terry and her child, "[his] baby and [his] baby boy," and field work as the "life's work" that has turned him into a "a man of the earth" (94–97). Sal goes on drinking sprees with Terry's brother and their friend Ponzo, relishes in Mexican food and comes to consider himself 'Mexican' like the workers he is living with. He describes himself as hosted by and incorporated into a communal environment that fits his fantasies of the ideal American 'It.' At a moment of exhaustion, he prays for himself and the Mexicans whom he patronizes as "the little people I loved" (97). His descriptions of loud, disturbing night scenes in LA are also devoid of social content and are collapsed into a general description of the city as the "loneliest," "most brutal" of cities populated by "beats" (90). These descriptions give prominence to Sal's despondent mood and draw attention to what Toni Morrison calls, "the dramatic polarity" created by skin color or otherness, "the projection of the not-me," "a fabricated brew of darkness, otherness, alarm and desire that is uniquely American" (1992: 38). In contrast, Hernandez's partially omniscient narrator reflects a nuanced awareness of racial relations and the feminization of migrant labor in the city: He refers to the racial and ethnic tensions caused by Japanese attack on Pearl Harbor and the Zoot Suit Beatings (37). He also mentions Japanese flower sellers, Spanish-speaking nannies, Mexican supermarket and Irish factory owners, and women of diverse origins who queue up for jobs at sewing factories where they take their children (51, 52, 61).

Mañana also queries the integration of Jack among migrant workers and the hospitality of the Mexican American community that Kerouac's fictional alter ego claims in *On the Road.* In Hernandez's novel Jack is soon viewed with suspicion, not only by Bea's family and husband as the reason for her illicit relationship, but also by the workers as a possible *lechuza* (109, 142), a white person who has infiltrated the community, who might give Mexican workers away for deportation, or a possible union organizer whose presence would cause landowners to deport workers for fear of accusations of worker abuse.[10] Amidst a tense, fearful atmosphere, the novel features the beating and humiliation of Jack by a group of migrant workers led by Bea's husband, an incident that leads Bea to ask Jack to leave for New York where she will later join him. In *On the Road,* Kerouac devises a hasty closure of Sal's romance with Terry upon the sudden advent of the cold, an argument about Terry's supposed neglect of her child, Terry's arguments with her family, and Sal's general impression that "he was feeling the pull of his old life calling him back" and that "everything was collapsing" (98). Sal sees Terry as "resigned" to his departure and to the idea that "she would never make it" to New York (101). Contrary to this Terry's passivity, in Hernandez's counter-narrative Bea comes across as a proactive, resilient host who protects her lover by insisting on his departure, propels a major plot turn in the story, and is determined to travel to Denver and New York to meet him.

5 "Not Only in My Eyes Is Paradise:" the Failure of Multicultural Hospitality

The epigraph to *Mañana Means Heaven,* taken from Beatrice's words in Dante's *Paradiso* reads: "Turn and listen: not only in my eyes is Paradise" (4). In the context of Hernandez's novel, Beatrice's words entreat the reader to look beyond the love story as described by Sal Paradise, to free Bea's image from the gaze of Jack Kerouac, the writer, and Sal Paradise the character, and to listen to the intricacies of Bea's own story. Hernandez's immigrant road novel follows Bea's

---

10   The Bracero Program, established in 1941 as a response to labor shortages, kept wages low and prevented the creation of Mexican labor unions. Growers were interested in cheap labor, such as that provided by Mexicans and *Okies* (Oklahoma dust bowl immigrants). In 1941, growers broke the strike of the AFL: They made redundant the strikers and recruited dust-bowl refugees. The strike of the National Farm Workers Union in the mid-1940s was broken when DiGiorgio Fruit Company brought in undocumented workers (Rosales 2000, 218–219). Deportation raids only occurred when harvest time was over. In *Mañana Means Heaven* Bea's brother Alex tells Jack about the farmers' stratagems to avoid a raid when it was called before the fruit had been picked up: They called a blackout to prevent the migrants' deportation (130).

several journeys back and forth from Selma in the San Joaquín Valley, to LA, to Denver, and then back to Selma again. *Mañana Means Heaven* concludes with Bea's trip to Denver to work as a waitress and her excruciatingly fruitless search for Jack. After leaving her children behind, moving to the city, and trying to find him in vain, Bea realizes that Jack's face "might not have been what she wanted at all" (211) and goes back home, a wiser person, loyal to her children and herself, now finally able to understand the smile in her father's face upon his return to Mexico after deportation, a sign of the comfort of going back to the safety of home. Writing "beyond the [romantic] ending" (DuPlessis 1985, 4) and concluding his road narrative as a 'narrative of return,' *Mañana Means Heaven* is an initiation narrative or *Bildungsroman* in which the protagonist comes to terms with her position as a female worker of Mexican origin in the United States. The love for and engagement with Jack does not lead to the social mobility, freedom, and dissolution of boundaries promised by the road, the myth of multicultural hospitality or the "euphoric pole" (marriage) of the Bildungsroman plot (DuPlessis 1985, 4), but to Bea's renewed self-awareness of where her community, her family, and her place are. The novel thus brings to the foreground the discordant, irreconcilable sociocultural realities of Bea Franco and Jack Kerouac/Sal Paradise, and the failure of Jack/Sal to respond to the needs of a potential guest who has hosted him temporarily. The road, a space where social transgression, hospitality and the breakdown of barriers between guest and host occurred, becomes, in the last episodes of the novel, a lonely road Bea travels in her futile search for Jack in Denver. Jack's return to New York, his sparse correspondence, and ultimate silence reinstate the social, cultural, and gender barriers between the lovers.

The temporary encounter between Bea Franco and Jack Kerouac enabled the white college boy from the East Coast to boost his incipient career as a writer by publishing a story inspired by a short affair with a hospitable 'Mexican girl,' a fact that remained unknown to Bea Kozera until 2010. In the author's afterword to the novel, a section titled "Memory Belongs to the Rememberer" [*sic*], Hernandez tells us that, in his interviews with him, Kozera denied ever having seen or met Jack Kerouac (224). Her denial, in apparent contradiction to the consent she gave the author to fictionalize her story, stands as a coy gesture that may contain a denial of the ideal of multicultural hospitality implied in Kerouac's version of the story, a refusal to acknowledge the fantasy of love across class and ethnic boundaries that inspired Kerouac's episode, as well as a realistic, empowered affirmation of who she has become despite all odds. Through the fictionalization of what could have been Bea Franco/Kozera's take on the story, Hernandez both identifies and challenges Kerouac's fantasies of the Mexican Other underlying his celebration of American racial and ethnic diversity as well as the underlying ideal of multicultural inter-racial love. In doing so, he vindicates a literary legacy grounded in the silenced stories that buttress national literary myths and the American ideal of multicultural hospitality.

References

Ahmed, Sarah. 2000. *Strange Encounters: Embodied Others in Postcoloniality*. London and New York: Routledge.

Alarcón, Norma. 1981. "Chicana's Feminist Literature: A Re-Vision Through Malintzin/or Malintzin: Putting Flesh Back on the Object." In *This Bridge Called my Back: Writings by Radical Women of Color*, edited by Gloria Anzaldúa and Cherríe Moraga, 182–190. New York: Persephone.

Alarcón Norma, Ana Castillo and Cherríe Moraga. 1988. *Esta puente mi espalda: Voces de mujeres tercermundistas en los Estados Unidos*. San Francisco: Ism.

Anzaldúa, Gloria. 1987. *Borderlands: The New Mestiza*. San Francisco: Spinsters/Aunt Lute.

Anzaldúa, Gloria and Cherríe Moraga. 1981. *This Bridge Called my Back: Writings by Radical Women of Color*. New York: Persephone.

Brigham, Ann. 2015. *American Road Narratives: Reimagining Mobility*. Charlottesville: U of Virginia P.

Cresswell, Tim. 1993. "Mobility as Resistance: A Geographical Reading of Kerouac's 'On the Road.'" *Transactions of the Institute of British Geographers, New Series* 18 (2): 249–262.

Derrida, Jacques. 1993. *Aporias*. Stanford, California: Stanford UP.

DuPlessis, Rachel Blau. 1985. *Writing beyond the Ending: Narrative Strategies of Twentieth-Century Women Writers*. Everywoman: Studies in History, Literature, and Culture. Bloomington: Indiana UP.

Fuchs, Lawrence E. 1990. *The American Kaleidoscope: Race, Ethnicity and the Civic Culture*. Hanover and London: Wesleyan UP.

Gregory, Derek. 1994. *Geographical Imaginations*. Cambridge, UK: Blackwell.

Hernandez, Tim Z. 2013. *Mañana Means Heaven*. Tucson, AZ: U of Arizona P.

Hill, Jane H. 1998. "Language, Race, and White Public Space." *American Anthropologist* 100 (3): 680–689.

Holton, Robert. 1995. "Kerouac among the Fellahin: On the Road to the Postmodern." *Modern Fiction Studies* 42 (2): 265–283.

Illouz, Eva. 1997. *Consuming the Romantic Utopia Contradictions of Capitalism*. Berkeley and Los Angeles, CA: U of California P.

Illouz, Eva. 1998. "The Lost Innocence of Love: Romance as a Postmodern Condition." *Theory Culture & Society*. 15 (3–4): 161–186.

Illouz, Eva. 2012. *Why Love Hurts: A Sociological Explanation*. Cambridge, UK: Polity.

Kerouac, Jack. 1955. "The Mexican Girl." *The Paris Review* Winter (11): 9–32.

Kerouac, Jack. 1957. *On the Road*. New York and London: Penguin.

Lankshear, Colin and Michael Peters. 1996. "Chapter 1: Postmodern Counternarratives." In *Counternarratives: Cultural Studies, Critical Pedagogies in Postmodern Spaces*, edited by Henry A. Giroux, 1–40. New York and London: Routledge.

Manzanas Calvo, Ana María and Jesús Benito Sánchez. 2017. *Hospitality in American Literature and Culture: Spaces, Bodies, Borders*. New York and London: Routledge.

Melehy, Hassan. 2016. *Kerouac: Language, Poetics, Territory*. New York: Bloomsbury USA.

Moraga, Cherríe. 1983. *Loving in the War Years: Lo que nunca pasó por sus labios*. New York: South End Press.

Morrison, Toni. 1992. *Playing in the Dark: Whiteness and the Literary Imagination*. Cambridge, MA, and London, UK: Harvard UP.

Pratt, Mary Louise. 1991. "Arts of the Contact Zone." *Profession* 91: 33–40.

Riaño, Peio H., and Javier Cercas. 2013. "Empecé a escribir tarde por culpa de Borges." *El Confidencial* [Accessed online on August 8, 2017].

Rich, Adrienne. 1986. *Blood, Bread and Poetry: Selected Poetry and Prose 1979–1985*. New York and London: W.W. Norton & Company.

Rosales, F. Arturo. 2000. *Testimonio: A Documentary History of the Mexican American Struggle for Civil Rights*. Hispanic Civil Rights Series. Houston, Texas: Arte Público.

Thoreau, Henry David. 1882. *Walden*. Boston MA: Houghton, Mifflin and Company.

Turner, Fredrick Jackson. (1893) 2008. *The Significance of the Frontier in American History*. New York and London: Penguin.

CHAPTER 12

"Parasites in a Host Country": Migrants, Refugees, Asylum Seekers and Other Zombies in *The Walking Dead*[1]

Ángel Mateos-Aparicio and Jesús Benito Sánchez

Abstract

In an interview published by *Forbes* on December 26, 2016, Jared Kushner, Donald Trump's son-in-law and head of Trump's presidential campaign data management, explained how he used sophisticated computer tools to identify voter blocks by looking at what TV shows they were following. He mentioned specifically that his research had shown, for instance, that *The Walking Dead* TV series was popular among people worried about immigration, which consequently made them preferred targets for Trump's frequent anti-immigration rants.

Regardless of whether or not this information had a real impact on the 2016 presidential campaign, what this anecdote revealed is actually a new insight into the interpretation of the figure of the zombie, which has until now been associated mostly with the rebellion of mindless masses. Seen in this new light, the post-apocalyptic America in which *The Walking Dead* is set is a country under siege by hordes of immigrants whose main and only purpose would be to feed on American flesh. Significantly, the immigrants that in most cases entered the country as guest workers—itself an oxymoron, since a guest that is made to work ceases to be a guest—now slip into the position of parasites. Immigrants, refugees, and asylum seekers are often envisioned as guests of the host nation-state. The inadequacy of the immigrant as guest metaphor has been explored by Mireille Rosello in *Postcolonial Hospitality*. Immigrant workers, the critic clarifies, are not to be regarded as guests for they are simply hired (9). Although the concept of the working guest dismantles the image of migration as an uncontrollable tide or invasion at the threshold of the nation-state, the image of the migrant as parasite crystalized in the American imaginary throughout the twentieth century. The discourse of nativism, from Proposition 187 in California to campaign promises in the

---

1 This chapter is part of research project "Historia Crítica de la Literatura Étnica Norteamericana: Una Aproximación Intercultural" (FFI2015-64137-P) funded by the Spanish Ministerio de Economía y Competitividad and of the European Project "Hospitality and European Film" 2017-1-ES01-KA203-038181 directed by Prof. Ana Mª Manzanas Calvo.

2010's, create the image of the immigrant as parasite sponging off the welfare of the United States. All kinds of social illness, from this perspective, can be attributed to invasive foreign bodies (Inda 2000, 47). J.X Inda, for example, traces how nativist rhetoric transformed the Mexican immigrant in particular into a parasite intruding on the body of the host nation, "drawing nutrients from it, while providing nothing to its survival and even threatening its well-being" (47). The nation-state is thus depicted as a living organism that gracefully and generously allows the entrance of an alien, a zombie, who, in turn, endangers the wellbeing of the host, transformed into an abused and endangered host; or, more precisely, into a hostage. The alien Other, the stranger, the immigrant, Inda states, "are often construed as threats to the integrity of the nation" (2000, 48).

The few not-yet-transformed inhabitants have to survive in enclosed, walled communities that defend them from the 'walkers': Hershel's farm, the jail, Woodbury, Terminus, Alexandria. As the protagonists migrate from one to the other in their fight for survival, they encounter different groups of humans who either offer hospitality or show aggression: Hershel, Woodbury and the Alexandria community are societies seeking to incorporate and assimilate newcomers; whereas groups like the Terminus community and the 'Saviors' either reject or exploit others, zombies, and humans alike.

The aim of this paper is thus to delve into the series' representation of the diverse, complex attitudes to immigration based on the characters' readiness to show hospitality to its full consequences, and to establish an association with the US and worldwide immigration policies resulting from these conflicting ways of relating to others.

Keywords

zombies – hospitality – bare life – refugees – *The Walking Dead*

1 Introduction: Zombies at the Gates

In the very first episode of the popular TV series *The Walking Dead* (2008-), "Days Gone By" (S1 E1),[2] Sheriff Rick Grimes (Andrew Lincoln), the story's main character, wakes up alone in a hospital after a prolonged coma induced by a shot wound inflicted while on duty. As he comes out of the hospital, he is baffled by the images of death and destruction he sees as he roams the empty streets of his hometown in search of his family. Still unable to comprehend

---

2 In order to facilitate the references to the long list of seasons and episodes, we will henceforth follow this format: (S(eason)X E(pisode)X).

that the dead have come back to life, he is unaware that his life is at risk, as the zombies are dangerous predators, desperate for human flesh. He is saved by Morgan Jones (Lennie James), who takes him in and gives him shelter and food in his own home, where he lives with his young son Duane. Morgan soon realizes that he also must provide Rick with a detailed account of what has happened: the advent of the zombie apocalypse. Without this opening act of absolute hospitality, Rick would not have survived. By admitting a total stranger to his home, Morgan initiates a long list of acts of hospitality that pervade the narrative of the renowned AMC zombie show, as most characters find themselves personally accepting, offering, or denying hospitality both as individuals and as members of communities of survivors. Only in the first season, Rick also receives help from Glenn (Steven Yeun), who leads him to his group of survivors where Rick finally finds his wife and son. After living in what seems like a refugee camp, Rick's group travels to a government facility where they are taken in by the only surviving scientist, Dr. Jenner, who regales them with food, drink, hot showers, and warm beds, the very staples of good hospitality (S1 E6). In time, Morgan himself will become the guest of a man named Eastman in an episode where the theme of hospitality is paramount (S6 E4).

This initial act of hospitality is repeated in the following seasons, which follow this basic pattern and recurrently narrate Rick and his group's quest for a safe haven, a fortified enclosure where they can feel free from the zombie threat. Under the spectral invasion, the human survivors of the zombie apocalypse are driven out of their homes, thus becoming refugees in their own country, displaced people that are forced to migrate in order to stay alive. In their wanderings, Rick and the other members of his 'family'—as they refer to themselves in the show—will often confront walls, fences, and closed doors, as if they were unwelcomed refugees, immigrants who must suffer the hostility of the communities they encounter. On other occasions, they reach what they perceive as secure, empty, or vacated strongholds, or are alternatively taken in by other survivor communities who are not reluctant to admit strangers. Similarly, when established in relatively safe sanctuaries, Rick's group will often be compelled to decide whether to offer hospitality to strangers who have undergone the same ordeals or to begin a confrontation with other survivors that will inevitably lead to the loss of their community and the resumption of their wanderings in hostile territory.

The Walking Dead thus reflects the current debates on immigration in the relation between zombies and humans as well as in the interplay that the zombie threat triggers among the different survivor communities. The zombie is portrayed as an alter ego of the immigrant/refugee that both endangers and reinvigorates the sense of community among the surviving humans, whose exchanges are depicted as acts of (in)hospitality towards each other. This chapter will explore how, in the microcosm of the narrative, the constant interaction among the different survivor groups in the story symbolizes the complexity of international relations and population movements in the contemporary global scenario, thus complicating the easy, one-sided view of immigration. The repeated appeal to unconditional hospitality in the series plays a major role, insomuch as the story is a succession of encounters with strangers where offering and receiving hospitality is key to survival. The willingness to accept complete strangers into one's own home and family, we claim, symbolizes the public discussion of the policies towards incoming populations at national and global levels, as the human survivors alternate between their position as immigrants, refugees, or displaced people and their stance as members of safe and prosperous communities that reject aliens.

Interlaced with these collective acts of hospitality—and hostility—are a multitude of occasions where individuals help each other; nevertheless, we will explore mainly the narrative intervals where hospitality is offered or denied collectively, since a detailed description of all acts of individual welcoming and generosity would require more space than this chapter can provide. After a brief review of the different interpretations of the zombie as fictional expression of Western anxieties over capitalist exploitation, consumerism, and mass immigration, the discussion pursues the analysis of the main locations where collective hospitality is offered and accepted in the series—Hershel's farm, the prison, and Alexandria—as well as those that represent hostile attitudes to newcomers: Woodbury and Terminus.[3] It is our claim that the followers of *The Walking Dead* are exposed to a very complex and ambiguous representation of the debates over immigration and refugees. Even if they identify themselves with the major characters in the story—Rick and his 'family'—and reject any metaphorical link with the zombies due to their inhuman appearance, viewers have to witness the anxieties of a group of desperate, displaced refugees, and assess difficult decisions like killing a defenseless visitor because it poses a potential threat. Due to the variety of hospitable or hostile attitudes represented in the narrative, as well as to the continuous instability and reversibility of the roles of host and guest, viewers are not offered simplistic or definite solutions to the issue of how to deal with a stranger/immigrant/refugee/asylum seeker,

---

3 Other friendly communities like Hilltop and the 'Kingdom,' and the hostile party of 'Saviors' have been left out of this analysis mainly because the relationship between Rick's group and all these societies is still in progress and the interpretation may be subject to changes as new events may affect the narrative.

and are constantly challenged by and confronted with the consequences of the characters' decisions.

2 Children of the First Globalization: from the Zombie as Slave to the Zombie as Illegal Immigrant

Since its initial appearance in the film *White Zombie* (1932) the zombie has been represented in a variety of forms and in diverse cultural products and, as a consequence, has acquired a wide range of symbolic meanings and accumulated various unfixed interpretations. The zombies in this early movie are portrayed as reanimated corpses deprived of will that toil endlessly to do their master's biddings. These empty bodies are different from George A. Romero's depiction of the zombie as what Kevin Boon calls a "flesh eating ghoul" (2007, 35) and from their more recent version as raging, biting predators in the film *28 Days Later* (2002). These abundant and changing figurations and the diverse situations in which zombies appear are emphasized by Ryan Lizardi, who highlights the flexibility of the representation of zombies when he states that the zombie is a malleable figure that can be described as a "universal signifier" (2013, 89) that can convey a diversity of meanings, and also as a "utility tool" (91) that can be used with different critical intentions, not all of them counter-hegemonic. Kevin Boon has proposed up to seven categories of zombies according to a variety of characteristics—mainly their ability to reason and speak (2007, 36), but the representation of the zombie changes continuously, altering the perception of what they signify, so that no reading of the zombie has become dominant or final. Like most monstrous figurations of the human, the zombies mirror (exaggeratedly) human behavior and are born in the context of the encounters with other peoples fostered by colonialism (Slusser and Rabkin 1987, viii). The zombies also appear in liminal situations, where a culture—perhaps still unconsciously—perceives a disquieting threat, regardless of whether the menace is posed by human enemy or a natural, supernatural, or notional entity. Insomuch as this chapter focuses on the reactions of the humans confronting the aliens rather than on the zombies' potential inner realities, no reference to speaking or articulate zombies will be made. Only the mindless, soulless versions will be contemplated, as they tend to symbolize the exploitation, oppression, and subjugation of humans by other humans: the zombie slave, the zombie ghoul, and the apocalypse zombie, all of which converge, we will argue, on the zombie as immigrant, which is predominant in *The Walking Dead*.

The zombie has been read first and foremost as a representation of the capitalist exploitation of the working classes. This is the initial, widely accepted interpretation of the zombie as slave that is evident in the critical approach to the film *White Zombie* (1932). The story is set in the West Indies (presumably Haiti) where a local mogul, Legendre, uses an army of revived corpses as zombie workers. At this stage, the undead are domesticated workers, automatons who will never be aware of their precarious existence, symbols for worker exploitation under capitalism. As Kyle Bishop states, in *White Zombie* the undead represent the "unthinking, unaspiring, non-threatening" laborers that are the object of desire for the capitalist ethos (2008, 146).

The analyses by Steve Shaviro and Stephen Harper delve into this interpretation of the zombie as a slave worker. In "Capitalist Monsters" (2002), Shaviro describes zombies as a "modern myth" (282), perfectly suitable to illustrate the "human face of capitalist monstrosity" (288). As a metaphor for the proletariat, zombies represent the capitalist alienation, exploitation, and sub-humanness of the working class; their putrefying bodies symbolize the prolonged spiritual decay of the lower classes. In "Zombies, Malls and the Consumerism Debate" (2002), Harper contends that zombies can also be interpreted as consumers, and points out that the presence of the monster reveals the "exploitation that enables consumerism" (7). Both works, however, focus not on the examination of *White Zombie*, but mainly on George A. Romero's *Dawn of the Dead* (1978). The second of Romero's zombie movies is set in a shopping mall, hence the reference to consumerism. Romero's zombies crave human flesh; their voracious appetite will begin to represent the Western mindless and unstoppable desire for material goods. Taking into account that in the modern, globalized world the alienated producers are located mainly in the Third World, Shaviro suggests that the zombie may represent the duality of most First-World inhabitants: on the one hand, they are alienated by the capitalist system as workers; on the other, they consume what vast masses of poorly paid workers in Third-World countries produce and are therefore unwilling, unaware accomplices of their exploitation. Romero's version of the zombie may thus be seen as a decomposing retaliation of Third-World subjugated workers against First-World mindless consumers.

It is therefore quite evident that the birth of the zombie as a myth should not be understood outside the postcolonial context, as Bishop argues in "The Sub-Subaltern Monster: The Imperialist Hegemony and the Cinematic Voodoo Zombie" (2008). Bishop suggests that "the creation of the zombie is a direct result of imperialism and cultural synthesis—the natives of French and West Africa and emancipated slaves from the United States were relocated to the West Indies [...]; their tribal beliefs were 'integrated' with Western Christian ideology" (2008, 147). The decaying, horrific, undead ghouls, Bishop points out, can and must be analyzed as products of the colonial gaze and of imperialist ideology and discourse within the framework of the representation of otherness.

This vision of the zombie as a representative of oppressed and exploited otherness, however, is neither fixed nor permanent. As on other occasions, the flexibility of the zombie as a symbol endures. In their "Zombie Manifesto" (2008) Lauro and Embry claim that the flesh-eating ghouls are hybrid entities perfectly equipped to undermine the humanist notion of the subject, as well as global capitalism and its colonial undertones. For Lauro and Embry, zombies are boundary figures that threaten the stable notions of subject and object, living and dead, master and slave (2008, 90). In this sense, they believe that the zombie is a much more threatening and unsettling figure than Haraway's notion of the cyborg (a hybrid between human and machine), which clearly inspires their analysis. The zombie would, therefore, be the epitome of the post-colonial, post-modern, posthumanist human being, an unabating challenge to traditionally contradictory notions such as the mind/body, the individual/collective, the master/slave, and the (re)producer/consumer dichotomies.

Other than referring back to colonial and postcolonial experiences, one could add that the invading zombies could also represent the masses of immigrant workers, refugees, and asylum seekers that turn up at the gates of affluent northern countries. The connection between immigrants and zombies is a recurrent motif in popular culture, as Fillol et al. have recently shown in "El imaginario del zombie cinematográfico" (2016), which focuses on recent films that depict the conditions of the Calais camps populated by immigrants and refugees who await their opportunity to cross the Channel and settle in the UK. These migrants describe themselves as zombies, neither really alive nor completely dead. In Papastergiadis's "Hospitality and the Zombification of the Other" (2013), the guest workers of the West appear as spectral individuals outside the social contract, who haunt the host nation as zombies. The anxiety over the migrant's arrival, Papastergiadis claims, is refigured as an invasion of the home country, with the subsequent fear that "migrants, like zombies, possess an insatiable appetite and predatory behavior that will destroy all forms of social control" (155). In "Alien-Nation: Zombies, Immigrants, and Millennial Capitalism" (2002), Comaroff and Comaroff delve into how the notion and the term "zombie" has been used in post-apartheid South Africa to refer to guest workers, who are perceived as a threat to domestic labor due to their readiness to accept extremely hard living conditions—akin to Agamben's notion of "bare life" (Agamben 1995). While zombies seem to be born, at least in the first instance, of colonial encounters—where local worlds engage and interact with imperial economies—the contemporary immigrant experience is clearly the child of the rapidly changing conditions of work under capitalism, "conditions which rupture not just established relations of production and reproduction, but also received connections of persons to place, the material to the moral, private to public, the individual to the communal, past to future" (Comaroff and Comaroff 2002, 796). In "Zombie Trouble: Zombie Texts, Bare Life and Displaced People" (2011), Jon Stratton reinforces and expands the relationship between the zombie monsters and migrant populations, since the zombie metaphor should include, the author contends, not just the illegal immigrants that reside in rich countries, but also asylum seekers, refugees and all kinds of displaced people. Stratton suggests that the growing "anxiety over border protection" and the "fear of being overwhelmed by displaced people" (266) is represented metaphorically in the fictional depiction of the human groups who defend their space against the zombie invading hordes. Whereas the zombie might emerge as a representation and response to the social and material disturbances triggered by the colonial encounter, the contemporary view of the immigrant as threat, as foreign invader, responds to the new conditions of production and circulation of capital and workers resulting from the rapid rise of neoliberal capitalism on a global scale. Whether interpreted as metaphors of cheap labor, illegal immigrants, refugees, or asylum seekers, zombies are monstrous representations of the oppression and exploitation resulting from colonialism and the global expansion of the capitalist economic mentality, which, as David Harvey suggests (2000) repeatedly generates inequalities among the different regions and countries so that the global market may survive (60).

The recent revival of the invasion narrative in the US, whether openly as zombie narrative, or more elusively connected to the presumed immigrant threat, shares the view of the national self as constantly under siege by invisible and spectral forces, namely parasites, which are already present in the national territory. Rather than merely conveying the fear of occupation or conquest of the national territory by external forces, these narratives reflect on the risk of contamination from within, of the self-losing its humanity and being reduced to 'bare life.' Most formerly stable categories of identity—like the binaries of live vs dead, us vs them, citizen vs stranger, host vs guest—collapse, demanding a re-entrenchment of the self against a massive, formless, rootless invader already present within us. This invader as parasite threatens to undermine the national self from the inside, draining its rapidly diminishing resources.

Zombies have the ability to proliferate like a virus, like a parasite that infects the host and destroys its individuality, turning the host into a multitudinous replication of itself. After Romero's version of the zombie, it is conventional knowledge that if bitten by a zombie, humans will be inescapably *zombified*. In this sense, the zombie disease provokes the dissolution of difference and the assimilation of otherness through contagion: once returned from a death caused by what appears to be an infection, all zombies are radically equal. Individualism and questions like race, gender, ethnicity no longer matter in the zombie mentality. The zombie bodies decay and do not show signs of difference. As Edward Comentale suggests, the zombie is the very expression of "disincorporation, decentralization and dissemination" (2014, 278). Like a virus, they cannot live without the host. Like a virus, they modify the host's nature in order to survive. The term "diasporic virology," coined by Comentale, describes the way zombies expand, as if they represented an "African infection" (2014, 308) that will contaminate the West. Zombies are "disabled, diseased, displaced" (Perron qtd in Hamilton 2013, 55), and desperate (for human flesh); and yet, their numbers never seem to diminish.

As a similar image of viral infection, the representation of the migrant as parasitical invader crystalized in the American imaginary throughout the twentieth century. The discourse of nativism, from Proposition 187 in California to campaign promises in the 2010s, created the image of the immigrant as parasite sponging off the welfare of the United States. All kinds of social illness, from this perspective, can be attributed to invasive foreign bodies. J.X. Inda, for example, traces how nativist rhetoric transformed the Mexican immigrant in particular into a parasite intruding on the body of the host nation, "drawing nutrients from it, while providing nothing to its survival and even threatening its well-being" (2000, 47). In the presence of the parasite, "the host is himself the food," slowly consumed by the intruder (Hillis Miller 1979, 219). Papastergiadis claims the refugee, in particular, fits the image of "dangerous parasite" who "not only carries unknown health risks, but also has an insatiable appetite for welfare payments" (2006, 433). The nation-state is thus depicted as a living organism that gracefully and generously allows the entrance of an alien, a guest of sorts, who in turn endangers the well-being of the host,[4] transformed into an abused and endangered victim; or, more precisely, into a hostage. The alien Other, the stranger, and the immigrant, Inda states, "are often construed as threats to the integrity of the nation" (2000, 48). The allegedly parasitized country is a particular kind of nation-state, based on a stable vision of who is always at home and who is not. Racialized nativism, from this perspective, creates the image of the immigrant as a threat to the welfare of the population.

---

4 The biological sense of host as plant or animal having a parasite dates back to 1857. Significantly, Spanish uses the word *huésped*, 'guest,' to refer to plants or animals hosting or harboring a parasite, testifying to the instability and reversibility of the roles of guest, host, and parasite. Both the host and the parasite form part of a symbiotic relationship that dismantles stable categories and establishes new forms of exchange.

According to this rhetoric the immigrant always gains in the exchange, where the host nation-state always loses (Inda 2000, 51), for immigrants are customarily depicted as unstoppable waves of parasitic aliens "set on (ab)using our social services, refusing to 'assimilate,' and adding to the crime and social pathologies" (Suárez Orozco qtd in Inda 2000, 50) of the countries in which they arrive.

But what is a parasite? As defined by the *Online Etymology Dictionary*, a parasite is "a hanger-on, a toady, person who lives on others," from Middle French *parasite* (16c.) or directly from Latin *parasitus* 'toady, sponger,' and directly from Greek *parasitos* "one who lives at another's expense, person who eats at the table of another," from noun use of an adjective meaning "feeding beside," from *para*—'beside,' and *sitos* 'food.' 'Para,' J. Hillis Miller explains, is an antithetical prefix "signifying at once proximity and distance, similarity and difference, interiority and exteriority, something inside a domestic economy and at the same time outside it, something simultaneously this side of a boundary line, threshold or margin, and also beyond it, equivalent in status and also secondary or subsidiary" (1979, 219). This ambiguity at the linguistic level echoes in the liminal position of the parasite, in and out, occupying a space that dispels the traditional opposition between outside and inside. The host and parasite create a new exchange and order through a new symbiotic relationship, for "there is no parasite without a host. The host and the somewhat sinister or subversive parasite are fellow guests beside the food, sharing it" (Hillis Miller 1979, 220). Parasitism for M. Serres is the central fact of existence. Without the interruption of the parasite, a system would be entirely closed from the outside. Without the parasite, there is no relation (1982, 8). This is the symbiotic relationship we focus on and explore in the analysis of *The Walking Dead* in the next section.

The invaders, whether ostensibly as undead zombies, or elusively as an undefined mass of immigrants, provide the opportunity for the American ideology to test itself. As parasitical Others flood the spaces of the American (individual and national) self, unlikely hosts are displaced and forced to occupy the position of hostages. The zombie, as representation of the immigration fear, is the invasive foreign body who contaminates the secure spaces of the nation-state. Lacking in national or ethnic markers, zombies know no boundaries, yet their placeless mobility blurs the secure boundaries of others. Under their intervention, the secure emplacement of the self is revealed under erasure. Ideas of home and belonging are equally suppressed, and the individual is made to feel unhomed, homeless, or trapped in "an unbounded state of global roaming" (Papastergiadis 2013, 166). The zombie subverts the biological and political notions of American individuality, while questioning the American capacity to respond adequately to the presence of the Other within, to give hospitality to an alien Other whose nature is threatening and unknown.

3 'I'm Going to Ask You Three Questions': the Apocalypse, Zombies, Parasites and the Law(s) of Hospitality in *The Walking Dead*

The post-apocalyptic world of *The Walking Dead* envisions the United States as a country in which a myriad of zombies has occupied the territory, overthrown the government, and forced the remaining surviving humans to abandon their homes and cities and become refugees. The long-feared infiltration by innumerable, desperately hungry, barely alive immigrants has suddenly become a reality. In the series, the zombies have actualized the hypothetical scenarios that appear in the debates about nationalism and immigration. The zombies behave like parasites that have occupied a host country and survive by literally consuming its previously abundant resources, as well as like a viral infection that has transformed the individual cells of the national body into replicas of the virus. Curiously enough, the very term used to refer to the zombies in the series, 'walkers,' is quite revealing, as it is related to notions such as 'wanderer,' 'wayfarer,' 'exile,' or 'immigrant.' Furthermore, one of the major consequences of this contagion/consumption/invasion is that the locals have become 'walkers' themselves, expelled from their homes, unable to enroll in productive activities anymore, and forced to survive by scavenging. It is uncertain whether the phrase *The Walking Dead* is applied to the zombies or to the human survivors, who would in time also come to regard themselves as 'walkers,' as Rick Grimes himself points out: "This is how we survive. We tell ourselves we are the walking dead" (S5 E10).[5] Together with the fact that all humans in the story learn that they will inevitably turn into zombies when they die, the identification of both humans and zombies as 'walkers' is aimed at avoiding readily-made, simplistic assumptions about the radical otherness of the undead. The walkers have spread everywhere in the United States of *The Walking Dead*, and are shot on sight by the survivors, thus literalizing Eduardo Mendieta's vision of the US-Mexico border as a "killing zone" (2017, 95) and his suggestion that the border has expanded to occupy the whole notional territory of the United States. As he explains, "[t]he border has become virtual, deterritorialized, and introjected into the homeland" (2017, 89).

---

5 Patrick Hamilton, who analyzes mainly the graphic novel on which the television series is based, notes that this is also a significant moment in the book's story (2013, 49).

The series' walkers are not the fast running ravenous monsters of Danny Boyle's *28 Days Later* (2002) nor the undead that show a tiny spark of intelligence and ability to handle tools in George Romero's *Land of the Dead* (2005), which seem to represent better the "millennial" zombies that emerge after 9/11 and are connected to a "crisis culture" that has dominated the beginning of the twenty-first century (Birch-Bayley 2012, 1137). These twenty-first-century undead have proved to be attuned to the quick pace and bleak outlook of a *zeitgeist* dominated by anxieties over mass immigration, contagion, contamination, terrorism and biological warfare, or the fear of natural disasters. The zombies that cause the collapse of the US government and society in *The Walking Dead* are slow and dumb and show neither individuality nor initiative. In this sense, they continue to represent the First-World worker/consumer and the Third-World tame worker/threatening immigrant dichotomies. But they also are products of their time and draw attention to the zombie apocalypse and to the social dynamics of the human survivors after the zombie apocalypse. In fact, in "The Zombie as Barometer of Cultural Anxiety" (2007) Peter Dendle suggests that the coming of the zombie apocalypse should not be understood only negatively, since it also appeals to 'fantasies of liberation' like the survivalist movement (2007, 53–54) and responds to a discontent with the status quo.[6] In this sense, the zombie apocalypse would seem to be like the opportunity to escape from modern anxieties and begin a new, simpler life. Bishop (2009), Sutler-Cohen (2011), Kozma (2013) and Comentale and Jaffe (2014) mention, with variations in their analyses, this influence of the survival narrative in millennial zombie stories. Nevertheless, this somewhat positive reading of the collapse of "technological modernity and transnational capitalism" (Canavan 2010, 434) is countered by an interpretation of the rise of the undead as a philosophical (and therefore intellectual) failure (Vacker 2013, 160), an interrogation of the 'future' of late capitalist hegemony (Canavan, 433), a technological renunciation (Kozma 2013, 142), a preparation for the realities of harder lives for the new generations (Bishop 2015, 20), or even a collapse of the utopian/dystopian binary (Moreman and Rushton 2011, 117).

It is therefore clear that the 'millennial' zombie narratives have shifted the focus of attention onto those who have survived the end of the world. This has reinforced the active reflection on the nature of social, political, and economic organization, as the audiences follow the struggle of the human survivors to rebuild a viable society. Without the protection of the national government,

---

6   The interpretation of disaster as an expression of discontent with reality is one of the staples of the genre and was suggested in one of the first critical approaches to disaster fiction. See Susan Sontag, "The Imagination of Disaster" *Commentary* 40.4 (Oct 1965), 42–48.

however, the US social structure splits into a mosaic of wandering groups and settled, fortified communities that constitute a microcosm for the representation of the tensions between asylum seekers and the individuals belonging to prosperous societies. As Daniel Drezner suggests in *Theories of International Politics and Zombies*, "[n]arratives about the living dead use small communities and families as their unit of social analysis" (2011, 15).

The individual and collective acts of hospitality in the series are thus aimed at providing a deeper insight into the individual and social implications of the encounters with Others, a reflection on the pertinence of the national laws of hospitality, and finally a meditation on the connection between these specific laws and a more universal, global, ethical, and unconditional Law of hospitality. This conceptual distinction between the 'laws' and the 'Law' of hospitality is one of the tenets of Jacques Derrida's reflection on the question of hospitality. The fictional world of *The Walking Dead* seems to actualize the Derridean duality and to erase the distinction, as the lack of a political structure makes the 'laws' of hospitality inapplicable or irrelevant. All encounters in the series are trapped between the impossible Law of unconditional hospitality and the absent laws in the face of a disappearing state. In this situation, the individuals' reactions to the presence of the Other is neither regulated by established laws, nor deterred by the fear of legal reprisals. The characters have to either act out of respect for a universal, absolute, self-imposed ethics, or they must assess the potential hostility of the foreigner on an individual basis, as there are no guidelines to distinguish between desirable and undesirable strangers provided by the government. Their responses vary from a generous willingness to help the strangers, to a form of cannibalistic hospitality, epitomized by the inhabitants of Terminus. Similarly, accepting hostile visitors means embracing the possibility that they become parasitical guests in the community that offers them hospitality. What is perhaps original in the series is that the narrative recognizes the humanity of the groups of desperate displaced refugees, so that the variety of hospitable or hostile attitudes represented in the narrative, as well as the continuous instability and exchangeability of the role of host and guest, complicate simplistic, unethical solutions to the question of how to deal with an immigrant/refugee/asylum seeker. The viewers are urged to understand that the role of host can be easily substituted by the role of guest, the guest thus becoming the host's host or, as Derrida would put it, "[t]hese substitutions make everyone into everyone else's hostage. Such are the laws of hospitality" (Derrida [1997] 2000, 125).

When on the road, Rick and his 'family' move like refugees that have escaped from a zombie invasion (as it happens in Hershel's farm) or from human attack (as it occurs in the prison), and behave like displaced people looking for a safe haven that would put an end to their wanderings. When confined inside what they perceive as secure locations, they introduce strict rules for admitting other humans into their sanctuary. After Rick is welcomed to the party of campers where his wife Lori, son Carl, and friend Shane have been trying to survive, the group abandons their original camping location and begins a journey to a governmental facility that is unable to provide shelter. In the meantime, Rick is accepted and will finally become the leader at a great price: he is forced to kill his rival Shane (S2 E12).

The confirmation that the government has collapsed puts the group on the road again, where they will first experience collective hospitality as they become guests at Hershel's farm. The way Rick and his group 'penetrate' the boundaries of Hershel Greene's (Scott Wilson) property is purely unintentional: one of Hershel's relatives accidentally shoots Rick's son Carl, who is taken in and saved from death by Hershel himself. As a benevolent landowner, Hershel offers hospitality to Rick's party, who set up camp and are allowed access to water and food. Curiously enough, Hershel's land has not been invaded by the walkers, as if to represent American exceptionality—the farm itself may be read as a symbol for the traditional, rural America. Nevertheless, conflict soon arises, as Hershel does not allow firearms on his property, something Rick's group sees as a mistake due to the zombie threat. When pushed by the others to convince Hershel, Rick repeatedly retorts: "This is his land," and also "We're guests here" (S2 E4). Although Hershel warns Rick that there may be an end to hospitality when he states, "I need you and your group gone by the end of the week" (S2 E2), the group finally take control of Hershel's farm. In the end, the farm is overrun by walkers and Hershel's surviving family joins Rick's group—therefore as guests—in their wanderings. Hershel complains, "It's my farm," to which Rick replies, "Not anymore" (S2 E13).

A similar pattern of hospitality can be found in the ensuing fortified homes occupied by Rick's group. After vacating the farm, they find a building complex where security is guaranteed: a prison. Although initially its connotations diverge from the notion of hospitality, as it implies a forced seclusion, the prison offers Rick and his group the fences and the strong walls they think they need to keep the undead at bay. Ironically, it is a fortified place, a gated community that promises freedom inside (Canavan 2010, 436), or an allegory of modern life (Lizardi 2013, 98). Nevertheless, the jail is not vacant, as a company of inmates still survive inside thanks to a pantry full of food and medical supplies. Rick and the others soon take over the prison—disregarding the inhabitants' rights—killing one of the prisoners who seems hostile to the newcomers, and making the prison their home. The unfriendly prisoner complains, "It's my house, my rules," to which Rick retorts: "We took down those walkers, this prison is ours" (S3 E2). In fact, their own appropriation of the prison, like their attitude on the farm, can be considered as a parasitical invasion.

Once settled in the prison, however, Rick's community seems to open up to the possibility of offering hospitality to others. A group of wanderers that includes important characters like Tyreese (Chad L. Coleman) and Sasha Williams (Sonequa Martin-Green) find their way into the prison, where they find shelter. The question of whether they should be offered hospitality initiates a conflict inside Rick's 'family.' Hershel, who still represents the good Southern host, tries to convince Rick that they should be allowed to stay, even if it seems dangerous to accept strangers inside their stronghold. But Rick is adamant, and sends them on their way—a decision he will regret later on. Tyreese and his party, on the other hand, had considered taking over the prison for a while, but Tyreese is reluctant to abuse the hospitality already received and speaks about defending 'decency' (S3 E9). As a consequence, Tyreese and the others, once rested and fed, leave the prison and find hospitality in Woodbury, the community that acts as a mirror of Rick's society in the third season. The Governor's hospitality, however, is not genuine but perverted, as we will discuss in more depth below. At the end of the third season, Tyreese and the other citizens of Woodbury, the Governor's stronghold, are taken in by Rick's society and are received in the prison as a group of refugees. Consequently, season four depicts a community of 'citizens' living in the prison, where they become increasingly threatened both from the inside (an infectious disease) and from the outside (increasing numbers of walkers at the fences). It is during their period in the prison that Rick's group devises the 'three questions' they use to evaluate anyone who they think could or should be accepted.[7]

The last example of a hospitable and sympathetic community in the series is Alexandria. Even the name has a utopian appeal. As was the case with Hershel's farm, the community living in Alexandria had escaped unscathed from the zombie apocalypse due to their isolation and to the fact that they have strong walls. Alexandria is again the representation of an affluent society in the context of deprivation that the series depicts and has implemented a policy of active search for refugees that qualify as members of this community, strongly

---

[7] The three questions are: 'How many walkers have you killed?' 'How many humans have you killed?' 'Why?' The 'candidates' are not expected to answer negatively to the second question, as they would seem insincere; nevertheless, their motives for killing other human beings are crucial. This ritual seems to mock Derrida's notion of absolute, unconditional hospitality: "Pure hospitality consists in welcoming whoever arrives before imposing any conditions on him, before knowing and asking anything at all, be it a name or an identity 'paper' " (Derrida 2005, 7).

supported by Deanna Monroe (Tovah Feldshuh), leader of this clean and well-supplied community. One of Alexandria's members, Aaron, goes on errands with the sole purpose of offering hospitality (shelter, food, security) to wanderers he finds outside the town's walls. Rick's group is initially distrustful of Alexandrians' real intentions, possibly as a result of their previous experience with other communities like Woodbury and 'Terminus,' where the offer of hospitality and sanctuary had become a nightmare. Offers of hospitality have to be weighed and cannot be readily accepted, as Rick explains to Deanna: "[out there] It's survival at any cost [...] They measure you by what they can take from you. By how they can use you to live" (S5 E12). In contrast, Deanna's attitude is optimistic and represents a hospitality without objections or limits, as she is willing to risk everything in order to integrate Rick's 'family' into their community. Conversely, Rick appears rather as a parasitical guest. In a conversation with Carl, who expresses doubts about Alexandrians' ability to defend itself, he declares: "If they can't make it, then we'll just take this place" (S5 E12).

Planning to appropriate the host's possessions is just an example of the abuse of extreme, pure, impossible hospitality, one that will turn the guest into the host. Rick's newcomers progressively take over Alexandria. In the story, this is presented in a positive light, as Alexandrians do not seem ready to cope with the brave, new, violent world of zombie infestation. In this sense, the willingness to offer hospitality and accept refugees and immigrants is seen from a constructive point of view, as it makes the communities—Hershel's family, the prison, Alexandria—more flexible and better adapted to the changing and threatening outside conditions. In contrast, societies like Woodbury and Terminus, which imprison or exploit newcomers, have to face destruction and dissolution. As it happened in the prison, the demise of Alexandria is caused by the coincidence of a zombie and a human threat: a great horde of walkers appears and puts pressure on the walls while a group of predatory, parasitical survivors who call themselves the 'Saviors' discover the community and intend to assimilate it.

If Hershel's farm, the prison, and Alexandria are considered temporary safe havens by Rick's group, the communities presented negatively in the series are those that deny or pervert the custom and the right to hospitality. During the time Rick's 'family' dwell safely in the prison, another prosperous community acts as a counterpoint to the jail: Woodbury. Run by a sadistic, dictatorial leader who calls himself the 'Governor' (David Morrissey), the Woodbury community finds and offers hospitality to Andrea, one of the members of Rick's group stranded after the zombie's attack on Hershel's farm. The prospect of a safe, clean, and well-supplied community is initially appealing, until Michonne realized that Woodbury is more a prison than an open community.

The Governor's crooked sense of hospitality is a sign of his inner perversion, as well as of the corruption of Woodbury, which resembles a totalitarian state where torture, rapine, and exploitation are commonplace. The town is run by fear of a zombie attack on the walls. In a sense, Woodbury may be read as a dictatorship founded on the acceptance of ever more restrictive regulations on liberties and civil rights caused by a constant anxiety over border protection and terror of inner threats. As an example, when the conflict between the Governor and Rick's group arises, the former calls Rick's friends 'terrorists' (S3 E8). The application of repressive policies does not only include newcomers, but ends up affecting everyone in the community. Woodbury is, therefore, an example of feigned hospitality, one that conceals exploitation and coercion of strangers by an oppressive system that commits the biggest crimes against hospitable behavior: denial of the right to continue the journey and appropriation of the guest for the host's benefit. The contrast with Hershel's generosity and Alexandria's solidarity is quite evident and revealing.

The most inhospitable social attitude in the series, however, lies in another of the various communities to be found by Rick's group in their wanderings: Terminus. Perhaps intentionally named after the Roman god that marked and protected the borders of the Roman Empire from barbarians (Manzanas 2007, 1–5), the community that populates Terminus is sinister and terribly inhumane. When the prison is attacked by the Governor and finally overrun by zombies, Rick's 'family' are forced to escape and disband. The different units soon begin looking for each other. They see the Terminus posters and come to the conclusion that if the others have seen them, their most probable destination would be this seemingly hospitable community. Terminus placards advertise an offer of hospitality. They promise that Terminus is a 'Sanctuary for all' and that 'Those who arrive survive.' Together with these mottos, posters display a map with the route to follow. The prospect of a friendly reception and a hearty meal, no questions asked, must have seemed irresistible to the multitude of wanderers in search of a safe haven. The Terminus community probably counted on this, as their intention is to lure as many human survivors as possible to their trap. As soon as the newcomers arrive to find open gates, they are led to a railroad freight wagon—reminiscent of the Nazi trains that transported the victims of the death camps—where they are incarcerated until slaughtered and consumed. Unaware of this, but distrustful of the Terminus people, the remains of Rick's group trespass the stronghold's fences, where they are offered a warm welcome only to be violently confined in the wagon soon afterward. The cannibalistic hosts of Terminus reverse the tradition of hospitality: instead of opening up their collective space to the visitor, allowing the guest to enter and leave at will, the people at Terminus deliberately plot to imprison them; instead of offering the guests a meal, the guests themselves become the meal.

When they discover the truth, Rick and the others deny the cannibals' humanity. Daryl (Norman Reedus) declares: "They ain't people" (S5 E1). According to the series logic, this is not too far from the truth. If the essential difference between humans and zombies is that walkers eat human flesh, then the division between the Terminus inhabitants and the undead can be overlooked: the Terminus people are but a specular image of the zombie. The Terminus community deliberately and calculatedly advertises its hospitality to attract refugees, migrants, and other displaced people with the sole intention of remorselessly exploiting them, as if to represent how the First World first promises sanctuary to migrant populations that later find themselves consumed, abused and cannibalized. The perversion of the laws of hospitality is complete: rather than be parasitized by unidentified visitors, Terminus citizens are hostile hosts that devour the guests regardless of whether they are inimical or friendly.

If welcoming the unknown that comes from the outside is what allows both the self and the nation to define themselves, *The Walking Dead* reflects on the politics of incorporation and rejection of the *unheimlich*, the spectral Other that enters the community and "threatens to contaminate or dissolve its identity" (McNulty 2007, viii). As the expression of anxiety over mass immigration and as allegories of a complex and controversial reality, the zombies in the *Walking Dead* confront viewers with the fear of the arrival of thousands of immigrants and refugees at the borders of developed countries. The series plays with the double nature of the immigrant, as life-force and death threat, as cannibalized Other and parasitic invader, both encapsulated in the single image of the contemporary zombie. Figuring the invasive others as unconscious zombies, rather than working migrants, allows for a more complex exploration of the American politics of hosting and hostility in the welcoming of others. Followers of AMC's renowned show must confront the harsh if fictional consequences of denying hospitality and evaluate, after a more cautious reflection, the real and potential risks of more relaxed immigration policies.

References

Agamben, Giorgio. 1995. *Homo Sacer*. Stanford: Stanford UP.
Birch-Bayley, Nicole. 2012. "Terror in Horror Genres. The Global Media and the Millennial Zombies." *Journal of Popular Culture* 45 (6): 1137–1151.
Bishop, Kyle. 2008. "The Sub-subaltern Monster: Imperialist Hegemony and the Cinematic Voodoo Zombie." *Journal of American Culture* 31 (2): 141–152.

Bishop, Kyle. 2009. "Dead Man Still Walking: Explaining the Zombie Renaissance." *Journal of Popular Film and Television* 31 (1): 16–25.

Bishop, Kyle. 2015. "The New American Zombie Gothic: Road Trips, Globalization and the War on Terror." *Gothic Studies* 17 (2): 42–56.

Boon, Kevin Alexander. 2007. "Ontological Anxiety Made Flesh: The Zombie in Literature, Film and Culture." In *Monsters and the Monstrous: Myths and Metaphor of Enduring Evil*, edited by Niall Scott, 33–43. Amsterdam: Rodopi.

Canavan, Gerry. 2010. "We Are the Walking Dead: Race, Time and Survival in Zombie Narrative." *Extrapolation* 51 (3): 431–453.

Comaroff, Jean and John Comaroff. 2002. "Alien Nation: Zombies, Immigrants, and Millennial Capitalism." *The South Atlantic Quarterly* 101 (4): 779–805.

Comentale, Edward and Aaron Jaffe. 2014. "Introduction." In *The Year's Work at the Zombie Research Center*, edited by Edward Comentale and Aaron Jaffe, 1–58. Bloomington: Indiana UP.

Comentale, Edward. 2014. "Zombie Race." In *The Year's Work at the Zombie Research Center*, edited by Edward Comentale and Aaron Jaffe, 276–314. Bloomington: Indiana UP.

Dendle, Peter. 2007. "The Zombie as Barometer of Cultural Anxiety." In *Monsters and the Monstrous: Myths and Metaphor of Enduring Evil*, edited by Niall Scott, 45–57. Amsterdam: Rodopi, 2007.

Derrida, Jaques. (1997) 2000. *Of Hospitality: Anne Duformantelle Invites Jaques Derrida to Respond*. Translated by Rachel Bowlby. Stanford: Stanford UP.

Derrida, Jacques. 2005. "The Principle of Hospitality." *Parallax* 11 (1): 6–9.

Drezner, Daniel W. 2011. *Theories of International Politics and Zombies*. Princeton: Princeton UP.

Fillol, Santiago, Glòria Salvador Corretger and Núria Bou i Sala. 2016. "El imaginario del zombie cinematográfico de los desamparados: del esclavo del clasicismo hollywoodense al inmigrante de la contemporaneidad europea." *Communication and Society* 29 (1): 53–67.

Hamilton, Peter. 2013. "Simulating the Zombie Apocalypse in Popular Culture and Media." In *Thinking Dead: What the Zombie Apocalypse Means*, edited by Murali Balaji, 45–61. Lanham: Lexington.

Harper, Stephen. 2002. "Zombies, Malls and the Consumerism Debate: George Romero's *Dawn of the Dead*." *Americana: Journal of American Popular Culture (1900-Present)* 1 (2): n.p.

Harvey, David. 2002. *Spaces of Hope*. Edinburgh: Edinburg UP.

Hillis Miller, J. 1979. "The Critic as Host." In *Deconstruction and Criticism*, edited by Harold Bloom, Paul de Man, Jacques Derrida and Geoffrey H. Hartman. New York: Continuum.

Inda, Jonathan Xavier. 2000. "Foreign Bodies: Migrants, Parasites, and the Pathological Nation." *Discourse* 22 (3): 46–62.

Kozma, Alicia. 2013. "Leave It All Behind: The Post-Apocalyptical Renunciation of Technology in *The Walking Dead*." In *Thinking Dead: What the Zombie Apocalypse Means*, edited by Murali Balaji, 141–158. Lanham: Lexington.

Lauro, Sarah Juliet and Karen Embry. 2008. "A Zombie Manifesto: The Nonhuman Condition in the Era of Advanced Capitalism." *Boundary 2* 35 (1): 85–108.

Lizardi, Ryan. 2013. "The Zombie Media Monster's Evolution to Empty Undead Signifier." In *Thinking Dead: What the Zombie Apocalypse Means*, edited by Murali Balaji, 89–103. Lanham: Lexington.

Manzanas Calvo, Ana María. 2007. "Introduction. Border Dynamics: From Terminus to Terminator." In *Border Transits: Literature and Culture across the Line*, edited by Ana María Manzanas, 1–5. Amsterdam: Rodopi.

McNulty, Tracy. 2007. *The Hostess: Hospitality, Femininity, and the Expropriation of Identity*. Minneapolis: U of Minnesota P.

Mendieta, Eduardo. 2017. "The U.S. Border and the Political Ontology of 'Assassination Nation': Thanatological Dispositifs." *The Journal of Speculative Philosophy* 31 (1): 82–100.

Moreman Christopher M. and Cory J. Rushton. 2011. "Introduction. They're US: Zombies, Humans/Humans, Zombies." In *Zombies Are Us: Essays on the Humanity of the Walking Dead*, edited by Christopher M. Moreman and Cory J. Rushton. Jefferson (NC): McFarland.

Online Etymology Dictionary, Available at: http://etymonline.com.

Papastergiadis, Nikos. 2006. "The Invasion Complex: The Abject Other and Spaces of Violence." *Geografiska Annaler. Series B, Human Geography* 88 (4): 429–442.

Papastergiadis, Nikos. 2013. "Hospitality and the Zombification of the Other." In *The Conditions of Hospitality: Ethics, Politics, and Aesthetics on the Threshold of the Possible*, edited by Thomas Claviez. New York: Fordham UP.

Seed, David, 2007. "Constructing America's Enemies: The Invasions of the USA." *The Yearbook of English Studies* 37 (2) Science Fiction: 64–84.

Serres, Michael. 1982. *Parasite*. Translated by Lawrence R. Schehr. Baltimore: Johns Hopkins UP.

Shaviro, Steve. 2002. "Capitalist Monsters." *Historical Materialism* 10 (4): 281–290.

Slusser, George and Eric Rabkin. 1987. "Introduction." In *Aliens: The Anthropology of Science Fiction*, edited by George Slusser, and Eric Rabkin, ii-xxi. Carbondale: Southern Illinois UP.

Sontag, Susan. 1965. "The Imagination of Disaster." *Commentary* 40 (4): 42–48.

Stratton, Jon. 2011. "Zombie Trouble: Zombie Texts, Bare Life and Displaced People." *European Journal of Cultural Studies* 14(3): 265–281.

Sutler-Cohen, Sara. 2011. "Plans Are Pointless; Staying Alive Is as Good as It Gets: Zombie Sociology and the Politics of Survival." In *Zombies Are Us: Essays on the Humanity of the Walking Dead*, edited by Christopher M. Moreman and Cory J. Rushton. Jefferson (NC): McFarland.

Vacker, Barry. 2013. "Space Junk and the Second Event: The Cosmic Meaning of the Zombie Apocalypse." In *Thinking Dead: What the Zombie Apocalypse Means*, edited by Murali Balaji, 159–179. Lanham: Lexington.

Multimedia

Darabont, Frank et al. 2010-. *The Walking Dead*. Various directors. New York: AMC.

Garland, Alex. 2002. *28 Days Later*. DVD. Directed by Danny Boyle. London: DNA Films.

Romero, George A. 1978. *Dawn of the Dead*. Beijing: Laurel Group.

Romero, George A. 2005. *Land of the Dead*. Los Angeles (CA): Universal Pictures.

Russo, John A. and George A. Romero. 1968. *Night of the Living Dead*. DVD. Directed by George A. Romero. Beijing: Laurel Group.

Weston, Gareth. 1932. *White Zombie*. Web. Youtube. Directed by Victor Halperin. Victor and Edward Halpering Productions.

Index

African American   31, 65, 68, 69, 70, 72, 73,
   140, 156–157, 167–168
Agency   7, 8, 12, 38, 46–48, 51–55, 148, 184, 189
   linguistic   12, 38, 51, 55
Ahmed, Sarah   196, 198, 199, 203, 205
   Strange Encounters   199
   "stranger fetish(ism)"   196, 203
Alexie, Sherman   25, 26, 31–33
   Flight   11, 25, 31–33
Alien   11, 16, 122, 159, 188, 214, 215, 219–220
   resident alien   11, 23–24, 26–28, 32–33
Alienation   30, 63, 83, 130, 216
Allegory   102, 103
Anagnorisis   24–27, 29, 31, 33, 185
Angel Island   79, 81
Arendt, Hannah   15, 116, 117, 120, 128
Asian-American   91, 136

Bakhtin, Mikhail   120, 122
Bancroft, George   109
   History of the United States from the Discovery of the American Continent   109
Barriocentric narrative/novel   13, 59, 64
Baudrillard, Jean   83, 149
Bildungsroman   208
Bilingualism   61, 64, 67, 68
   bilingual creativity   88, 91
Border   2–3, 5–7, 50, 52, 58, 62, 67, 82, 115, 119, 156, 177, 184–185, 199, 221, 227, 228
   gendered border   50
   linguistic border   82
Brigham, Ann   197–199
   American Road Narratives   197–199
Buber, Martin   116
Buddhism   136, 147, 148, 151

Caldwell, Taylor   157, 161, 163–164, 165, 166, 169
   Captains and the Kings   157, 161, 163–164, 165, 166, 169
Cannibalism   15, 83, 149, 152
Capitalism   185, 216, 217, 218, 222
Caribbean   16, 74, 177, 181, 182n7, 183n10, 191
Chicana/o   59–61, 66, 87, 195, 196, 196n3, 200
Cisneros, Sandra   9, 12, 13, 38, 40, 43, 44, 48, 50, 53–55, 59–61, 74

The House on Mango Street   12, 13, 36, 38, 42–51, 52–55, 59–61
Code-switching   9, 13, 59, 61, 65–67, 69
Colonization   21–22, 96, 101, 108–110, 187
   Decolonization   12, 22–25, 28, 31–33
Comaroff, Jean and Comaroff, John   186, 217–218
Communication   8, 9, 61, 135, 141, 151, 181
Community/ies   3–5, 9, 10, 40, 43, 48, 52, 53, 55, 59, 60, 62–68, 70–71, 72–74, 78, 95, 102, 120, 123–125, 129, 131, 136, 140–143, 145–146, 150, 151, 162, 169, 171, 173, 179, 180, 190, 191, 199, 203, 204, 206–208, 213–214, 214n, 222–228
   speech communities   10, 65
Conrad, Joseph   84, 85, 87
Consumerism   16, 214, 216
Counternarrative   197, 198, 198n
Critical Judgement   117

Damai, Puspa   4, 6, 22, 160, 165, 170
Dependent nations   21
Derrida, Jaques   4–8, 10, 13, 23–24, 80, 82, 83, 84, 86, 90–91, 95–96, 105, 107, 115, 116, 117, 119n3, 124, 129–130, 135, 137, 144–145, 146, 152, 156, 162, 177, 179, 189, 191, 196, 199, 223, 225n
   arrivant   196, 197, 199. *See also* guest
   Monolingualism of the Other   80, 86, 90
   Of Hospitality   23
Dialogism   14, 116, 119–121, 126, 130, 185
Díaz, Junot   9, 12, 38, 40–42, 44, 45, 49, 52, 55, 86
   This is How you Lose Her   12, 38
Dikeç, Mustafa   39, 42, 58
Douglas, Mary   135, 141
Dwelling   5, 8, 80, 82–87

Eating   135, 141, 145n. *See also* food
Empathy   8, 114, 117, 120, 127, 128, 135, 139, 141, 150
Ethics   3, 5, 6, 11, 26, 38, 74, 115, 117, 120, 137, 140–141, 142, 147, 148–149, 151, 196n3, 199, 223
Exclusion   2, 3, 16–17, 50, 58, 59, 60, 63, 65, 67, 69, 71–74, 160, 188, 191, 197

INDEX

Exile   14, 81, 83, 85, 87, 103, 105, 109, 160, 178, 187, 197n, 221

Fairclough, Norman   38, 47, 51
Food   15, 135–141, 142, 143, 146, 147, 148, 150, 151, 206, 213, 219, 220, 224, 226. *See also* eating
Foucault, Michel   41, 109, 181, 187, 189

Gatekeeper   38, 45, 47, 48, 51, 52, 55, 66, 184
Ghettoized neighborhood   58, 59. *See also* marginalized neighborhood
Gordon, Mary   157, 160, 165
   The Other Side   157, 160, 166, 171–173
Guest   4, 6, 8–10, 12–14, 16, 24, 27, 29, 33, 38–43, 45–48, 51, 53–54, 55, 58, 60, 65, 68, 73, 80, 83, 85, 86, 87, 90, 102, 106, 107–109, 135–136, 138, 140–141, 142, 144–147, 148, 151, 164, 167, 171, 173, 177, 179–183, 185, 197–199, 201, 203, 205, 208, 213, 214, 217–220, 223, 224, 226–228. *See also* guest-host binary/relationship; parasitical guest; Jaques Derrida: *arrivant*
Guest-host binary/relationship   6, 11, 12, 15, 24–25, 33, 39, 42, 55, 68, 177, 197, 199. *See also* guest; host; insider-outsider dynamic

Hawthorne, Nathaniel   10, 14, 94–110
   "Endicott and the Red Cross"   14, 95, 97, 103–106, 109
   Mosses from an Old Manse   97
   Provincial Tales   97
   Seven Tales of my Native Land   97
   "The Gentle Boy"   14, 95, 100, 106–108, 110
   "The May-Pole of Merry Mount"   14, 97, 98, 100–102, 108, 109
   The Story Teller   97
   Twice-Told Tales   97, 98, 103, 106
Hernández, Tim Z.   16, 195, 196, 197, 199, 200, 201, 203, 206, 208–209
   Mañana Means Heaven   16, 195–198, 200–209
Historical Fiction   94, 99, 103
Holy Land   118, 119, 121
Hospitality   4–11
   conditional   6, 15–16, 23–24, 62, 70, 95, 125, 127, 129, 137, 146, 162, 163, 167, 191
   from below   4, 11, 12, 24–25, 28, 29, 33
   Law of   148, 140, 157, 162, 163, 167, 223
   laws of   5, 137, 138, 156, 157, 162, 163, 167, 223
   linguistic   8, 13, 80, 82, 86, 87. *See also* linguistic boundaries; linguistic exclusion
   multicultural   16, 139, 196, 197, 204, 208, 209
   unconditional   6, 6n, 11, 15–16, 23–24, 28, 30, 95, 107, 115–116, 119–120, 126–130, 132, 135, 143, 143, 146, 157, 159, 162, 163, 171, 173, 184, 214, 223, 225n
Host   4–17, 21, 23–29, 33, 38, 40–41, 43, 46–48, 50–51, 54–55, 58–60, 65–69, 71, 73, 80, 82–83, 85–87, 90, 101, 102, 106, 107, 109, 115, 120, 126, 135, 138–148, 151, 177, 179–183, 197, 198–201, 203, 205, 207, 208, 214, 218–220, 219n, 223, 225, 226, 227, 228. *See also* guest-host binary/relationship
   host country/community   13, 39, 40–42, 45, 47, 58, 59, 61–63, 65, 74, 75, 156, 157, 160, 161, 162, 165, 166, 169, 170, 171, 173, 177, 187, 217, 219–220, 221
   hosted host   12, 16, 38–49, 51, 52, 55
   displaced host   10, 14, 95, 105–106, 109, 110
Hostage   5, 45, 79, 87, 90–91, 187, 219, 220, 223
Hostility   3, 4, 6, 7, 11, 15–17, 58, 60, 61, 65, 71, 90, 123, 130, 135, 142–143, 148, 150, 156, 163, 173, 177, 180, 184, 188, 191, 213, 214, 214n, 223, 224, 228
Hostipitality   6, 6n, 16, 80, 84, 95, 137, 139, 140, 150, 191
Hybridity   61, 67, 69, 74, 80, 85, 86, 87, 88, 90, 91, 157

Ignatiev, Noel   15, 155–159, 165, 167
   How the Irish Became White   15, 155, 157
Illouz, Eva   197, 199–202
   "romantic competence"   201
Infection   189, 219, 221. *See also* parasite
Inner cities   60, 61, 68, 74
Insider-outsider dynamic/self-other dynamic   60, 196n3. *See also* guest-host binary/relationship
Interhuman
   encounters   117
   hatreds   30, 115

Invasion   6, 90, 143, 147, 163, 213, 217–220, 221, 223, 225, 228
Irish-American   15, 156, 158, 169, 171–173. *See also* Irish migrant

Japan   136, 138, 140n7, 150, 151
Jerusalem   15, 118, 121, 123, 124
Jin, Ha   13, 78–91

Kachru, Braj B.   80, 88n, 89
Kant, Immanuel   4–5, 6, 14, 102, 110, 119n3, 148
  Perpetual Peace   4, 6, 14, 95, 106
Kerouac, Jack   16, 195–196, 196n2, 197n, 200–202, 205, 206–207, 208
  On the Road   16, 195, 197, 200–207
  "The Mexican Girl"   16, 195, 203
Knowledge   9, 12, 39–41, 46, 47–48, 50, 54, 140
Krevel, Mojca   148

Language   7–10, 12–14, 16, 21, 38–40, 46, 48–50, 52–55, 58–75, 80–91, 96, 118, 124, 128, 159, 181–182, 184, 191, 197n, 199, 204.
  agency   8, 12, 38, 46–48, 50–55
  hospitable   7, 82
  inhospitable   80, 82
  interaction   8–10, 12–13, 38, 46–47
  linguistic boundaries/language barriers   13, 37, 55, 65–68. *See also* linguistic exclusion; linguistic hospitality
  linguistic exclusion   60, 63, 67, 69, 71–74. *See also* linguistic boundaries; linguistic hospitality
  low status   59, 68–69
  radicalization of   59, 62, 64–68
  space   9, 12, 38, 47, 50, 57, 62
Levinas, Emmanuel   3–8, 12, 14, 58, 95, 110, 117, 120, 140–142, 147, 151, 157
Literature   80, 84, 87–88, 91, 96, 98, 106, 147, 151, 160
  Native American   22–33
  translation   8–10, 82–88
Love   100, 116, 122, 197–198, 199–209
  interracial   208–209
  multicultural   198, 209

Manzanas, Ana and Benito, Jesús   4, 7, 10, 86–87, 90, 137–138, 138n, 149, 161, 163, 170–171, 197–198

Marginalized neighborhood   59, 61, 63, 71, 74. *See also* ghettoized neighborhood
Marshall, John   21
McCourt, Frank   157, 161–162, 164, 166, 168, 173
  'Tis   162, 164, 166, 168–169, 173
Melville, Herman   11, 14–15, 114–129, 190
  Clarel: A Poem and Pilgrimage in the Holy Land   14–15, 114, 117, 119–130
    Rolfe   117, 125–129
  Moby-Dick   15, 116, 120–122, 126, 130
    Ishmael   116, 122, 126, 129, 130
    Queequeg   116, 122, 129
Migration   2–3, 6–7, 16, 26, 58, 64, 78–79, 156, 159–160, 165, 177–179, 184, 188, 197n, 198, 201, 205, 213–214, 220, 221–222, 228. *See also* mobility
migrant   2, 5, 7, 11–17, 21, 23–28, 30–31, 37–40, 43–45, 49, 51–52, 55, 58–68, 74–75, 78–82, 84–85, 87, 90, 99, 101, 115, 156–163, 166–167, 169–173, 177–191, 198–199, 206–207, 211–228.
  Asian   30, 79, 156
  Caribbean   15, 16, 74, 177–191
  Chinese   31, 78–80, 81, 90
  Irish   15, 99, 155–173, 206
  Latino   38, 40–55, 60–75, 180
  Mexican   2–3, 26–29, 60–64, 195–198, 200, 203–208, 219
Mobility   50, 59, 64, 73, 75, 142, 160, 190, 197–208, 220. *See also* migration; road; travel
  in American road narratives   197–208
Monolingualism   9, 13, 59, 60, 62, 80, 82n3, 85–88, 90–91

Nabokov, Vladimir   84–87
Nativism   162–167, 211–212, 219
New England   21, 94–98, 101–102, 104, 106–107, 167

Other, the   3, 5–10, 12–13, 15–17, 26, 30, 38, 55, 58–59, 73, 84, 86–87, 90, 95–96, 105, 114–117, 118, 119, 120, 122–126, 129–130, 135–138, 140, 144, 147–148, 151, 156, 157, 159, 162–167, 173, 177, 184–185, 191, 196, 198–199, 203–204, 208, 217, 219, 220–223, 228. *See also* stranger
  fantasy/ies of   16, 202, 203, 204, 208
  incorporation of   203

INDEX

Other, the (cont.)
   hospitable Other 203
   otherness 15–17, 115, 148, 156, 157, 166–167, 173, 184–185, 191, 206, 217, 219, 221
Ozeki, Ruth 15, 136–151

Palestine 118–119, 121
Papastergiadis, Nikos 217, 219–220
Paper daughters/sons 79, 91
Parasite 16, 143, 144–146, 159, 218–221, 228. *See also* infection
   parasitical guest 16–17, 169, 220, 223, 226, 228. *See also* guest
   parasitism 134, 147, 220
Postcolonial theory 22–24, 33
Power 5, 8, 9, 10, 12–13, 16, 38–48, 52–55, 58–68, 71, 73–75, 82–83, 144–157, 169–170, 182–183, 198–199
   power relations/dynamics 9, 12, 16, 38, 46, 52–53, 58, 68, 73, 182–183, 199
Prejudice 60–61, 64, 68–69, 71–74, 100, 118, 140, 161–167
Puerto Rican 65–74, 168, 168, 190–191
Puritanism 10, 14, 96–117

Quakerism 107–108, 110

Race 7, 15–16, 27–28, 42–43, 59, 68–69, 72, 156–159, 162–163, 167, 197, 206, 219
   racial labeling 89, 159, 163, 167, 169, 204
Return 63, 173, 208
   narrative of 198, 208
Ricoeur, Paul 8, 80, 82, 86–87
Ridge, John Rollin *See* Yellow Bird
Road 16, 195–208, 223–224. *See also* mobility
Romero, George A. 215–216, 218, 222

Salem 96–97
Serres, Michel 134, 145, 220
Silko, Leslie Marmon 25, 26, 28–32, 33
   Ceremony 11, 24–26, 28–29, 31
Slavery 167–168, 180–181, 184–190, 215–217
Sociolinguistic approach 12, 14, 58–75
Spanglish 61, 67, 69
Spivak, Gayatri C. 4, 11–12, 23–33, 185
Stranger 4–6, 10, 15, 17, 21, 60, 62, 64, 71, 83, 95, 107, 109, 120–125, 130, 135–145, 147–148, 162, 169, 186, 198–199, 203–204, 212–214, 218–219, 223, 225, 227. *See also* the Other

Tagore, Ravindranath 23
   Gora 23–24, 31
Television 136–138
Telfer, Elizabeth 135, 141
Thomas, Piri 68, 70, 72, 74
   Down These Mean Streets 13, 59, 64–75
Threshold 12–13, 58, 60, 64–65, 71, 75, 197, 199, 220
Travel 118, 129, 187, 197n, 205. *See also* mobility

Undead 216, 220–222, 224, 228. *See also* zombie
Unheimlich 228
Universal Wail 122, 130
United States 21–22, 27–28, 33, 63–64, 67, 70, 73, 78–81, 86n, 91, 106, 137, 159–161, 163, 167, 170, 171, 177–178, 184, 216, 219, 221.
   Civil War 119
   Postbellum US 119, 119n, 121

van Dijk, Teun 9, 40, 41, 46, 47, 48
Virus *See* infection

Walking Dead, The (TV series) 16, 212–228
Wall 58, 71, 79, 121–122, 124–125, 129, 156, 213, 224–227
Whiteness 16, 29–30, 68–74, 156–159, 163–164, 167–169, 171, 183, 203–204
Whitewashing 156, 170, 173
White Zombie (film) 215–216
Wild justice 24, 26, 28, 31, 33
Williams, Roger 21–22, 103–104
Writer 7, 97
   exiled 81, 85–86
   hyphenated 91
   migrant 80–91

Xenophobia 59, 71–72, 115

Yellow Bird 24–28, 33
   Life and Adventures of Joaquin Murieta 11, 24–26, 27–28, 31

Zombie 16–17, 189, 212–228. *See also* undead
   "Zombie Manifesto" 217

Printed in the United States
By Bookmasters